SCOTLAND'S GOLF COURSES

The Author

Robert Price was born in Cardiff, Wales. After taking degrees in geography and geology in the University of Wales (B Sc) and Edinburgh (Ph D) he lectured in American universities for two years and carried out research in Alaska. In 1963 he was appointed lecturer in geography at Glasgow University and subsequently held appointments as Senior Lecturer and Reader at Glasgow. His main research interests have been glaciers and glaciated landscapes: he has published three books and over thirty papers in scientific journals. In 1984 he was awarded the degree of D Sc for his contributions to the study of glacial environments past and present.

A keen golfer, Dr Price has been a member of Kirkintilloch Golf Club for 20 years. During 30 years of travelling throughout Scotland in connection with his work he has taken the opportunity to play on 60 different golf courses and has visited over 400.

Scotland's Golf Courses

Robert Price

ABERDEEN UNIVERSITY PRESS

First published 1989
Aberdeen University Press
A member of the Pergamon Group

© Robert Price 1989

British Library Cataloguing in Publication Data

Price, Robert
    Scotland's golf courses
    1. Scotland, Golf Courses
    I. Title
    796.352'06'8411

ISBN   **0 08 036591 4**

PRINTED IN GREAT BRITAIN
THE UNIVERSITY PRESS
ABERDEEN

CONTENTS

LIST OF TABLES

LIST OF FIGURES

LIST OF BLACK AND WHITE PLATES

LIST OF COLOUR PLATES

All the above colour photographs are by Peter Davenport.

Front cover illustration:
St Andrews golf courses. Aerial photograph by Peter Davenport.

Back cover illustration:
Tobermory golf course, Isle of Mull.

PREFACE

'Hearing a man who has only recently discovered the game of golf
holding forth on the beauty of what I should have thought to be
a comparatively ordinary course, I fell to marvelling at the
extraordinary variety of experience offered by this singular game
and the extraordinary reluctance of the average player to take
advantage of it.

Every other game is played on the same kind of pitch the world
over. One football field is like another; one cricket pitch like the
next, except that in one case the background may be the village
chestnuts and in another the gasometers.

Yet not only is every golfing pitch different from all others, but
it consists of 18 little pitches within itself. Thus an almost
inexhaustible supply of golfing problems presents itself.

How strange, therefore that men of imagination in other walks
of life so lack that quality as golfers that they will cheerfully play
month by month, year by year, decade by decade, over the same
18 holes.

Ten to one, too, that they play with the same people every
Sunday at the same hour, make the same remarks on the first tee,
and what is more, play a four ball. Human ingenuity could
scarcely devise golf in a duller form.'

from *The Best of Henry Longhurst*,
M W Wilson and K Bowden (eds) (Collins, 1979), pp 174–5.

Apart from the last paragraph, the above quotation is a very apt
justification for the writing of a book which attempts to explain why
every 'golfing pitch is different from all others'. However, my interest
in golf stems from the fact that for the past twenty years there has
been a very important entry in my diary for 6 p.m. every Monday
evening throughout the summer months—'Four-ball match at
Kirkintilloch Golf Club'. This book is dedicated to the members of that
foursome: Ian Campbell, Graham Cruickshank and David Shaw; the
other 160,000 golf club members in Scotland, and to all visitors who
wish to know more about the variety of landscapes to be found on
Scotland's golf courses.

In the early stages of research for this book it became evident that a complete list of all the golf courses in Scotland did not exist. The various published lists did not agree with each other and as fieldwork was undertaken it was discovered that not only was the same course often referred to by different names but that courses existed which had never been referred to in published lists. By 1986 it was necessary to draw up a final list on which to undertake statistical analyses and for this reason that list has been adhered to, although a few additional courses have been 'discovered' by the author since that date and new courses have been opened (see chapter 2). There are many new 'golf developments' in the planning stage in Scotland and we may well see a new era of expansion in the game in this country. However, this book is concerned with the list of 425 Scottish golf courses completed by the author in 1986. Inevitably there will be factual errors in such a large quantity of data assembled from a wide variety of sources. The author extends his apologies to the reader for any such errors. In order to assemble and present the data systematically, Scotland has been divided into four regions (A,B,C,D—see appendix) based on either single or multiple administrative regions. Each golf course has been assigned a regional number which is used in the text, on maps and in the appendix.

Robert Price
Glasgow

ACKNOWLEDGEMENTS

During the past four years of work on this project I have received a great deal of help and encouragement from many people and organisations. I offer my sincere thanks to:

Numerous golf club secretaries who have provided information about their clubs.

Mr R A L Burnet, Historian and Librarian of the Royal and Ancient Golf Club of St Andrews.

My family—Mary, David and Catherine who have tolerated my attempts to visit all of Scotland's golf courses and who have assisted with the preparation of the manuscript and illustrations.

Mrs D Briggs, who typed the original manuscript.

Mrs H Davies, who prepared the index.

Miss Y Wilson and Miss M Hodge who produced the maps and diagrams.

Dr G W Allan, Mr G Menzies and Prof J Rooney, who read and commented on the text.

Mr C MacLean and his staff at the Aberdeen University Press.

Golfers who have shared my enthusiasm to play on as many different golf courses as possible: Ian Campbell, Peter Carr, Chalmers Clapperton, Graham Cruikshank, Norrie Lawson, Mary Price and David Shaw.

Chapter 1

THE HISTORY OF THE GAME OF GOLF

Although this book is primarily concerned with golf courses, it is necessary to provide some historical background about the origins and evolution of the game, the equipment and golfing societies (clubs). Scotland can rightly claim to be the 'home of modern golf' in that it was here, between 1740 and 1900, that all the major developments in the game, its equipment and administration took place. It was also from Scotland that the rules, players and course designers spread throughout the world. Many of the game's traditions started on the classic links courses of Scotland. The pre-eminence of the Royal and Ancient Golf Club of St Andrews as rule-maker and administrator of the game both for professionals and amateurs and the 'export' of golf course architects and professional players to all corners of the globe demonstrate the importance of Scotland to the game of golf.

Many books have been written about the history of golf. This author will confine himself to a brief discussion of four phases in the development of the game:

1. Pre-1735—historical references to the game of golf and connections between Scotland and the Low Countries;
2. 1735-1849—early Scottish Golfing Societies (clubs) and golfing equipment;
3. 1850-99—the expansion of golf in Scotland, the organisation of the sport and the development of balls and clubs;
4. 1900-86—the 'modern' era.

The reader requiring more detailed information on the history of the game of golf is referred to the Bibliography, in particular those books marked *.

GOLF IN SCOTLAND BEFORE 1735

If golf is defined as a game involving the driving of a ball with a club over a long distance into either a hole in the ground or against a

1

small post, tree or door, then close links with *colf*, played in the Low Countries between the fourteenth and eighteenth centuries and the game of gouff, (or 'gollfe' or 'golf') played in Scotland between the fifteenth and eighteenth centuries, can be established. Van Hengel, (1985), has made a detailed study of manuscripts and paintings (450 paintings between 1500 and 1700) in the Low Countries which not only provide information about the game of *colf* but which clearly establish close trade and political connections between the Low Countries and the east coast of Scotland between 1485 and the mid seventeenth century. Large quantities of *colf* balls were exported from Holland and Zeeland to Scotland and in the mid seventeenth century Scottish wooden clubs were exported to and used in Holland. Van Hengel (1985 p 11) states 'There is absolutely no doubt that *colf* was an early form of golf'.

The first documentary evidence of *colf* in the Low Countries is dated at around 1360, while the first documentary evidence which refers to golf in Scotland was in an Act of Parliament of 1457 which forbids the playing of 'Gouff'. There are various references to Scottish golf being played in the churchyards and streets in the sixteenth century and the game may well have been similar to *colf*. Throughout the period 1550–1650, there are records of the game being played mainly on the links land along the east coast of Scotland, and also at Perth, Forfar and Glasgow (Fig 1.1 and Table 1.1). Many of these early records are only passing references to golfers and the earliest description of the Scottish game of golf is to be found in a Latin Grammar for Aberdeen schools produced in 1632. This work refers to bunkers, iron clubs, holes and sand for teeing up (Hamilton D, 1985).

It seems highly likely that during the sixteenth and seventeenth centuries the Scottish game of golf moved out of the streets and churchyards either to common ground known as 'greens' or on to the coastal links land. By 1650, the links at Gullane, Leith, St Andrews, Carnoustie, Montrose, Aberdeen, Banff and Dornoch were golfing grounds, and the seeds of modern golf had been sown in the sands which would remain such a strong feature of the Scottish golfing landscape. Little is known about the way in which the game of golf was actually played in the sixteenth and seventeenth centuries. Not until 1721 is there an eye-witness account of the game being played. This is contained in a poem published by James Arbuckle, a Glasgow University student. Hamilton (1985) states: 'That the poem should contain a section on the game of golf suggests that the game was then a familiar feature of Glasgow life. Arbuckle describes a game between fairly skilful players, and the poem shows that the match was played on the Glasgow Green'. Glasgow Green was a relatively small area on

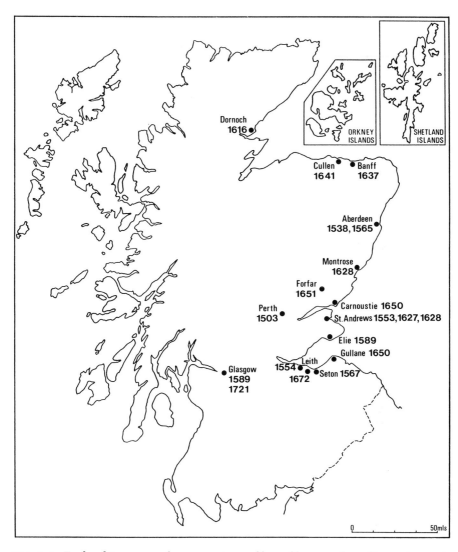

FIG 1.1   Early literary references to golf, golfers and golf equipment 1503–1721.

TABLE 1.1 LIST OF EARLY REFERENCES TO GOLF, GOLFERS AND GOLF EQUIPMENT
IN SCOTLAND

1457	James II (Parl. 14, cap. 64) Act of Parliament discouraging football and 'Gouff'.
1503	King James IV bought clubs from a bow-maker in Perth (D Hamilton, 1982).
1538	Golfers at play in Aberdeen—Aberdeen Burgh Records—1538 MS Vol XVI.
1552	St Andrews charter: The Document reserves to the Provost and Town Council and townspeople the right of using the links for 'golfe, futeball, shuting and all games . . .'.
1554	Reference to a dispute between the cordiners (cobblers) of the Cannongate and the cordiners and gouff ball makers of North Leith. The inference is that cobblers were stitching leather balls but we do not know what they were filled with (The Chronicle of the Royal Burgess Golfing Society).
1565	Golf included in a list of unlawful games in Aberdeen.
1567	Mary Queen of Scots was charged with playing golf and pall mall at Seton House, East Lothian, a few days after the murder of her husband. (Inventories of Mary Queen of Scots, Preface p lxx, 1863).
1589	Glasgow Kirk Session ruled that there be 'no golf' in the High at the Blackfriars Yard, Sunday or weekday'. (James Colville, The Glasgow Golf Club, 1907, p 1).
1616	Records of golf being played at Dornoch (D Hamilton, 1982).
1627	James Pitt recorded as clubmaker of St Andrews.
1628	Memoirs of the Marquis of Montrose, Mark Napier, Edinburgh. T G Stevenson 1856 gives account of golfing expenses at St Andrews, Leith and Montrose.
1636	David Wedderburn's—The Vocabula—a description of the game of golf— Aberdeen. (D Hamilton, 1985).
1637	Banff—record that a boy was hanged for stealing, among other things, two golf balls.
1641	Record of golf at Cullen.
1650	Record of golf at Carnoustie.
1650	Gullane: the weavers of Dirleton played the weavers of Aberlady on Old Handsel Monday (A Baird, 1982).
1651	Non-documented claim that golf played at Forfar.
1721	Description of the game of golf by a Glasgow University Student, James Arbuckle (D Hamilton, 1985).

the north bank of the Clyde, to the west of the only bridge over the river. It was a gravel terrace where a summer crop of grass was grown and sold by auction. The game described by Arbuckle took place in winter. Summer golf was almost impossible throughout Scotland in the sixteenth and seventeenth centuries because the links and commons upon which it was played yielded an important grass crop during the summer. It is likely that the courses upon which golf was played at this time were natural landscapes consisting of links land or river terraces. Such land was well-drained and, at least outside the summer months, had close-cropped turf. Such courses may have consisted of only a few holes and the locations of these may have been changed from time to time.

There can be little doubt that golf was well established in Scotland by the middle of the seventeenth century. All the available records suggest that, apart from Glasgow and Perth, the game was mainly played on the east coast links. It was played by all classes of society. According to Archie Baird, Gullane's golf historian (Baird, 1985, p 7), 'As far back as 1650, the weavers of Dirleton played the weavers of Aberlady annually on Old Handsel Monday'. However, the wooden clubs and the 'feathery' ball used in the seventeenth century were relatively expensive and it is more likely that these could be more easily afforded by merchants and the aristocracy. Whether the poorest golfers played with the same expensive equipment is not known. However, there is no doubt that the next stage in the development of the game of golf in Scotland, the formation of Golfing Societies or clubs, was very much in the hands of wealthy merchants, landowners, professional men and academics.

EARLY SCOTTISH GOLFING SOCIETIES (CLUBS) 1735-1849

The arranging of matches, wagers and dining facilities eventually led to the formation of Golfing Societies or clubs. The earliest days of these organisations are shrouded in mystery. Two Edinburgh Golfing Societies—the Royal Burgess and the Honourable Company of Edinburgh Golfers—both began in the early decades of the eighteenth century. It is believed that the Royal Burgess Golfing Society was founded in 1735, but the earliest documents in the club's possession go back no further than 1773. However, it is clear from the Minutes that golf was being played by members of the Society for some considerable time before that date. The Society played golf at Bruntsfield links, then moved to Musselburgh and then to Barnton in 1895.

In the early eighteenth century golf was played on Leith links. It was following a request to the Magistrates and Council of Edinburgh from a group of Leith golfers, described as 'gentlemen of honour skilful in the ancient and healthful exercise of the golf', for a silver club to be played for annually, that the first rules of golf were drawn up. The 13 rules of the Gentlemen Golfers of Leith (later to become the Honourable Company of Edinburgh Golfers) laid down for the inaugural competition for the silver club were as follows:

'Articles and Laws in Playing at Golf' 1744:
1. You must tee your ball within a club's length of the hole.

2. Your tee must be upon the ground.
3. You are not to change the ball which you strike off the tee.
4. You are not to remove stones, bones or any break club for the sake of playing your ball, except upon the fair green, and that only within a club's length of your ball.
5. If your ball comes among watter, or any wattery filth, you are at liberty to take out your ball and bringing it behind the hazard and teeing it, you may play it with any club and allow your adversary a stroke for so getting out your ball.
6. If your balls be found anywhere touching one another you are to lift the first ball till you play the last.
7. At holling you are to play your ball honestly for the hole, and not to play upon your adversary's ball, not lying in your way to the hole.
8. If you should lose your ball, by its being taken up, or any other way you are to go back to the spot where you struck last and drop another ball and allow your adversary a stroke for the misfortune.
9. No man at holling his ball is to be allowed to mark his way to the hole with his club or any thing else.
10. If a ball be stopp'd by any person, horse, dog, or any thing else, the ball so stopp'd must be played where it lyes.
11. If you draw your club in order to strike and proceed so far in the stroke as to be bringing down your club; if then your club shall break in any way, it is to be accounted a stroke.
12. He whose ball lyes farthest from the hole is obliged to play first.
13. Neither trench, ditch or dyke made for the preservation of the links, nor the Scholars' Holes or the soldiers' lines shall be accounted a hazard but the ball is to be taken out teed and play'd with any iron club.

John Rattray, Capt

Although the game of golf had been played for hundreds of years on an informal basis, the rules laid down by the Gentlemen Golfers of Leith in 1744 mark the beginnings of the formalisation of the game— membership fees, clubhouses, club secretaries and committees were soon to follow.

Ten years after the formation of the Honourable Company of Edinburgh Golfers, twenty-two gentlemen met in St Andrews and each contributed five shillings for a silver club to be competed for annually. Thus was formed the St Andrews Golfing Society in 1754 and they adopted the rules devised by the Leith Golfers. The St Andrews Society played over a links course of 11 holes out and the same number back. The course was very narrow and lay between dense banks of whin. In 1764 it was decided to make the first four holes into two and since the same fairways and greens were used going out and back, the round was thus reduced to 18 holes which then became the standard round.

Seven other Golfing Societies were established in Scotland before the end of the eighteenth century; Bruntsfield Links 1761; Musselburgh 1774; Aberdeen 1780; Crail 1786; Glasgow 1787; Port Errol (Cruden Bay) 1791; Burntisland 1798. Members of these ten golfing societies were expected to wear the appropriate 'uniform' while playing the game, participate in wagers and attend dinners after a game. For the social activities the 'Golf House' at Bruntsfield, which was a tavern owned by a club maker, one Thomas Comb, and the Golf House at Leith, constructed by the Gentlemen Golfers at a cost of £760 in 1767, were the fore-runners of modern clubhouses.

Between 1800 and 1849 a further thirteen golf clubs were established:

> 1810 Montrose (Royal Albert); 1815 Kingsbarns, Leith Thistle; 1817 Tayport (Scotscraig), St Andrews Thistle; 1820 Innerleven; 1832 North Berwick; 1841 Peterhead; 1842 Carnoustie, Royal Perth; 1843 St Andrews Mechanics; 1845 Barry Panmure; 1847 Leven.

Thus, during the first 114 years of 'organised' golf in Scotland only 23 Golfing Societies or clubs had been formed. Little is known of the early history of many of these clubs because of the absence of written records. This may reflect that masonic traditions of secrecy dominated the early golfing societies. Only when non-masons had joined the Golfing Societies in such numbers that the character of the clubs was changed, were formal records kept. It would appear that golf in Scotland was at a fairly low ebb at the beginning of the nineteenth century. The 23 clubs in existence by 1850 probably had a total membership of less than 500, although there is little doubt that informal golf was still played by non-members on the links land.

Apart from the courses at Bruntsfield (Edinburgh), Glasgow Green and the North Inch at Perth, all of the other Scottish courses were coastal links. Although there were 23 clubs in existence by 1849 this does not mean that there were 23 courses. At least three clubs were playing on the St Andrews links by 1843: St Andrews Golfing Society,

St Andrews Thistle and the St Andrews Mechanics. Similarly, more than one club played on both the Leith and Musselburgh courses. The links land was ideally suited to the game of golf. Well-drained and closely cropped turf (by sheep and rabbits) permitted the game to be played throughout the year. Play was curtailed in the summer months on the 'inland' courses of Bruntsfield, Perth and Glasgow because of the summer grass crop.

Each of the golf clubs had their own rules, but most of them closely followed the 13 rules drawn up in 1744 by the Honourable Company and subsequently adopted by the St Andrews Society. By 1830 the Honourable Company was in temporary decline and in 1834 the St Andrews Golfing Society became the Royal and Ancient Golf Club of St Andrews and so began its pre-eminence not only in Scottish golf, but on a global basis.

The earliest document relating to golf in St Andrews is a charter of 1552 which reserves to the Provost and Town Council and Townspeople the right of using the links for '. . . golfe, futeball, shuting and all games, as well as casting divots, gathering turfs (to roof their houses), and for the pasturing of their livestock'. No formal golf course existed in the sixteenth and seventeenth centuries. Even at the time of foundation of the Society of St Andrews Golfers in 1754 the course was a sterile wasteland of heather and whin with narrow fairways of short grass. There were many hazards and only crude 'greens' with rough, often deep 'holes'. Not until 1806 were green keepers employed at St Andrews. The matches, often accompanied by much betting, were decided by the number of holes won. Most matches were 'foursomes' in which members of each side played alternate strokes. Not until 1759 was stroke or medal play used to decide the winner of the silver club at St Andrews. It would appear that, in the mid eighteenth century, St Andrews had already become the Alma Mater of the Golf. The original minute book of the Society of St Andrews Golfers (later to become the Royal and Ancient) states:

> The noblemen and gentlemen above named being Admirers of the Anticient (sic) and healthful Exercise of the Golf, and have at the same time, having the Interest and Prosperity of the Ancient City of St Andrews at heart, being the Alma Mater of the Golf, did in 1754 Contribute for a silver club . . . having a St Andrew engraved on the head thereof to be played for on the Links of St Andrews upon the 14th Day of May of said year, and yearly in time coming.

It is indeed remarkable that by this declaration these 22 men laid the foundations for the establishment of St Andrews to become the world's headquarters of golf administration.

In the latter half of the eighteenth century golf was a relatively expensive game to play. The clubs and balls used were expensive and only the wealthy were members of the Golfing Societies. The 'feathery' ball was made of leather and filled with a 'top-hat full' of boiled goose or chicken feathers. The leather cover was soaked in alum water before being filled with feathers so that when it dried it shrank but the feather stuffing expanded, hence producing a hard ball. These balls cost between two shillings and sixpence and four shillings each. About 1800, the feathery ball had a standard size of about $1\frac{1}{4}$ inches in diameter and weighed between 26 and 30 drams.

Because the 'feathery' ball was easily damaged by iron clubs, irons were only used in ruts or bunkers. It is very likely that the first makers of wooden clubs were bowmakers. The first record of the purchase of golf clubs is dated 1502 when James IV of Scotland purchased clubs from a bowmaker in Perth. The first Royal warrant holder was William Mayne (1603), Bower Burgess of Edinburgh, who was appointed Clubmaker to James I of England and VI of Scotland. Clubmakers were associated with the early golfing centres at Bruntsfield, Leith, and Musselburgh (see Henderson and Stirk, 1985). The heads of the early wooden clubs were long, narrow and shallow and the face was concave. The shafts were ash or hazel and the heads were made of beech, apple, pear or thorn. The early clubs had no grips but sheep skin was used as a grip from about 1800.

Early irons were made by blacksmiths and were heavy and cumbersome. Throughout the 'feathery' era only two irons were used—the sand iron with a large concave face and the rut iron which had a very small head. There were no 'sets' of clubs, the individual player ordering his clubs to suit his particular preference and no two clubs were the same.

Although the St Andrews Golfing Society became the Royal and Ancient Golf Club in 1834, both the town of St Andrews and the links went through hard times during the 1840s. J K Robertson (1974, p 48) states: 'The town was in debt to the tune of £10,000 . . . a vast sum then for a small community that was dwindling every year. The University had sunk to a handful of students, there had even been talk of moving it to Perth. By 1848 the links, the townspeoples' heritage, had been illegally sold to the neighbouring landowner, Mr George Cheape, of Strathtyrum. Cholera, the black plague, had hit the town'. However, two things happened between 1845 and 1850 which were to transform both the fortunes of St Andrews and other golfing centres and the future of the game of golf—the arrival of the railway and the making of a new golf ball. In 1845 it was proposed to route a railway line through the links at the Burn Hole. The Royal and Ancient was successful in having the line re-routed alongside the links and the line was opened in 1851. The railway era was to have a marked effect on the growth of the game of golf in Scotland throughout the second half of the nineteenth century.

There is some debate as to who was the first person to make and use a golf ball made of gutta percha (see Henderson and Stirk, 1985). It is believed that in 1843 a Dr Paterson of St Andrews University, received a large black marble idol of Vishnu from Singapore which was wrapped in gutta percha. His son Robert made a golf ball from this malleable material and used it on the Old Course in the early hours of an April morning in 1845. Subsequently Robert's brother made a batch of these balls and sent them to London in 1846 under the name of 'Paterson's Composite Golf Balls'. Allan Robertson, the St Andrews ball maker was not interested in the new ball because he was afraid it would ruin his trade in 'feathery' balls, but his assistant Tom Morris decided to open his own shop to make and sell the cheaper and more durable golf ball. There are other claims for the making of the first gutta percha ball, but wherever it originated it transformed the game of golf. Because of its cheapness (one shilling each) it opened up the game to artisans and peasantry. Between them, the railway and the gutta ball brought a new prosperity to St Andrews and allowed the game to expand both in terms of numbers of players and numbers of clubs and golf courses, throughout Scotland and the rest of the United Kingdom.

EXPANDING GOLFING HORIZONS 1850–99

Between 1850 and the end of the century the number of golf clubs in Scotland increased from 17 to 195. There were two distinct facets to this expansion. Between 1850 and 1880 only 26 new clubs were formed but between 1880 and 1900 nearly 150 new clubs were established. This was a period of industrial growth in Scotland which was accompanied by a rapid increase in the urbanisation of the population. For example, the City of Glasgow doubled its population between 1851 and 1901 (329,000 to 761,000) while the region of West-Central Scotland increased its population from 900,000 to 1,900,000 over the same period. This rapid population increase, associated with industrial prosperity provided a new, relatively well-off, middle class who were reasonably mobile as a result of the expanding railway network. It is therefore not surprising that leisure activities, such as golf, also underwent considerable growth. The factors affecting the number of golf courses and their location in Scotland will be discussed in more detail in Chapter 2.

By 1880 the dominance of links courses in Scottish golf was coming to an end and by 1900 about half the courses were on inland sites with many of them in suburban locations around the main population centres of Glasgow and Edinburgh.

The *Golfers Handbook* of 1881 lists 49 clubs in Scotland with a total membership of over 3,800 but there are some notable gaps in the membership data. It is likely that there were over 5,000 golf club members in Scotland by 1881, by which date the Royal and Ancient had a membership of 750. It is probable that by the end of the century there were some 20,000 golf club members in Scotland and many others who played the game without joining a golf club.

Throughout the second half of the nineteenth century the clubs and balls changed very little. Long-headed wooden clubs were carried loosely by the player or caddy. The first canvas golf club container was not used until 1890. The gutta percha ball, made in moulds, was replaced by the gutty, which was a composite ball, in the 1880s. Both of these types of balls cost about one shilling to buy while, throughout the period, wooden clubs cost between four and five shillings and iron clubs about three shillings and sixpence. During the latter part of the nineteenth century the condition of golf courses was steadily improved. By the beginning of the 1880s teeing areas were being separated from the greens, $4\frac{1}{4}$ inch diameter hole cutters were being used and grass cutting and weeding being undertaken. The significance of the use of grass cutting machinery will be discussed in Chapter 2.

The Royal and Ancient built its first clubhouse in 1854 and organised a foursomes championship in 1857. In 1860 the first Open Championship was held at Prestwick and in 1865 Tom Morris was appointed as the Royal and Ancient's first professional. In 1873 the Open Championship was played at St Andrews. This was the era of widespread recognition of the game of golf. Players, professionals and equipment-makers were responsible for taking the game to England, to Europe and to North America. Although Scots had taken the game to London in the early seventeenth century, the first club, Blackheath, was not founded until 1766 and other clubs were not established until the 1860s (Westward Ho! 1864, London Scottish 1865, Royal Liverpool 1869). The first club in Europe was at Pau in France (1866) and Scots immigrants carried the game to Canada (Montreal 1873, Quebec 1874, Toronto 1876). There are records of golf clubs and balls being exported from Leith to Charleston, South Carolina in 1743, and

1.1   Golf Club House and Grand Hotel with Tom Morris at the tee *c.* 1896. GWW photograph courtesy of GWW Special Collection University of Aberdeen.

1.2   Golf on St Andrews Links—'Holingout' *c.* 1890. GWW photograph courtesy of GWW Special Collection University of Aberdeen.

1.3 Golf on St Andrews Links—'A Bad Bunker: Act of Play' *c* 1890. GWW photograph courtesy of GWW Special Collection University of Aberdeen.

1.4 Golf on St Andrews Links—'Driving' *c.* 1890. GWW photograph courtesy of GWW Special Collection University of Aberdeen.

the South Carolina Golf Club was founded in 1786 and the Savannah Golf Club in 1795. The new era of golf in the United States is associated with the foundation of the St Andrews Club in Yonkers in 1888 and Shinnecock Hills Golf Club in 1891. It was the early successful Scottish golfers who travelled to instruct others how to play the game and to advise on how to lay out a course. Tom Morris travelled from St Andrews to Westward Ho! to lay out their course in 1864. Large numbers of Scots crossed the Atlantic and became golf professionals and course architects. It is said of Tom Bendelow, who designed over 600 courses in the American Mid-West, that his only qualification to be a golf course architect was his Scottish accent. The most famous Scottish-born golf course architect to work in the United States was D J Ross of Dornoch, who learned club making at Forgan's Shop in St Andrews and was taught his golf by 'Old' Tom Morris. In 1893 he returned to Dornoch as greenkeeper and professional and then emigrated to Boston in 1898. He was involved in designing over 500 courses in the USA and Canada, including Pinehurst.

Within Scotland there was certainly variety in the types of golf clubs which emerged during the big expansion between 1880 and 1900. By the very nature of Victorian society there was inevitably a social stratification within the private clubs. Many clubs became predominantly male preserves (e.g. the Royal and Ancient). The first ladies' golf competition was held in Musselburgh in 1810 and the first ladies' golf club was established in St Andrews in 1867. That club had 500 members by 1886. The ladies often played on separate short courses. In Scotland, however, unlike England and the United States, the concept of the common links land was retained and persons not belonging to any golf club could play a game on the links. It is remarkable that any resident of St Andrews had the right of playing on the Old Course, free of charge, until 1946, and even visitors did not have to pay a fee until 1913. Similar circumstances prevailed on other links at Carnoustie, Montrose, Aberdeen, Gullane and North Berwick. This tradition was strengthened in the large cities such as Edinburgh, Dundee and Glasgow where municipal golf courses provided facilities for non club members. It is therefore not surprising that the game of golf in Scotland has been enjoyed by all classes of society for the past two hundred years.

At the end of the nineteenth century golf was an established part of Scottish life and landscape. The Championships gave it publicity among the non playing public. The Royal and Ancient was becoming the centre of administration for the game—it issued the Rules of Golf to all clubs in 1888 and was given the sole control of the Rules of Golf Committee in 1897. Golf was already playing an important part in the newly emerging tourist industry of Scotland, but no-one could have guessed what a significant role was yet to be played by the 'Home of Golf' as the new century began. (Pls. 1.1, 1.2, 1.3, 1.4).

THE MODERN ERA   1900–86

About half of Scotland's golf courses of today were in existence by the turn of the century. A further 130 were opened by 1930, mainly in suburban locations in central Scotland but also in tourist areas in the south-west and north-east of the country. A further 45 courses were opened between 1930 and 1970. It is rather remarkable that only 24 courses have been opened since 1970. The underlying pattern of the distribution of the 425 golf courses in Scotland had been clearly established by 1930. The reasons behind this distribution pattern will be discussed in Chapter 2.

Two important technical developments which took place during the first 30 years of this century had important impacts on the game of golf both in Scotland and throughout the world. In 1902 a rubber-cored ball—the Haskell—was made in America by the Goodrich Tyre and Rubber Company of Akron, Ohio. By the mechanical winding of elastic thread or tape, a core was formed which was then covered by gutta percha. This ball went further when hit properly, and even if miss-hit it still performed better than the previous gutta percha balls. The widespread adoption of this ball did much to stimulate the growth and spread of the game of golf.

Various experiments had been made with steel-shafted golf clubs prior to the First World War. The USGA ruled that they could be used in their competitions in 1924 but they were not approved by the Royal and Ancient until 1930.

By 1930, therefore, Scotland contained 330 golf courses and Scottish players had access to both good quality mass-produced golf balls and clubs. For the next 30 years golf in Scotland was largely a participatory sport played by a wide cross-section of society. Professional golfers were based in many local clubs, and National and even Open Championships received only minimal media coverage. When the Open Championship was held in St Andrews in 1900 there were 81 entrants. When it was played at Carnoustie in 1931 there were 215 entrants, but when it returned to St Andrews in 1960 there were 410 entrants and it was won by Kel Nagle of Australia. By 1984 there were 1,413 entrants for the Open at St Andrews. These few statistics are a measure not only of the development of the professional game on a global scale but also of the popularity of the game at all levels. Whether measured by the earning capacity of the top professional golfers (e.g. Jack Nicklaus has won over five million dollars in prize money), or by the annual sales of golf balls (24 million balls per year in Britain; 240 million balls per year in the USA), or by the number of golf club members throughout the world (over 25 million), the past two decades have seen a transformation in the status of the game.

In what ways have these remarkable changes affected the golfing scene in Scotland? The Royal and Ancient, as both the world-wide ruling body and the administrator of one of the great international professional tournaments, has had to make many adjustments. Many Scottish golf courses have been improved as their membership lists have lengthened and their incomes increased. Investment in the improvement of courses has resulted from the higher standards demanded by players. Membership and green fees have increased but for many thousands of golfers in Scotland golf remains a relatively cheap sport. Major golfing centres such as St Andrews, Gleneagles and Turnberry are part of a world-wide golfing market. An economic study undertaken when the Open Championship was held in St Andrews in 1978 estimated that over £3 million were spent in the area during one week (excluding gate money). The Scottish nation owes a great debt to the pioneers of the game of golf. Their recognition of the golfing potential of both the links and inland landscapes of Scotland has not only produced a fine selection of golf courses for the Scots people, but has also laid the basis for a very significant international tourist market. The economic significance of this resource—the golf courses of Scotland—is as yet appreciated only to a limited extent. The remainder of this book is concerned with the description and explanation of the character of these golf courses.

Chapter 2

THE LOCATION OF GOLF COURSES—WHERE AND WHY

Scotland's 425 golf courses occupy approximately 45,000 acres of land. At present day prices these courses, club houses and related facilities probably represent a capital investment in excess of £300 million. However, many of these courses were created for a few hundred pounds and even today it is possible to develop a basic nine-hole course in a rural area for about £50,000. The cost of ground purchase and subsequent development into a championship course with associated high quality facilities in an urban or suburban area may be several million pounds. Scottish golfers, along with the many thousands of golfers who visit Scotland each year, owe a great debt to the pioneers of the modern game in Scotland who established so many golf courses between 1880 and 1920 when land was relatively cheap.

This chapter attempts to explain the distribution pattern of Scottish golf courses over the past 250 years. The present distribution pattern (Fig 2.1) reflects a variety of controls which affect the provision of golfing facilities. Many of the traditional, long-established golfing areas have been supplemented by the creation of large numbers of courses in response to a demand from the residents of urban areas in the Central Belt—about half of Scotland's golf courses are to be found in the urbanised central belt stretching from the Ayrshire coast to Dundee. In terms of the regional subdivision used in the subsequent chapters of this book (Table 2.1), it is not surprising that Regions B and C contain over half of Scotland's golf courses. About one-third of Scotland's golf courses are of nine-holes and two-thirds of 18 holes.

The rural areas of the south of Scotland contain a fairly even spread of courses. In the north-east, courses are mainly situated along the coast and in the Spey and Dee Valleys. The north-west Highlands are a golfing desert.

A particular characteristic of Scottish golf courses is that 70 courses (16 per cent) are designated Public Courses, i.e. they are open to all members of the public regardless of whether or not they are members

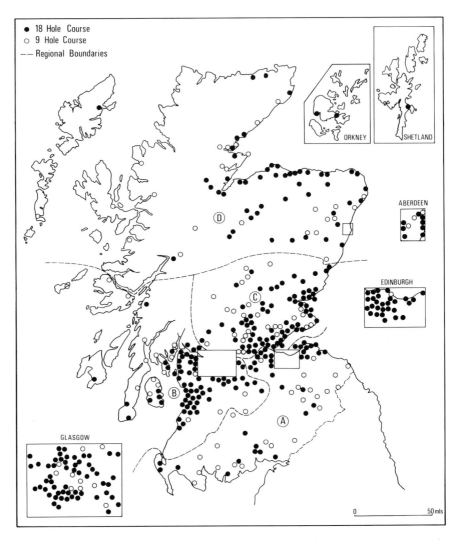

FIG 2.1 The distribution of nine-hole and 18-hole courses. Region A: Dumfries and Galloway, The Borders, Lothian. Region B: Strathclyde. Region C: Central, Fife and Tayside. Region D: Highland, Grampian and the Islands

TABLE 2.1

THE NUMBER OF NINE-HOLE AND 18-HOLE COURSES, COST PER ROUND AND ACCESSIBILITY TO VISITORS, IN EACH REGION

Region	No of 9-Hole Courses	No of 18-Hole Courses	Total No of Courses	Cost per Round[1] % in each category						Accessibility to visitors[2] % in each category			
				A	B	C	D	E	F	U	WD	I	M
A Galloway Borders Lothian	27	63	90	13	55	22	9	—	1	77	9	7	7
B Strathclyde	30	121	151	23	41	27	4	2	3	52	20	11	17
C Central Fife Tayside	28	68	96	15	50	24	6	2	2	72	26	1	—
D Grampian Highland Islands	25	63	88	13	76	7	4	—	—	87	8	5	—

NOTES

1. Cost per round—1987 prices
Based on cost of a weekday round not introduced by a member.
Play on weekends and Bank holidays may be more expensive.
Day Tickets may be available.

Category A—less than £3   B—£3-6
          C—£7-10   D—£11-14
          E—£15-18   F—over £18

2. Accessibility to visitors
   U Unrestricted
   WD Weekdays only
   I Introduction required: Letter from own club or membership
      card or handicap certificate
   M Visitors may only play with a member
At all courses certain periods may be allocated for members
competitions and visiting parties.

of a golf club. This is true of such famous courses as those at St Andrews (including the Old Course, although the player must now have an official handicap—a limitation introduced only in 1986), Carnoustie, Gleneagles and Turnberry. Many of the public courses are administered by District Councils and there are some 40 such courses where a round of golf costs less than £3. Other public courses are administered by Golf Course Trusts or Links Management Committees, while others are part of hotel complexes. Although many of the 355 private courses in Scotland are mainly restricted to play by their own members, a letter of introduction from one's own club secretary or an introduction by a local member usually facilitates use of most of the courses by a visitor. Many private clubs welcome visitors without formal introduction. This is particularly true of clubs in rural areas and in the principal tourist resorts.

In comparison with other countries (Table 2.2), Scotland has a very high level of provision of golf courses. The figures speak for themselves. Not only is the number of courses per head of population high, but the cost of a game of golf in Scotland still remains relatively cheap when compared with other parts of the United Kingdom and with the rest of the world. On only half a dozen of the Scottish courses does a round of golf cost over £18, while on some 100 courses the cost per round is between £7 and £14, and there are still over 200 courses where a round of golf costs between £3 and £6. It is still possible to find the occasional unsophisticated nine-hole course where the deposit of a one-pound note (or coin) in an honesty box entitles you to play the course.

The remainder of this chapter is concerned with the description and

TABLE 2.2

THE NUMBER OF GOLF COURSES PER THOUSAND PEOPLE IN VARIOUS COUNTRIES

Country	Courses per '000
Scotland	1 course per 13
USA	1 course per 17
Ireland	1 course per 18
Wales	1 course per 25
England	1 course per 36
Sweden	1 course per 47
Japan	1 course per 82
West Germany	1 course per 302
Spain	1 course per 366
France	1 course per 373

TABLE 2.3

NUMBER OF NEW GOLF COURSES OPENED IN EACH DECADE (1730–1980) IN EACH REGION,
AND THE NUMBER OF PERSONS PER GOLF COURSE IN SCOTLAND

	A	B	C	D	Total	Cumulative Total	Decade %	Cumulative %	Persons per golf course
1730–39	1	—	—	—	1	1	0.25	0.25	
1740–49	1	—	—	—	1	2	0.25	0.50	
1750–59	—	—	1	—	1	3	0.25	0.75	
1760–69	—	—	—	—	—	—	—	—	
1770–79	1	—	—	—	1	4	0.25	1.50	
1780–89	—	1	1	1	3	7	0.75	1.75	
1790–99	1	1	—	1	3	10	0.75	2.50	
1800–09	—	—	—	—	—	—	—	—	
1810–19	—	2	—	—	2	12	0.50	3.00	1:150,000
1820–29	—	1	—	—	1	13	0.25	3.25	
1830–39	1	—	—	—	1	14	0.25	3.50	
1840–49	—	2	—	1	3	17	0.75	4.20	
1850–59	1	3	3	—	7	24	1.75	5.95	1:120,000
1860–69	3	—	3	—	6	30	1.50	7.45	
1870–79	1	3	5	4	13	43	3.25	10.70	1:79,000
1880–89	11	11	4	15	41	84	10.25	20.95	1:44,000
1890–99	25	46	22	18	111	195	27.75	48.70	1:20,000
1900–09	13	29	15	14	71	266	17.75	66.45	1:16,000
1910–19	5	5	8	2	20	286	5.00	71.45	1:16,000
1920–29	11	18	9	7	45	331	11.25	82.60	1:15,000
1930–39	4	7	4	3	18	349	4.50	86.50	1:14,000
1940–49	3	—	1	1	5	354	1.25	87.75	1:14,000
1950–59	1	4	3	2	10	364	2.50	90.25	1:14,000
1960–69	1	5	2	4	12	376	3.00	93.25	1:13,800
1970–79	1	6	3	5	15	391	3.75	97.00	1:13,300
1980–86	—	2	4	3	9	400	2.25	99.25	1:12,750

Note: A, B, C, D refer to regions as defined in Chapters 5, 6, 7 and 8.

explanation of how, when and where Scotland's golf courses came
into existence. Collecting information about the chronology of golf
course development is not an easy task. The one date which most golf
club secretaries can readily provide is the date of foundation of their
club. However, that date does not necessarily coincide with the
opening of the course they presently play over. Some clubs (e.g.
Glasgow Golf Club and the Honourable Company of Edinburgh
Golfers) have played over several different courses throughout their
long history. Conversely, several clubs play over the same course,
while other clubs have never had a course of their own. However, in
the majority of cases the foundation date of a golf club coincides with

the opening date (plus or minus a couple of years) of its own course. Therefore, since the date of foundation of a club is the most readily available information, unless other information suggests that a particular course pre-dates the foundation of the club, most of the analyses which follow are based on the published date of club formation. If more than one club has regularly used a particular course then the date of the foundation of the oldest club has been used.

It has been possible to determine the date of opening of 400 out of the 425 golf courses/clubs in Scotland. Table 2.3 summarises this information for each of the four regions (A, B, C, D) and for each decade from 1730 to 1980. Although it has been established in Chapter 1 that golf was played in at least 15 locations in Scotland (Fig 1.1) in the sixteenth and seventeenth centuries, little is known about the character of the courses used or about the organisation of the game. It is only after the formation of the Golfing Societies and golf clubs in the mid eighteenth century that information about Scotland's golf courses becomes available.

THE OLD LINKS COURSES (FIG 2.2)   1730–1849

Although golf was almost certainly continuously played from the seventeenth century on the various links sites shown on Figure 1.1, formal records of golf clubs using specific courses indicate only three golf courses in existence in Scotland by 1750—Bruntsfield Links in the centre of Edinburgh (1735), Leith Links (1744), and St Andrews (1754). A further seven clubs came into existence by 1800: the Thorn Tree Club at Musselburgh (1774), the Society of Aberdeen Golfers (1780), Crail (1786), Glasgow (1787), Port Errol—Cruden Bay (1791), Dunbar (1794) and Burntisland (1797). A total of ten courses were in existence by the end of the eighteenth century. Eight of these occupied coastal links land and therefore continued the Scottish golfing traditions of the sixteenth and seventeenth centuries, while two courses were found in the very centre of expanding cities on common land used for a variety of purposes.

During the first half of the nineteenth century, the coastal links tradition was maintained with clubs/courses being established at Montrose (1810), Tayport–Scotscraig (1817), Leven (1820), North Berwick (1832), Peterhead (1841), Carnoustie (1842) and Perth (1842). The use of the North Insch at Perth by the Royal Perth Golf Club continued a tradition of golf being played on the gravel terraces beside the Tay which goes back to the sixteenth century.

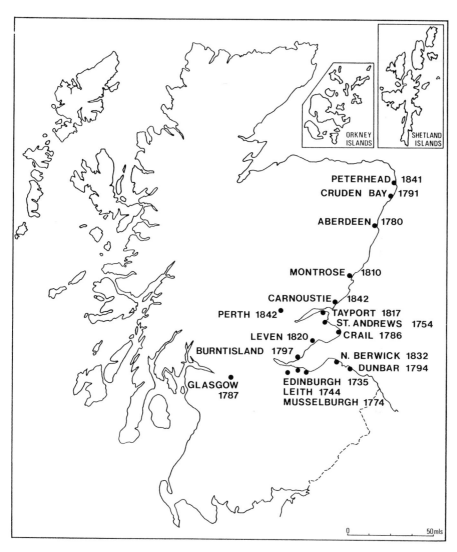

FIG2.2 The location of golf courses: 1730–1849.

EARLY EXPANSION 1850-79

This period saw the beginning of the expansion of golf throughout Scotland. A further 26 courses were opened between 1850 and 1879 (Fig 2.3). The railway reached St Andrews in 1851, the Royal and Ancient clubhouse was built in 1854 and the first Open Championship was held in 1860. The population of Scotland also increased at a steady rate: 1800—1.6 million; 1850—2.9 million; 1880—3.4 million (Fig 2.4). After 1850, the growth in urban population was a significant contributor (50–60 per cent) to the total population with the population of Edinburgh increasing by 30 per cent, and that of Glasgow by nearly 60 per cent between 1850 and 1880. This was also the railway era in Scotland. By 1860 the rail links between Glasgow and Edinburgh, Glasgow and Carlisle, Edinburgh and North Berwick, Edinburgh and Carlisle, Glasgow/ Edinburgh and Stirling, Perth, Dundee, Aberdeen, Fraserburgh, Elgin, and Inverness had been completed. By 1880 the network had been extended to Oban in the west and Wick and Thurso in the north-east. The opening up of Scotland by the provision of a rail network coincided with a marked change in attitude to the Highlands. The area became fashionable as a place to take a holiday or buy property. Such attitudes stemmed from the decision by Queen Victoria to buy the Balmoral Estates in 1852 and to undertake numerous regal tours in Scotland. The period 1860–80 saw the foundations of the modern Scottish tourist industry being laid. The provision of golf courses in rural areas was no longer to depend only on local demand as there would be a desire by visitors to play golf as part of a holiday. The relentless impact of the Industrial Revolution was beginning to produce a relatively wealthy upper middle class who were mobile and had sufficient free time to engage in sporting activities. The main impact of visiting golfers was yet to come but the signs of its beginnings can be seen in the spread of golf courses up to 1879.

Of the 26 courses opened between 1850 and 1879, 18 were on coastal sites—most of them links courses on the east coast of Scotland (Fig 2.3). Courses at Prestwick (1851), Machrihanish (1876) and Troon (1878) heralded the expansion of golf around the shores of the Firth of Clyde. There were also signs of the first serious attempt to play golf at inland sites. Of particular interest is the opening of a course at Lanark in 1851. The course was located on a spread of fluvioglacial sand and gravel with an irregular surface topography of ridges, mounds and hollows. The site would have been well-drained and would have had many of the characteristics of true links land (see

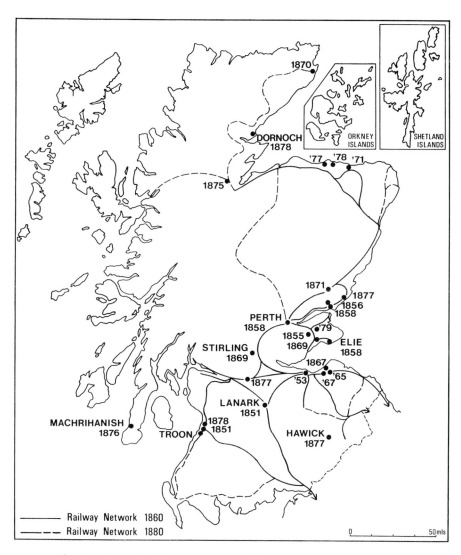

FIG2.3 The location of golf courses opened between 1850 and 1879 and the railway network in existence in 1860 and 1880.

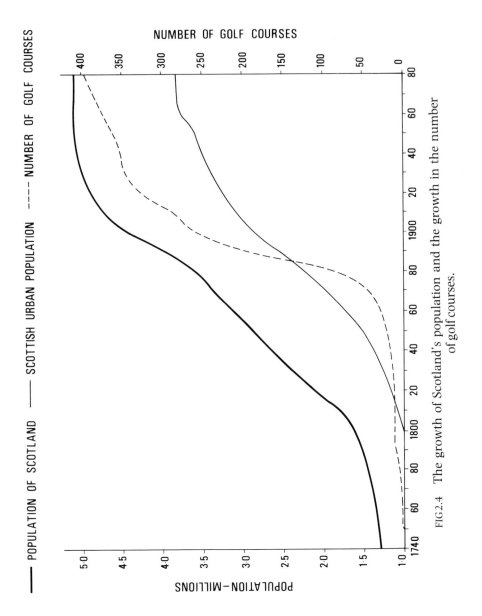

FIG 2.4   The growth of Scotland's population and the growth in the number of golf courses.

Chapter 3). Other inland courses existed at Perth (1858) on the gravel terrace at the North Inch on the banks of the Tay, at Haddington (1865), Stirling (1869), Forfar (1871), Hawick (1877), Airdrie (1877) and Ladybank (1879) in Fife. Little is known about the early character of these courses. The first publication which lists Scottish golf courses is *The Golfers Manual* by 'A Keen Hand', published in 1857. It contains one or two pieces of information which indicate some of the problems faced by the golfers of this period. With reference to the Bruntsfield links in Edinburgh the author states: 'The Links, situated on the outskirts of Edinburgh, possesses a clay sub-soil, with grass which grows too luxuriantly for good play during summer, but during other seasons of the year, the course is in pretty good order.' Referring to the course on the North Inch at Perth the author states '. . . from the thick growth of the grass, mole-heaps, and absence of hazards, the play is very monotonous. The principal time for play is autumn and spring'. This publication also provides information about the dates on which medal competitions were played on each of the courses. The most common months for such competitions were April, May, September and October. On some of the links courses, medal competitions were also held in July and August. It must be remembered that golf courses of the period were more or less in their natural state. The fine grasses of the links land, cropped by rabbits and sheep could be played on throughout the year but would be at their best in spring and autumn. The turf of inland courses would produce longer grass and would be less suitable for play in July and August. On many courses there was little formal management of the fairways and greens. Old Tom Morris was appointed Green Keeper to the Royal and Ancient in 1865, a hole cutter was patented in 1869 and iron bands were purchased for the holes on the Elie course in 1874. The committee of the Earlsferry and Elie Golf Club authorised on 17 August 1877, the purchase of a lawnmower for the putting greens (A M Drysdale, 1975). This was a major investment because the total income of the club for 1871–2 was £28. 1s. 0¼d., of which the wages of the greenkeeper accounted for £5. Expenditure was £27. 9s. 1d., leaving a surplus for the year of 11s1 1¼d.

It would appear that by the 1870s the first serious attempts at improving the conditions of both fairways and greens had begun. The part played by mowing machines in the improvement of golf courses is rather difficult to establish. The first grass cutting machine was invented in 1830 and the manufacture of such machines began in 1832. By 1852, Ransomes had produced some 1,500 machines, although in a publication describing the history of the company they

2.1 The 'Old Course', St Andrews. First, 17th and 18th fairways and the Swilken Burn.

2.2 The North Inch, Perth: one of Scotland's earliest inland golfing grounds.

state, 'Surprisingly, mechanised grass cutting was not generally accepted by golf courses until about 1890.' They produced their first horse drawn machine in 1870. It would appear that the Elie Golf Club committee were a very progressive group. There is an interesting photograph in the booklet *Ransomes—A Great Tradition—150 Years of Grasscutting Technology 1832–1982*, of the first Ransomes motor mower purchased by the Royal and Ancient in 1911. Behind the somewhat cumbersome machine can be seen the bridge over the Swilken Burn on the 18th fairway and there are numerous sheep grazing the fairway. There are letters in the Royal and Ancient archives from the early 1890s from the Town Clerk of St Andrews offering the pasturage of the Links to the Secretary of the Royal and Ancient (himself!). It would appear that sheep grazing plus rabbits were the main means of keeping the grass short throughout the period 1850–79. However, there are signs that both grass cutting by hand and by machine, along with other improvements in the course, had begun to take place. The management of both greens and fairways was a greater requirement on the inland courses than on the coastal links land.

By 1879 there were at least 43 golf courses in Scotland and some 50 golf clubs with some 4,000 members (including at least two ladies' clubs—St Andrews Ladies 1867 and Dunbar Ladies 1873). The first golf books had been published: *The Golfers Manual*, 1857; *Golfers Year Book*, 1866; *Golfers Handbook* 1880. The Royal and Ancient had built its clubhouse, appointed its first professional/greenkeeper and was beginning to develop its role as the administrator of the game of golf. The game had started to be played on inland sites and the foundations had been laid for the rapid expansion of the game which would take place during the next three decades (Pl. 2.1).

THE GOLFING BOOM   1880–1909

This was the period of great expansion of golf in Scotland. Two hundred and twenty-three golf courses (56 per cent of all of today's Scottish courses) were opened—180 of 18 holes and 43 of nine holes. The distribution of these golf courses (Fig 2.5) was such that apart from the Western Grampians and North-West Highlands all other parts of the country had at least one golf course within a 25 mile radius of any major settlement. The largest increase in the number of golf courses was in Strathclyde Region (Table 2.4) where 86 courses were opened between 1890 and 1909. More specifically, there were 47 new courses opened in and around Glasgow and 18 in and around Edinburgh.

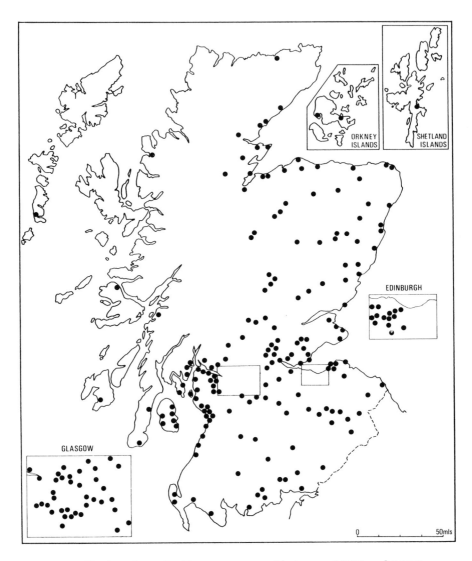

FIG 2.5   The location of golf courses opened between 1880 and 1909.

TABLE 2.4

NUMBER OF COURSES OPENED EACH YEAR IN EACH REGION 1880–1909.
NUMBER OF NINE-HOLE COURSES IN BRACKETS

	A	B	C	D	Total
1880	4(1)	2(1)	—	—	6(2)
1881	—	—	—	—	—
1882	—	—	—	—	—
1883	(1)	—	—	2	3(1)
1884	3	—	—	—	3
1885	—	—	1	(1)	2(1)
1886	(1)	—	—	—	1(1)
1887	(1)	3	2	1	7(1)
1888	—	3	—	5	8
1889	—	3(1)	1	5	9(1)
1890	2	3(1)	3(2)	6	14(3)
1891	1	5(1)	3(1)	2(1)	11(3)
1892	7(1)	7(1)	—	1	15(2)
1893	3	3	1	1	8
1894	4(2)	3	3(1)	3(2)	13(5)
1895	(1)	10(1)	4(3)	2(1)	17(3)
1896	4(2)	8(2)	—	(1)	13(5)
1897	2(1)	4	2	—	8(1)
1898	(1)	1	2(1)	2(1)	6(3)
1899	(1)	1	2(1)	5(2)	9(4)
1900	1	4(1)	1	1	7(1)
1901	—	2	3	1	6
1902	2(1)	—	1	—	2(1)
1903	2	3	2(1)	1	8(1)
1904	(1)	4	2	2(1)	9(2)
1905	(2)	7	1	1	11(2)
1906	3	4	—	1	8
1907	1	4	—	1	6
1908	1	3	2	3(3)	9(3)
1909	1	2	2	2	7
					223(43)

Two distinct aspects of this rapid expansion require discussion. Firstly, this period saw the movement of golf away from predominantly coastal locations to inland sites. Of the 223 new courses, 157 were on inland sites and 66 on coastal sites. Secondly, the growth of the urban population in Scotland by nearly one million between 1870 and 1909 led to a great demand for suburban golf courses. The population of Scotland increased by one million between 1881 and 1911 with the population of Glasgow almost doubling (587,000 to 1,000,000) and Edinburgh's population increasing by 30 per cent (295,000 to 400,000) during the same period. By 1901 Scotland's urban population was 2.9 million (65 per cent) with 44 per cent of the total population living in west-central Scotland. It is therefore not at all surprising that the provision of golf courses in and around these rapidly growing areas was a major characteristic of the growth of golf in Scotland during this period. Although the majority of the new courses were related to the foundation of new private golf clubs primarily catering for the upper middle and upper classes, some 22 public courses existed in Scotland by 1909.

The growth of the urban centres of Greater Glasgow and Edinburgh was only partly responsible for the distribution pattern on Figure 2.5. It is not surprising that with the development of both land and water communications, numerous courses were opened around the Firth of Clyde. Similarly, the development of tourism in Dumfries and Galloway, the Borders (particularly the Tweed valley) and in the Grampians (particularly the Tay, Dee and Spey valleys) led to the creation of new golf courses.

The pattern of growth in the number of golf courses opened between 1880 and 1909 was not even (Fig 2.6, Table 2.4). The major expansion took place between 1890 and 1894 with 61 new courses with a further 49 being opened between 1895 and 1899. The largest number of new courses opened in any one year—17 was in 1895.

Certain important growth points in Scottish golf were established during this period. The large number of courses established in and around Glasgow and Edinburgh has already been noted. East Lothian doubled its number of courses, and St Andrews added two additional courses alongside the Old Course. The basis of the modern map of Scottish golf courses had been clearly established by the end of the first decade of this century.

The expansion of the inland courses not only reflected a major increase in demand for courses, but a major improvement in the ability of greenkeepers to control the condition of the course. It was not necessary to be totally dependent on rabbits and sheep to keep the fairways and greens in reasonable playing condition. No longer was it necessary to be totally dependent on the dune ridges, intervening hollows, sand spreads and other natural phenomena for the creation of a golf course. While coastal links land was relatively well-drained, many inland sites required some drainage. While the position of tees and greens had evolved over many years on the old links courses many of the new courses had various possibilities to offer both in lay-out, landform modification, removal of trees and bushes and the creation of hazards. Such decisions were to be made by experienced and successful players of the game. The winners of championships

NUMBER OF NEW GOLF COURSES : 1880—1909

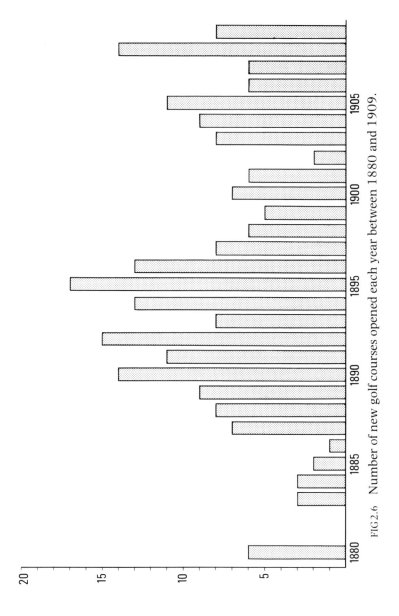

FIG.2.6   Number of new golf courses opened each year between 1880 and 1909.

became the designers of the new golf courses. The profession of golf course architect was beginning to emerge. F W Hawtree (1983) in his book *The Golf Course—Planning, Design, Construction* provides an interesting account of the history and philosophy of golf course architecture. He clearly establishes that at least until the 1920s all golf course designers accepted the natural landforms of the site chosen for a new course—the art consisted in making the best use of the natural landscape for the enjoyment of the game of golf. He states (p 6), 'Before horses and scoops were called in, all insisted that their first duty was to employ fully all the natural features of the site.'

Since the game of golf had developed almost entirely on coastal links land up until 1880 it is not surprising that on many of the inland courses at least some of the characteristics of those links were 'transported' to inland sites. Specifically, the creation of sand-filled bunkers became a part of the inland golfing landscape even if they were entirely artificial.

A wide variety of landforms was utilised by the designers of the new inland courses between 1880 and 1909 (see Chapters 3 and 4). It is probable that very little modification of the natural contours took place, and we know little of the way in which actual sites were chosen. Presumably a group of golfers would decide to establish a club and try to obtain, either by lease or purchase, the most suitable available piece of ground in their neighbourhood. They themselves might decide on the positioning of tees, fairways and greens, or they might invite a golf 'professional', on the basis of his wide experience and proven golfing skills, to advise on the best lay out. Two names dominated golf course design in Scotland at the turn of the century— Tom Morris ('Old Tom') 1821–1908, and Willie Park Jnr, 1864–1925.

Thomas Morris was born in St Andrews in 1821 and was apprenticed to Allan Robertson at the Old Course from 1839 to 1851. He had a major dispute with Robertson over the use of the gutta percha ball, so he moved to Prestwick as greenkeeper and professional, where he remained until 1865. He then returned to St Andrews, where he was the first professional appointed by the Royal and Ancient, which he remained until his retirement in 1904. Morris won the Open Championship on four occasions (1861, 1862, 1864, 1867). His son 'Young Tom' also won the Open four times before he was 22 years old, but he died at the age of 25. 'Old Tom' Morris advised on the design of the following Scottish golf courses: Askernish (South Uist), Barry, Carnoustie, Crail, Dornoch, Dunbar, Elie, Glasgow-Killermont, King James VI—Perth, Ladybank, Luffness New, Machrihanish, Muirfield, Prestwick, Royal Burgess—Edinburgh, St Andrews—New, Stirling and Tain.

Willie Park Jnr was born in Musselburgh in 1864 and died at the age of 61 in Edinburgh. From 1880 to 1894 he served as assistant greenkeeper and professional with his uncle, Mungo Park, at Ryton in England. He then returned to Musselburgh to join his father (Willie Park Snr who had won the first Open Championship in Prestwick in 1860) in the club and ball making firm of W Park & Son. He won the Open Championship in 1887 and 1889 and was runner up in 1898. He subsequently designed courses in England (Sunningdale and Huntercombe) and in the United States (1895-8 and 1916-24). Sir Guy Campbell called him the doyen of course architects and credited him with setting the standards for the many designers who followed him. He designed over 70 courses in the USA and Canada and over 100 in Britain, including the following in Scotland: Baberton, Barnton, Bathgate, Biggar, Bo'ness, Bridge of Weir, Bruntsfield Links, Burntisland, Carnoustie, Crieff, Dalkeith, Duddingston, Forres, Gailes, Glasgow Killermont, Glencorse, Granton on Spey, Gullane, Innellan, Innerleithen, Jedburgh, Kilspindie, Melrose, Monifieth, Montrose, Murrayfield, Luffness New, Selkirk, Shiskine, St Boswells, Torwoodlee, Turnhouse.

Another great name in Scottish golf at this time was James Braid. Born in Earlsferry in 1870 he won the Open Championship in 1901, 1905, 1906, 1908 and 1910. He went on to make a major contribution to golf course design in the 1920s and 1930s, which will be discussed in the next section.

Undoubtedly, the condition of golf courses began to improve during the last decade of the nineteenth century. The employment of greenkeepers and general workmen along with the use of grass cutting machines and other implements must have radically changed the conditon of golf courses. Ransomes were selling lawnmowers to golf clubs throughout the United Kingdom during the 1890s. Initially they were designed for use on the greens and tees, but from 1870 horse drawn mowers were available which may have been used to cut fairways. A horse drawn machine, specially designed for cutting rough golf courses, was introduced by Ransomes in 1905. Ransomes also produced the world's first petrol driven lawn mower in 1902, and by 1903 they were producing four models—one with a 30 inch cut which was described as 'a specially powerful machine for steep inclines and golf links'. It is believed that the Royal and Ancient had purchased one of these motor mowers in 1911.

Not only had a great expansion of golfing facilities taken place at the turn of the century, but the quality of those courses must have improved dramatically as both man and machine were put to work both during construction and subsequent maintenance. Golf was no longer a casual game played on common lands. The era of the golf club committee, the club secretary and of income and expenditure accounts had arrived. Although still very dependent on the natural contours of the land, course design and course management had begun to change the character of the game of golf. Many of the suburban courses had to be designed to fit relatively small areas: quite often a single farm of approximately 100 acres would be purchased, and in order to provide 18 holes the lay-out required parallel alignment of fairways. In other circumstances, such as the utilisaion of the parkland of a large mansion, a more expansive approach was possible. Already the debate had begun as to whether inland courses could ever be regarded as a true test of golfing skill since they were so obviously different from the classic coastal links.

CONSOLIDATION 1910–49

There were 88 new courses opened during this 39-year period (Figs 2.7 and 2.8) and there were three distinct phases of development with two periods of stagnation.

The expansion in the number of golf courses which characterised the turn of the century continued between 1910 and 1913, when a further 18 courses were opened. The period of the Great War (1914–18) saw no new courses and several courses went out of existence. Parts of many other courses were used for agriculture. Between 1920 and 1930, 49 new courses were opened—22 of these between 1926 and 1930. A further 16 courses were added between 1932 and 1938. The advent of the Second World War (1939–45) meant that no new courses were opened until 1947. The pattern of this growth in the number of golf courses was very similar to that identified for the period 1880–1910. Of the 88 courses only ten were at coastal locations, with a large proportion (50 per cent) of the others being in the urbanised central belt—20 new courses in and around Glasgow and 12 new courses in and around Edinburgh. The demand for golf courses in suburban locations was still growing but total population growth had begun to lessen and the effects of two World Wars and the financial depression of the nineteen-twenties and early nineteen-thirties obviously took their toll.

It was during this period that the concept of the golf resort was introduced to Scotland. In one sense, St Andrews was the forerunner of this type of development, but it had developed in association with a public links course of great antiquity and tradition. Hotels had already been built by the turn of the century in St Andrews, as had also the

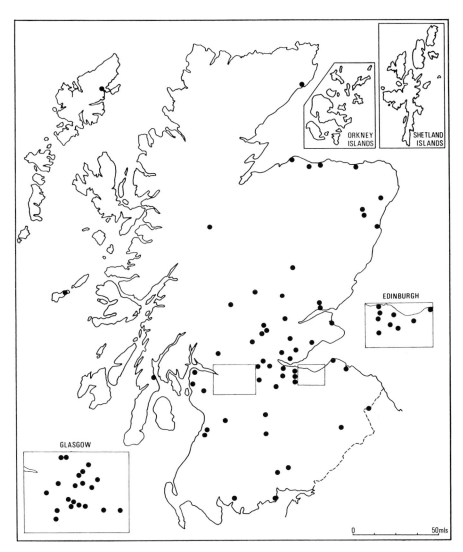

FIG 2.7   The location of golf courses opened between 1910 and 1949.

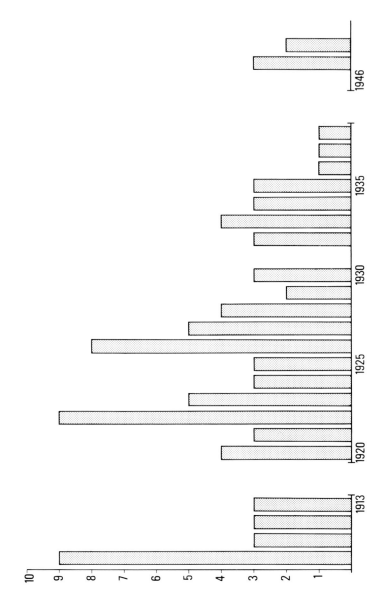

FIG 2.8   Number of new golf courses opened between 1910 and 1949.

New and Jubilee courses. The Eden course was added in 1912. The four courses and the general character of the university town began to attract many visitors. The first purpose-built golf resort was developed at Turnberry by the Glasgow and South Western Railway. A branch line was opened from Ayr, allowing frequent train services from Glasgow and a direct sleeper service from London. By 1907 Turnberry had become a recognised golfing centre with a first class hotel. During both World Wars the golf courses were requisitioned for military use. A similar development was undertaken at Gleneagles by the Caledonian Railway Company. The construction of the Gleneagles Hotel began in 1914 but was interrupted by the First World War. Work was resumed in 1922, with James Braid designing both the King's and Queen's courses which were opened in 1924. It is perhaps surprising that other golf resorts on the scale of Turnberry and Gleneagles have not yet been developed in Scotland.

One name above all others dominated the profession of golf course designer during this period. James Braid was born in Earlsferry, Fife, in 1870. He became an apprentice carpenter in St Andrews, played his first professional tournament in 1894 and was appointed Professional at the Romford Golf Club in England in 1896 before moving to Walton Heath Golf Club in 1906. Braid, along with Taylor and Vardon, were the 'Great Triumvirate' of competitive golf during the first 20 years of the twentieth century. After winning five Open Championships, Braid devoted a great deal of his time to golf course architecture but, because he hated travelling, many of his designs were based on the analysis of topographic maps from which he produced detailed and accurate working drawings. He designed some 60 courses in England and the following 38 courses in Scotland: Airdrie, Ayr Bellisle, Ayr Seafield, Balmore, Blairgowrie, Blairmore & Strone, Boat of Garten, Brechin, Brora, Carnoustie Burnside, Cawder, Cowal, Crow Wood, Dalmahoy, Deaconsbank, Dullatur, Edzell, Forfar, Forres, Glenbervie, Glencruitten, Gleneagles (King's and Queen's), Greenock, Hayston, Hilton Park, Kingsknowe, Powfoot, Rothesay, Routenburn, Preston Grange, Stranraer, Turnhouse, Monkton Hall, Crieff, Elie, Murcar and Nairn.

The number and distribution of golf courses in Scotland had been largely established by the turn of the century. In 1900 there was one course for every 16,000 people in Scotland. This had only changed to one for every 14,000 by 1950. The great diversity in golf course types will be discussed in subsequent chapters. The game of golf remained accessible to a very wide cross-section of the Scottish people. Large numbers of golf clubs in rural areas provided very cheap golf in relatively unsophisticated circumstances. Numerous public courses in the large cities provided similar golfing opportunities in the urban and suburban setting. At the same time, high quality courses associated with sophisticated clubhouse facilities were developed by some private clubs and by resort developers. This wide range in the character of golf courses remains one of the most distinctive features of Scottish golf. It is also a striking feature of Scottish golf courses that although during the period 1910–49 developments in earth-moving equipment gave much greater scope to the golf course architect to make changes in the land surface on which courses were being laid out, the vast majority of Scottish courses show little sign of landform modification. While the detailed morphology and position of tees, greens and bunkers may reflect the work of man and machine, most Scottish golf courses owe their general character to the long history of geological and biological processes which had created the landscapes utilised by golf course architects.

STEADY GROWTH   1950–86

There were 46 courses opened in Scotland during this period, spread fairly evenly over the entire country (Fig 2.9). This was a period of slow but steady growth (Table 2.3). There were no new courses opened in and around Edinburgh, and only one in Dumfries, Galloway and the Borders. There were ten new courses opened in and around Glasgow—four of them associated with the new town developments at East Kilbride and Cumbernauld. The new towns at Glenrothes and Livingston also had golf courses constructed. Two courses (the Princes and Glen Devon) were added to the Gleneagles golf complex, and additional courses were opened at St Andrews (Balgove) and Carnoustie. Industrial developments at Fort William and Invergordon saw courses opened close to each of these towns and attempts to encourage additional tourism saw courses opened on Mull, Skye, and in the Spey Valley. The most northerly course on mainland Scotland was opened at Thurso in 1964. Two hotel-based projects were opened during this period—one at Gleddoch House (1974) to the west of Glasgow, and the other at Murrayshall (1980) to the east of Perth. It is interesting to note that 12 of the 46 new courses were public courses primarily provided and administered by municipal authorities.

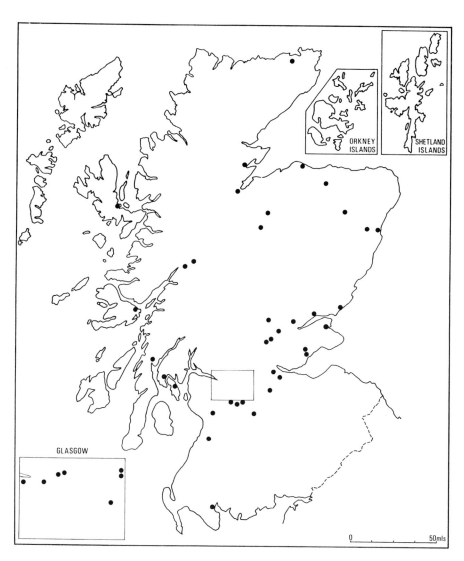

FIG 2.9   The location of golf courses opened between 1950 and 1986.

RECENT DEVELOPMENTS AND PLANS FOR THE FUTURE

A few golf courses have opened since 1986 and numerous press statements have referred to projects which, if they all materialise, will involve a total investment of some £600 million in golf-related projects in Scotland. In 1987 a £1.5 million hotel and golf course development was opened at Letham Grange near Arbroath. At the other end of the golfing spectrum, three nine-hole courses are planned in Argyll, at Dalmally, Taynuilt and Inverary. The total investment for the three courses is only of the order of £150,000, but they will be an excellent addition to the golfing scene in Argyll, both for residents and tourists. The course at Dalmally was opened in 1987.

Only one genuine new 18-hole golf club course has emerged in recent years. The Newmachar Golf Club at Hawkshill, 8 miles north of Aberdeen was founded in 1979 in response to long waiting lists for membership of the other Aberdeen courses. In 1981, 135 acres of land were purchased and Dave Thomas designed a 6,782 yard, par 72 course. The total investment in this project was about £500,000. The course will be opened for play in 1989.

Many of the large-scale projects consist of hotels, leisure centres, time-share units and up-market housing associated with one or more new golf courses. One of these is at Cumbernauld: the new course was designed by Dave Thomas in association with Seve Ballesteros. A 50-bedroom hotel and 400 houses will be built alongside the golf course with a total investment of £40 million. Other similar projects have been announced for Archerfield near Muirfield in East Lothian, and at Dunbar and Livingston. Plans for a golf course village consisting of 200 luxury houses, a 150-bedroom hotel and a tournament-class golf course at Cardrona near Peebles have been published, the estimated investment being £30 million.

As part of a wider development of public golf facilities, a consortium consisting of the PGA European Tour, McAlpines and the Wholesale Co-operative Society plan to build five golf courses incorporating housing developments throughout Britain, each project involving an investment of £30 million. It is proposed that one of these developments be in Scotland at Irvine. Other golf developments in the west of Scotland are planned at Loch Lomond, Fintry (north-east of Glasgow), Ochiltree in Ayrshire and Kilmartin in Argyll.

St Andrews also has some major developments planned to cope with the ever increasing demands on its golf facilities. The Jubilee course has been extended to 6,700 yards by golf architect Donald Steel, with the construction of eight new greens and 12 new tees. There is to be a new clubhouse, on the right side of the first fairway of the Old Course, along with a 250-space car park. The Eden course is also to be improved and a new 18-hole course is to be constructed at Strathtyrum, along with another new clubhouse and driving range. Plans are also well in hand to build the first British Golf Museum adjacent to the R and A Clubhouse, although this project has run into some controversy over the architectural character of the new building. The total investment in these projects is of the order of £5 million. Some would argue that such developments are long overdue if St Andrews wishes to continue its role as one of the outstanding golf resorts in the world.

Assuming that most of the above proposed developments materialise during the next decade, about 12 new golf courses will be constructed in Scotland. The justification for these new developments is the increasing demand both by residents and tourists for good quality golf courses. It has only been during the past few years that there has been a growing realisation of the importance of golf in the Scottish economy. The first serious study of the golfing industry in Scotland, with particular reference to the development and marketing of golf facilities, was undertaken recently by the Scottish Tourist Board. The results of that investigation were published by the STB in 1988 under the title 'Golf, Staying Ahead of the Game'. The Board recognise that golf is now big business in Scotland with over 2 million rounds of golf played by visitors rather than local members in 1986, and these visitors generated over £6 million of income. It is estimated that golfers visiting Scotland on organised tours generate £5 million of income to the carriers and hoteliers. The STB also recognise that, 'Whilst golf plays a crucial role in Scottish Tourism, it has to be recognised that, with few exceptions, courses have not been developed for tourism but for the local resident population.' It is in this context that many of the new developments 'are being planned to cater for the visiting golfer'. The potential for attracting North American, European and Japanese visitors to the 'Home of Golf' is indeed considerable. Unfortunately the 'honey pot syndrome' tends to produce over-crowding on the famous courses at St Andrews, Gleneagles, Turnberry, Muirfield and Troon. The Scottish people and the overseas visitors are now benefiting from the enthusiasm and foresight of the golfers of the late nineteenth and early twentieth centuries. Nowhere else in the world is there such a variety of golf courses in such a relatively small area.

Chapter 3

GOLFING ENVIRONMENTS

Although a golf course only occupies 100 to 150 acres of land its character is greatly influenced by the physical environment of its particular location. This physical environment consists of rocks, landforms, soil, vegetation and weather. The golf course architect may have created a few bunkers or mounds and constructed elevated tees or plateau greens, but the general character of a golf course is usually strongly related to its natural environment. Many of Scotland's golf courses were laid out before mechanical earth-moving equipment was available and therefore tend to incorporate many natural features. Not only the course itself but the surrounding scenery (or landscape) and the weather conditions all contribute to the golfing environment. This chapter is concerned with how these golfing environments originated and how they vary within Scotland.

Despite being a small country, Scotland (total area 28,000 square miles) has a great many different physical environments and therefore there is considerable variety in the available golfing environments. To understand how these environments have been created it is necessary to look back into the geological history of Scotland because the present environment has evolved over many millions of years. The early geological history of the country was responsible for the arrangement of rock types and structures which constitute the basic framework of the country. The erosional work of rivers carved valleys in the upland areas while the same rivers transported the eroded material to the lowlands and the coast. Major changes in the landforms of Scotland were brought about, during the past two million years, by the events collectively known as 'The Great Ice Age'. On numerous occasions the climate of Scotland cooled to such an extent that glaciers developed and merged into great ice sheets which buried the land surface. The last glaciers only disappeared some 10,000 years ago and the erosional and depositional activities of glacier ice and its associated meltwaters were responsible for many of the landforms and surface deposits seen in Scotland today. As the ice sheets expanded and retreated relative sea level around the Scottish coastline rose and fell by as much as 300 feet and the position of the coastline changed. After the last ice sheet retreated the new land surface was colonised by plants and animals. By 9,000 years ago much of Scotland was covered by forests—birch and oak in the lowlands and in the south and west, and by pine and birch in the north and on high ground. The earliest evidence, in Scotland, of man's colonisation of the natural environment dates to about 8,000 years ago. In the subsequent period both natural and man-induced changes have led to the destruction of much of the natural woodland and to the creation of vast areas of peat and heather moorland.

Before examining how the geological and vegetational history of Scotland have influenced the character of it's golf courses it is necessary to clarify the meaning of several terms. The natural environment is produced by the operation of natural processes. The type of natural processes which operate in any area are largely controlled by the climate of that area. The climate determines the type of geological processes which create landforms and the range of animal and plant species which occupy an area. Together, the surface forms, drainage and natural vegetation comprise the natural landscape. When a natural landscape is occupied and used by man it can be extensively modified and the adjective 'natural' has to be removed. Scotland's present landscapes are far from natural. Even though the landforms, which constitute a major part of any landscape, are entirely the product of natural processes there are few parts of Scotland where man's use of the land has not modified the vegetation, the soil and the general appearance of the landscape.

THE GEOLOGICAL FRAMEWORK

There is a strong north-east to south-west trend in several important geological structures in Scotland (Fig 3.1). These structures are related to the Caledonian earth movements which occurred some 500 million years ago. Three major faults divide the country into four distinct geological regions: the Southern Upland Boundary Fault, the Highland Boundary Fault and the Great Glen Fault.

Much of the area to the south of the Southern Upland Boundary Fault consists of closely folded sedimentary rocks which have been eroded to produce the smooth, rounded slopes of the Southern Uplands. There are also important masses of granite in the south-west.

The so-called 'Midland Valley' of Scotland is bounded by major faults both to the north and south. This geological region is not one single valley as its name implies but consists of a series of sedimentary

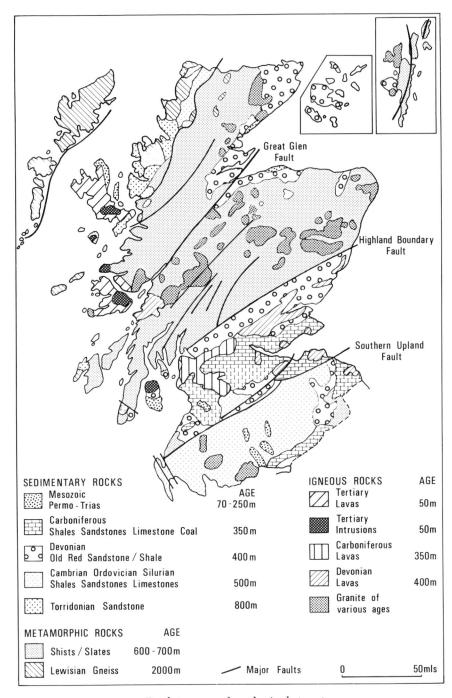

FIG 3.1   Rock types and geological structures.

basins, mainly of Carboniferous (coal bearing) and Devonian age which form both lowlands and plateaux, separated by upland areas consisting of volcanic rocks. The volcanic rocks (mainly basalt) of Carboniferous age underlie the upland areas to the south and south-west of Glasgow and form the Kilpatrick and Campsie Hills. Volcanic rocks of Devonian age form part of the Pentland Hills, Ochil Hills and Sidlaw Hills.

North of the Highland Boundary Fault the geology is very complicated. Large parts of the Highlands are underlain by very ancient metamorphic rocks which, when eroded, tend to produce rather rugged scenery. There are important granitic masses in the eastern Grampians (e.g. the Cairngorms) and important areas of relatively recent volcanic rocks (Tertiary age: about 60 million years ago) in the west on the islands of Skye, Mull and Arran. The far north-west of Scotland and the Outer Hebrides are underlain by very ancient Lewisian metamorphic rocks. In great contrast to both the ancient metamorphic and more recent volcanic rocks are the stratified sandstones of Devonian age which underlie much of Caithness, Orkney and the areas around the Moray Firth.

Only in certain very specific circumstances can the solid rocks underlying a golf course directly influence the character of that course. The vast majority of golf courses are influenced by the unconsolidated sediments which usually cover the underlying solid rocks. However, in upland areas where glacial erosion has often laid bare the underlying solid rocks the character of those rocks certainly does influence the golfing environment. There are several courses in the Highlands where the rough metamorphic rocks give a rugged appearance to both fairways and rough. The most dramatic effect of a particular rock type on the character of golf courses is to be found in areas where the courses are built on land underlain by volcanic lavas. These lavas have a very distinctive 'layered' appearance and give the landscape a 'stepped' character. Because of the chemical character-istics of these lavas and their land-use history, golf courses built on these lavas are of the moorland type. Many such courses are to be found on the Clyde 'plateau basalts' around Glasgow. A most remark-able golf course built on the Tertiary lavas at Tobermory (Pl 3.1) on the island of Mull makes full use of both the relatively flat surfaces of individual lava flows and the steep cliff-faces produced by subsequent glacial erosion of the lavas.

It is in terms of the general landscapes in which golf courses are located that the underlying solid geology and structural history are of significance. Few golfers are so absorbed in their game that they are not aware of the scenery which surrounds them. The superb views

3.1 Tobermory, Mull. A moorland course on Tertiary lavas.

from the Tobermory course along the Sound of Mull or up Loch Sunart are very much a product of the geological history of that area—largely a volcanic landscape. The courses laid out on the sands and gravels of the Spey Valley have the marvellous backdrop of the granite massif of the Cairngorms. In the Southern Uplands many of the courses are to be found on valley-floors or valley-sides and yet it is the rounded hills so characteristic of much of this region which provide the scenic setting. Even on links courses it is the rock type and geological history of the landward margin of the wind-blown sand which give such courses their broader landscape characteristics.

THE IMPACT OF THE ICE AGE

No other geological event had a greater influence on golfing environments than the Ice Age. During the past two million years there have been major fluctuations in Scotland's climate. We now live in an Interglacial Period which, if geological history repeats itself, is coming to an end. There may have been as many as 20 glacial periods each lasting about 100,000 years, separated by interglacial periods each lasting about 10,000 to 15,000 years during the last two million years. During the glacial periods, average January and July temperatures in Scotland at sea level were lowered by at least 10° centigrade. Such changes in climate allowed much more precipitation to fall as snow and therefore glaciers were able to develop and expand into ice sheets. The last great ice sheet to develop in Scotland began to form about 27,000 years ago and finally melted away about 10,000 years ago. As the last ice sheet destroyed much of the evidence of its predecessors we know more about the impact of the last glaciation than we do about the many earlier ones. Because the last ice sheet had such a major effect on the Scottish landscape, and therefore on the character of the land used for golf courses, it is necessary to examine the history of the environmental changes brought about by that ice sheet.

The existence of a great ice sheet which covered Scotland in the recent geological past has been known since the middle of the last century (Price, 1983). Individual glaciers began in valley heads (corries) and expanded down valleys as snow accumulation increased. The main centres of ice accumulation were in the western Highlands and islands, the western Southern Uplands and eastern Grampians (Fig 3.2). Individual valley glaciers became thicker and longer and eventually over-topped the interfluves and spread out across the lowlands, and developed into a major ice sheet. It is highly likely that the surface of this ice sheet attained a maximum altitude in excess of 5,000 feet and over central Scotland the ice was probably more than 4,000 feet thick. By about 20,000 years ago the entire mainland and most, if not all, of the islands and much of the area now covered by less than 300 feet of sea water was buried by glacial ice.

Glacial ice moving forward under the force of gravity is capable of a great deal of erosion. Valleys that have been occupied by glaciers tend to be straight and steep-sided—such glacial troughs are widespread throughout the Highlands and Southern Uplands. The material eroded by the moving ice is incorporated in the ice and transported some distance only to be deposited as a sediment—known as till— when the ice melts. Much of the till, consisting of angular rock fragments in a clay/silt matrix is deposited beneath the glacier or ice sheet during ice wastage (melting). Till is a very widespread surface material in Scotland. It ranges from one to fifty feet in thickness and covers much of the lowlands and valley sides. Under certain circumstances the till deposits are built into hummocks or ridges known as moraines. When till is deposited while the ice sheet is still moving forward, a very distinctive landform known as a drumlin (Pl 3.2) is created. A drumlin is a streamlined hill shaped like half an egg. These elongated mounds are usually 30 to 100 feet high and 200

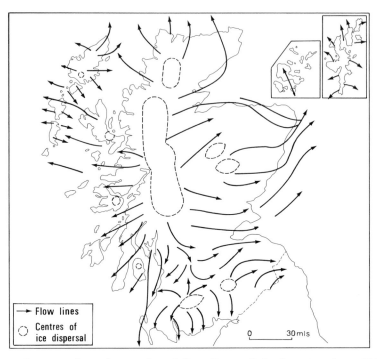

FIG 3.2   Centres of ice dispersal and flow lines of the last ice sheet (18,000 years before present).

to 1,000 yards in length. They often have steep slopes facing the former direction of ice movement and gentle streamlined tails. Drumlins often occur in groups or swarms (Fig 3.3) and therefore produce a very distinctive landscape with a strong lineation, quite steep slopes and often poor drainage conditions (heavy soils). There are numerous golf courses in drumlin landscapes around Glasgow (see Chapter 4).

  A period of glaciation means that large quantities of water are locked up in the glaciers and ice sheets. When the climate begins to warm up, vast quantities of meltwater are released in a relatively short period of time. These meltwaters are capable of eroding deep channels in solid rock and transporting large quantities of rock debris entrapped in the ice. This debris is released as the ice melts and the rapidly flowing meltwaters modify the rock debris to produce rounded gravel and sand (Pl 3.3). Large areas of Scotland are covered by these sand and gravel deposits, (fluvioglacial deposits). These deposits have a variety of forms depending on how and where they were deposited (Fig 3.4). Where valley systems debouch onto the lowlands, large fans

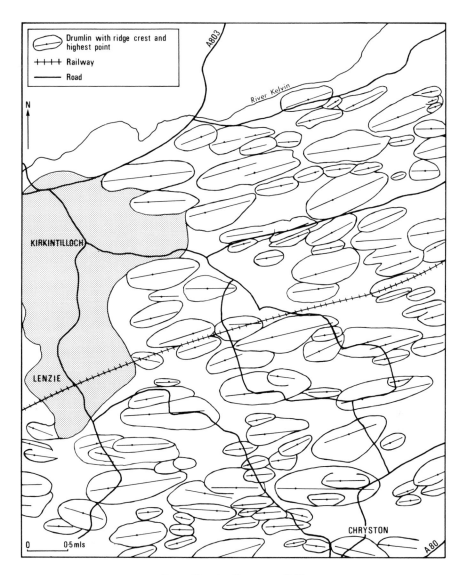

FIG 3.3 Drumlins to the east of Glasgow.

3.2   A typical drumlin north-east of Glasgow.

3.3   Fluvioglacial sand and gravel in a kame terrace in the Spey Valley.

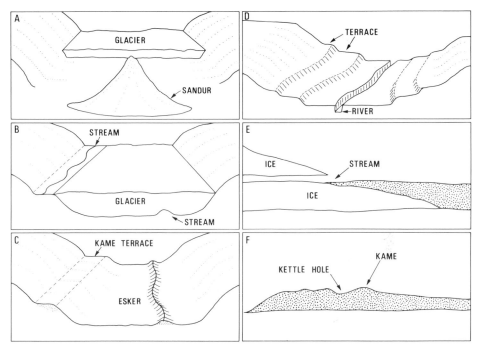

FIG 3.4   Landforms produced by the meltwaters of the last ice sheet.

A   The formation of an outwash fan (sandur) in front of a glacier.

B   Meltwater streams flowing along the lateral margin and in tunnels under the ice.

C   Lateral stream deposits (kame terraces) and tunnel deposits (esker ridges) after the glacier has melted.

D   River terraces produced by rivers cutting into sand and gravel deposits laid down on the valley floor by meltwaters.

E   A stream issuing from a glacier and depositing sand and gravel both on top of, and in front of the ice.

F   When the ice melts the spread of sand and gravel contains depressions (kettle holes) and mounds (kames).

of fluvioglacial sand and gravel have been deposited (e.g. near Blairgowrie). These gently sloping fans are known as outwash fans or sandar (an Icelandic term: singular = sandur). When the flow of meltwaters was confined by steep valley sides the floor of the valley became choked with sand and gravel which were later eroded by the river to produce river terraces. In some locations, fluvioglacial sand and gravel were deposited between a valley glacier and the valley side. When the glacier melted, the valley-side terrace was left abandoned—

these features are known as kame-terraces. Both on outwash fans and kame-terraces large blocks of glacier ice were sometimes buried by the fluvioglacial deposits and when the ice melted large enclosed depressions—kettle holes—were produced. When large quantities of glacier ice were buried by sand and gravel the subsequent melting of the buried ice produced a chaotic assemblage of mounds, ridges and depressions known as kame and kettle topography (Pl 3.4). Some large meltwater rivers were confined to tunnels in the glacier ice. When these tunnels became choked with fluvioglacial sand and gravel, long sinuous ridges known as eskers were produced (Pl 3.5). They are literally fossil river channel deposits which emerge after the glacier ice has melted.

These spreads, mounds, terraces and ridges, produced by the meltwaters of the last ice sheet to cover Scotland, have been extensively used as sites for golf courses. They represent the nearest inland equivalent to the classic links ground of the coastal golf courses. The similarities between windblown-sand landforms (links) and fluvioglacial sand and gravel landforms (sandar, kames, terraces, eskers) are numerous. Both sets of landforms are well-drained and support firm turf. Both sets of landforms are characterised by ridges and hollows and by short steep slopes which frequently change direction. Both sets of landforms consist of materials (sand and gravel) easily worked by man either with or without mechanical assistance. As was shown in Chapter 2, many of the early inland golf courses in Scotland were established on these relatively easily managed fluvioglacial deposits. It would appear that golfers and golf course architects have a considerable affinity for fine grained unconsolidated sediments whether they are deposited by wind or water.

Reference has already been made to the fact that a period of glaciation results in the 'locking up' of large quantities of water (precipitation) in the ice sheet. This water is extracted from the oceans and since it is stored in the ice sheet for long periods before being returned to the oceans, there is a world-wide fall in relative sea level (up to 300 feet) during periods of glaciation. However, the development of an ice mass several thousand feet thick on a land mass results in increased weight on the earth's crust beneath the ice sheet, which in turn produces a depression in the crust and a rise in local relative sea level. The manner in which these opposing tendencies operate during a period of glaciation to affect local relative sea level changes, need not concern us. The geological record around Scotland's coastline clearly demonstrates that such glacially-induced sea level changes have taken place. During the wastage of the last ice sheet (14,000–10,000 years ago) much of the land area of Scotland

3.4 Kames (mounds) and kettle holes (depressions) in sand and gravel deposits. The inland equivalent of links land.

3.5 Eskers: ridges of sand and gravel.

was still depressed by the weight of the last ice sheet and some of the oceanic waters of the world were still locked up in the large ice sheets which still existed in Northern Europe, North America and Antarctica. Relative sea level in the Firths of Moray, Tay, Forth and Clyde stood some 50–120 feet above present sea level. Marine cut platforms in Fife (Pl 3.6), and raised beaches in Jura (Pl 3.7), bear testimony to these former higher stands of sea level. Relative sea level continued to fall from these higher altitudes until about 8,500 years ago when the world's great ice sheets began to melt at such a rate that world-wide sea level began to rise rapidly. This sea level rise was sufficiently fast that it overtook the still rising land of Scotland and relative sea level rose around much of the Scottish coastline, reaching a maximum about 6,500 years ago. The relative rise in sea level was of the order of 15 to 40 feet depending on location. This rise in sea level, followed by the subsequent fall to present levels had a profound effect on the character of much of Scotland's coastline and on the provision of land subsequently used for golf courses. During the high stand of sea level, low lying areas particularly in the estuaries of the Tay, Forth, Clyde and Solway were inundated and large quantities of marine clays were deposited. When sea level later fell these marine clays were exposed to form the extensive flat-lands (carse lands) which now border the present shores of the Scottish estuaries. On more exposed coasts the high stand of the sea cut new cliff-lines and deposited raised beaches of sand and gravel (Pl 3.8). As the sea retreated from this old coastline (after 6,500 years before present) large sandy beaches (strands) were exposed. These intertidal sands became the source of vast quantities of sediment which could be picked up and transported by the wind to a new location further inland. The windblown sand was then spread across older raised platforms or raised beaches and frequently shaped into dune systems (Pl 3.9). One of Scotland's most distinctive golfing environments—the links—was therefore a product of changing sea levels which were in turn brought about by a period of glaciation.

Blown sand in the form of coastal dunes and 'links' occupy about 300 miles of Scotland's coastline (Fig 3.5). The total length of the Scottish coastline (including the islands) is about 7,500 miles, so the links only occupy four per cent. Although a small percentage, the links occupy four distinct regions, in only three of which have they been developed as golf courses. From North Berwick to Fraserburgh, links form a very significant part of the coastline and golf has a long history on many of them (St Andrews, Carnoustie, Aberdeen, Elie, Leven, Gullane). The second most important region is around the shores of the Moray Firth. The third region is in south-west Scotland

3.6 Raised marine platforms, Kincraig, Fife; evidence of former high sea levels.

3.7 Raised beach gravel over 100 feet above present sea level. West Loch Tarbert, Jura.

3.8   A post-glacial raised beach and abandoned cliffline, Kintyre.

3.9   Dune ridge (with marram grass), inter dune flat occupied by fairway and green, and former coastline (abandoned cliff behind white houses), Turnberry.

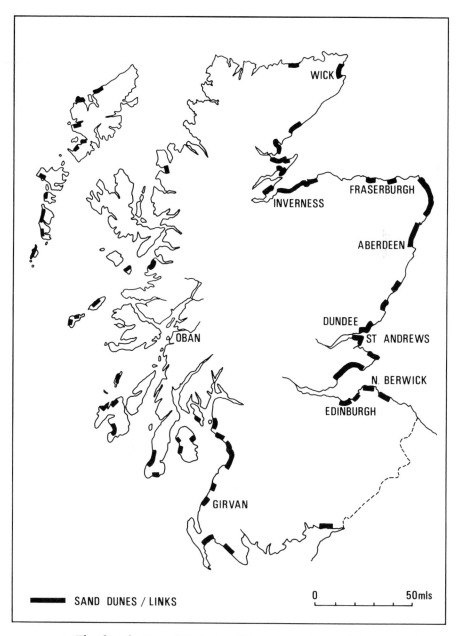

FIG 3.5 The distribution of 'links-land' (accumulations of blown sand).

around the shores of the Solway Firth and Firth of Clyde. The fourth region is made up primarily of the Inner and Outer Hebridean Islands and although there are many miles of links (known locally as machair) only in a few locations (Islay and South Uist) have they been used for golf courses.

Scottish links land occupies a relatively narrow zone (often less than one mile wide) along the coast. Since the source of the sand is the adjoining beach and the mode of transport is on-shore winds, the distance the sand extends inland is not great. It tends to accumulate in dune ridges which are usually 10 to 30 feet high, and, on average, blown sand rarely occurs higher than 75 feet above present sea level. There are limited cases, however, where blown sand occurs between 200 and 300 feet above sea level. The links land is, therefore, a narrow zone paralleling the present coastline where sand has accumulated in the form of ridges, hummocks and spreads. The zone is usually about half-a-mile wide and the ridges rarely more than 30 feet high. These sand accumulations are the product of aeolian transportation and subsequent deposition. The cause of deposition is related to a reduction of wind velocity as a result of the presence of colonising plants such as marram grass (*Ammophila arenaria*) and sea lyme (*Elymus arenarius*). The morphology of a links area is affected by the character of the depositional area (which is often a raised beach or raised marine-platform), wind strength and direction, the source and volume of blown sand, the nature of the vegetation cover and the local surface and subsurface drainage conditions. A typical links area has the following characteristics (Fig 3.6). Above the line reached by high water Spring tides, is the back shore where pioneer species begin to colonise the sand accumulations. The coastal dune, which is aligned parallel to the coastline and covered by long dune grasses (marram) may attain heights of between 10 and 40 feet in Scotland. It usually has a steeper seaward facing slope. The coastal dune may be succeeded inland either by a 'slack' separating it from an older dune ridge or by a gently undulating surface or 'links plain'. In some localities there may be more than one 'Old dune' ridge or there may be areas of sand hills or hummocks when dune ridges have migrated inland as a result of erosion in blow-outs. Since many of the links areas in Scotland are the product of the general fall in relative sea level, there is a series of parallel dune ridges with the oldest ridge (and often lowest) being on the landward margin of the system. Golf course architects have often taken full advantage of the sequence of ridges and depressions to be seen on links land. The fairways and greens are found on the short grass of the inter-dune areas (slacks or valleys) while the dune ridges and their tough marram grass form areas of 'rough'.

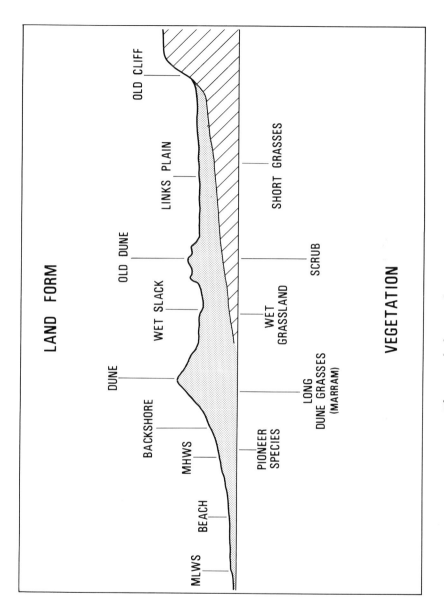

FIG 3.6   The morphology and vegetation of 'links'.

Links land has provided an ideal combination of variety of surface form and vegetation which together provide fairways and greens on firm short grass interspersed by rough grass (or heather or gorse) which may or may not be on steeper slopes. It is perhaps tempting to think of links land as a natural environment. However, the coastal links have been occupied by man for over 5,000 years and grazing of animals, the collection of whins, and in some cases intensive cultivation have led to extensive modifications to this environment. The golfers of the seventeenth and eighteenth centuries also acted as agents of erosion and no doubt initiated 'blow-outs' in dune ridges. It is often claimed that little modification by golf course architects and greens keepers has taken place on these 'natural' links when laying out golf courses. However, it should be remembered that even without mechanical aids the landforms of the links, which consist entirely of sand, were easily reshaped. At a very minimum, plateau tees and greens were constructed, bunkers excavated and in some cases dune ridges either removed or modified. Areas of rough grass, whin, heather and scrub were either trimmed or removed and new species of grass planted on tees and greens. One wonders just how much the present Old course at St Andrews has changed since the eighteenth century.

SCOTLAND'S VEGETATION

Although changing sea levels associated with the wastage of the last ice sheet in Scotland are of major significance to the character of coastal golf courses, other changes in the natural environment which followed the return to Interglacial (i.e. much milder climate) conditions are also significant. Within a thousand years of the last glaciers melting in the Highlands, much of Scotland was covered by trees. The forests in the south and in the Midland Valley were mainly of oak and birch. The forests at higher altitudes and throughout much of the Highlands were of birch and pine. There is no doubt that the earliest known human occupants of Scotland found it to be a wooded country even up to altitudes of 2,500 feet. Based on botanical records in the form of different species of pollen recovered from lake sediments and peat, it has been established that during the past 5,000 years a transformation in the vegetation of Scotland has taken place—the forests were gradually replaced by moorlands (heathlands), grassland, and arable land. Although there is much debate as to whether these vegetational changes were initiated by climatic changes (e.g. increased wetness), or by human activity in the form of creating woodland clearances for agriculture, or a combination of both, there can be little doubt that the forest cover declined in favour of the expansion of moorlands.

The decline of forests and increase in moorland is frequently associated with signs of human settlement and land cultivation. The Neolithic, Bronze Age and Iron Age populations certainly had an impact on the extent of forest cover in Scotland. Forests survived longest in the more remote regions. Further forest clearance was undertaken at the time of the Viking invasions in the first and second centuries AD and again in the sixteenth, seventeenth and eighteenth centuries when timber was in demand as charcoal for iron smelting. In the eighteenth and nineteenth centuries the increasing acreage of open country attracted sheep farmers and this development was the final act of forest destruction. The grass moors and heather moors are now a major feature of the Highlands, Islands, and Southern Uplands.

There are a few golf courses in Scotland where natural woodlands, either of oak or pine, are still present to give a distinctive character to the golfing landscape. There are many courses where the golfing landscape is dominated by heather moorland. It has also been common practice during the past 100 years to plant extensive acreages of imported pines. The fairways of many Scottish golf courses are lined by pine plantations or mixtures of Scots Pine, imported pines and birches.

After the major transformation from forest to moorland and/or cultivated land had largely been completed, it became fashionable for Scottish landowners to develop parklands around their large country houses in the eighteenth and nineteenth centuries. The essential characteristics of an area of parkland are that the area was enclosed by a fence and that there was a mixture of pasture land and woodland. Wealthy landowners employed landscape architects to plan their parklands so that pastures, elegant deciduous and coniferous trees, roadways lined with shrubs, lakes, lawns and flower gardens blended together to produce beautiful landscapes. Enclosure was the dominant idea so that in southern Scotland a fenced field of any description is often called a 'park'. The mixture of meadows and isolated trees (often oaks, elms or horse chestnuts) produces a landscape ideally suited to inland golf courses. Even where golf courses have been laid out in grassland (and even on moorland courses) trees have often been planted in an attempt to create a parkland landscape. However, the classic parkland courses are to be found in the grounds of large estates where changes in land use resulting from economic and social changes have led to the break up of the estate. In some instances fine Georgian or Victorian houses have been converted to golf clubhouses. Such parkland courses may now be found in suburban locations.

With few exceptions, the majority of inland golf courses in Scotland owe their landscape characteristics as much to their vegetation as to the landforms upon which they are built. Just over half of Scotland's golf courses (239) may be described as parkland courses.

The 126 coastal courses are primarily on links land but some are on high coastal platforms which have either a very thin cover of blown sand or none at all. In such circumstances a moorland vegetation with extensive areas of heather has developed. The vegetation of the coastal links courses has also been much modified by human interference. This has not always been a destructive influence because the addition of new grasses for greens and tees, the provision of fertilisers, irrigation and drainage, have all helped to stabilise some dune systems. Since most Scottish dune systems are less than 6,000 years old and since the dunes were often used as settlement sites by early man, it is likely that there has always been some human interference in the dune environment. Dunes are very rich in species of plants and animals. A survey of natural and introduced vascular plants on 43 of the more important dune systems in Britain showed that over 900 species occur on them (more than half of these species being introduced directly or indirectly by man). Because of the wide variety of habitats in a dune system there are quite rapid changes in vegetation across the system (Fig 3.6). There is little evidence of extensive natural woodlands on Scottish dunes but there have been numerous attempts at afforestation during the past two hundred years. Essentially the dune vegetation consists primarily of a variety of grasses and herbs, plus some scrub woodland.

From the few descriptions of the character of the early links golf courses there can be little doubt that they were very different to the manicured modern equivalents. Gorse and heather, marram grass and marsh plants have been controlled to constitute reasonable 'rough' and the tees and greens much improved by drainage, weeding, irrigation and re-seeding. The modern links course is hardly a part of nature's wilderness!

Although all aspects of the vegetation on Scotland's golf courses have been much modified by man, the trees, shrubs, grasses and herbs which do occur give particular characteristics to the courses. The rolling links land, where fairways of close-cropped grasses and herbs are separated by mounds or dunes covered by long marram grass, heather or gorse, are in great contrast to the inland parklands and moorlands. These vegetation patterns are themselves often related to variations in altitude which in turn produce some remarkable contrasts in local climate.

GOLFING WEATHER

Scotland has a cool, humid, temperate climate. At low altitudes extremes of heat or cold are rare and there are marked contrasts between the western and eastern parts of the country in wetness. A major characteristic of the Scottish environment is the variability in weather conditions from day to day and even on some occasions from hour to hour. There are few days in the year when a golfer can safely set out for a round of golf with the appropriate clothing for the conditions on the first tee and be certain that he will neither have to remove nor add items of clothing to adjust to changing weather conditions during the next three hours. A set of adequate rainwear and an umbrella are as important to a Scottish golfer as a set of golf clubs.

Golf is played throughout the year on most Scottish golf courses. The relatively mild and humid climate sustains the turf of fairways and greens throughout the year. The links courses of Ayrshire, East Lothian, Fife and north-east Scotland remain in the best condition and only periods of snow cover and/or intense frost cause the closure of such courses. Even in periods of heavy rain the sandy soil of these courses allows water to drain away fairly quickly. Inland courses may become water-logged during periods of heavy rain and become unplayable. Courses at higher altitudes—there are some 40 golf courses above 500 feet—have shorter playing seasons due either to excessive wetness, frost or snow. The Scottish climate deteriorates rapidly with increasing altitude and the maintenance of golf courses which are between 500 and 1,000 feet above sea level is both more difficult and more costly.

In addition to the condition of the course, weather conditions also determine the overall enjoyment of a game of golf and greatly affect the difficulty of the courses. Wind strength and direction are perhaps a greater influence on the character of a golf course than the landforms on which it has been built or the ideas of the golf course architect who built it. Since both wind strength and wind direction change from day to day or even within the period of one round of golf, the vagaries of weather add to the character of Scottish golf courses. On many links courses a relatively easy, par three hole of 175 yards may require only a seven iron in calm conditions but a three wood or even a driver when a strong wind is blowing in the golfer's face.

There are eight weather elements of particular interest to Scottish golfers: temperature, precipitation, hours of sunshine, fog, wind strength and direction, frost, and snow cover. Because there are some

TABLE 3.1

CLIMATIC DATA FOR A SELECTION OF SCOTTISH LOCATIONS

	Temperature Av. Daily Max °C		Gales	Bright Sunshine	Snow Lying	Precipitation m.m.			Two Driest Months
	JAN	JULY	Av No of Days	Hours per Year	No of Days	JAN	JULY	YEAR	
AYR	6.1	17.9	—	1333	6.1	83	81	918	March, April
GLASGOW	5.5	18.6	5.8	1266	9.7	94	74	982	March, April
LANARK	4.9	18.0	—	1227	28.0	67	73	813	April, June
EDINBURGH	5.9	18.6	—	1332	16.1	52	75	661	March, April
DUNBAR	—	—	—	1515	7.0	46	55	571	March, April
PERTH	5.3	19.2	—	1301	18.3	70	74	778	March, April
ST ANDREWS	—	—	9.5	1427	—	61	65	682	March, April
ABERDEEN	4.8	17.1	—	1376	3.8	80	83	847	March, April
NAIRN	5.7	17.7	—	1285	19.6	45	61	613	March, April
FORT WILLIAM	6.2	17.0	—	1055	—	191	149	2029	May, June
WICK	5.1	15.4	12.2	1264	19.2	82	63	788	April, May
TIREE	6.9	15.9	35.2	1420	4.5	115	85	1129	April, May

significant regional variations in each of these elements, a brief analysis of their characteristics will be given.

Temperature

The average daily maximum temperature in July at low altitudes is generally between 17° and 19° C (Table 3.1). In January mean daily maxima range between 6° C on the west coast and 5° C on the east coast. Winter golf can be quite pleasant so long as it is not raining, there is little or no wind, and the sun is shining.

Precipitation

There are some very marked regional contrasts in total precipitation received by different parts of Scotland with a distinct west to east gradient (Table 3.1 and Fig 3.7). The western parts of Scotland receive between 800mm (31 inches) and 3,000mm (120 inches) per year with only the Ayrshire coast and the Solway Firth coast receiving less than 1,200mm (47 inches). Large parts of the eastern

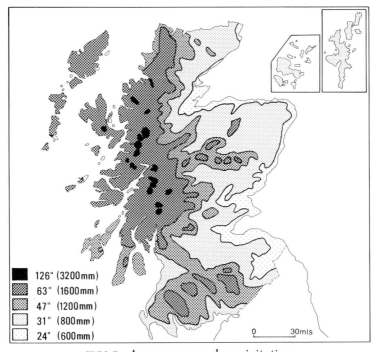

■	126" (3200mm)
▨	63" (1600mm)
▨	47" (1200mm)
□	31" (800mm)
□	24" (600mm)

FIG 3.7   Average annual precipitation.

half of the country receive between 800mm (31 inches) and
1,200mm (47 inches) but the east coast lowlands receive only 600-
800mm (24-31 inches). Throughout the country the three driest
months are usually March, April and May.

Hours of Sunshine; Fog

Scotland can hardly claim to be a sunny country (Table 3.1 and
Fig 3.8). Much of the country records less than 1,400 hours of bright
sunshine per year. In January nearly all of the country receives, on
average, less than one and a half hours of sunshine per day and this
rises to between four and five hours per day in July. The sunniest
places in Scotland are Dunbar (1,515 hours per year), St Andrews
(1,427 hours per year) and Tiree (1,420 hours per year), while west
coast locations tend to receive between 1,000 and 1,300 hours per
year. Many east coast locations would record much higher sunshine
figures if it were not for the development of coastal fog (locally known
as haar) during periods of calm, warm summer weather.

A feature of the summer in Scotland is the long period of twilight.

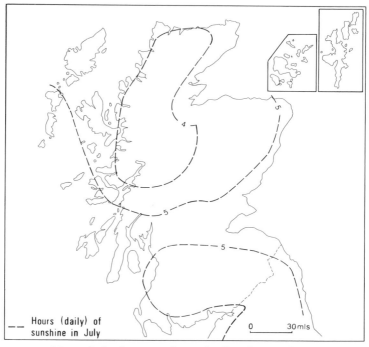

FIG 3.8   Mean daily duration (hours) of bright sunshine in July.

On the longest day there is no complete darkness in northern Scotland. For example, at midsummer, places in the Moray Firth area have more than 18 hours of daylight compared with about 16 hours at places in southern England. Throughout Scotland it is possible to play 18 holes of golf after 6 p.m. during the months of May, June, July and August.

Wind Strength and Direction

Over large areas of Scotland the average wind speed is about 8 to 10 knots (10 to 12 miles per hour) but along the west coast, in the Western and Northern Isles and at high altitudes, there is a much higher frequency of strong winds and gales. The strong winds are usually associated with the passage of winter depressions: even in the west and north of the country, prolonged periods of strong winds are unusual in summer. Gale force winds are recorded on average on six days per year in Glasgow, nine days per year in St Andrews, 12 days per year in Wick and 35 days per year on Tiree. At most locations the winds have a westerly component for about 50 per cent of the time and an easterly component for about 35 per cent of the time.

Frost

Frozen ground not only changes the character of a golf course but it inhibits plant growth and greens can be damaged by excessive use when they are frozen. Over much of Scotland, excluding the Western and Northern Isles, the coasts of the Firth of Clyde and the entire length of the east coast, frosts can occur at any time between mid-September and mid-May. The incidence of frost increases with altitude so that relatively high (over 300 feet) inland golf courses can experience frozen ground conditions for over half the year. When frost occurs on coastal links courses, which are generally very well drained, it may only last for a couple of hours after sunrise.

Snow Cover

With the exception of coastal lowlands (less than ten days per year) and areas of high ground over 2,000 feet (over 40 days per year) snow cover is experienced in Scotland on between ten and 40 days per year. The majority of golf courses are located in areas of relatively low frequency of snow cover—ten to 20 days per year.

Scotland contains a greater variety of golfing environments than any other country. The 425 golf courses reflect the complex environmental history of the country. Landscapes produced by ancient geological events contrast with those which were produced as a result of the events of the last Ice Age which only happened 'yesterday' in geological terms. Scottish golf owes much to the advance and retreat of the last ice sheet and the associated sea level changes. With human occupation of the recently deglaciated and newly forested landscape beginning some 8,000 years ago, man's impact was soon to modify nature's handiwork. Forests were cleared, farming began and eventually in the eighteenth and nineteenth centuries an urban industrialised society would evolve. Golf courses are to be found on wild moorlands, wind-swept links, elegant parklands, surrounded by housing estates and factories, and in suburban and periurban environments. The combination of nature and man has produced a remarkable variety in the environments available to the golfer in Scotland.

Chapter 4

THE CLASSIFICATION OF GOLF COURSES

It is possible to classify Scotland's 425 golf courses in a variety of ways. The tables in the Appendix provide a range of data upon which classifications can be based. The number of holes on a course— usually nine or 18 but occasionally 12—the length of a course and its degree of difficulty (standard scratch score) can be the basis for a simple statistical classification. Whether the course belongs to a private club (with or without facilities for visitors) or is a public (municipal) course and the cost per round of golf or a day ticket is of particular interest to visiting golfers. All this statistical information is available in books such as the Benson and Hedges *Golfers' Handbook* (published annually) and the *Golf Course Guide to the British Isles* by Donald Steel. Golf in Scotland is still relatively cheap. Based on the information listed in the 1988 *Golfers' Handbook*, a round of golf on a week-day costs less than £3 on 17 per cent of Scottish courses, £3 to £6 on 54 per cent of courses, £7 to £10 on 21 per cent of courses and over £10 on only 8 per cent of courses. The most expensive golf is inevitably associated with famous places such as Turnberry, Troon, Prestwick, Gleneagles, St Andrews and Muirfield.

The classification of golf courses used in this book is based on the landscape characteristics of the courses themselves. A landscape consists of the rocks, soils, landforms, vegetation and man-made structures. The previous chapter demonstrated that much of the landscape of a golf course is determined by the geology and landforms on which it is located along with its vegetation. The character of a golf course is the product of the morphology, soils, drainage and vegetation of the fairways and greens; the general landscape characteristics of the entire course (e.g. undulating parkland, moorland plateau or sand dunes/links) and the general scenic setting. The geological and botanical history, plus the history of land use by man, all contribute to the present landscape characteristics of a course. The surface geology is most important in determining the landforms, the soils and drainage of golf courses. The events associated with the last glaciation either directly or indirectly were responsible for creating the distinctive character of over 60 per cent of

71

Scotland's golf courses—directly through the deposition of glacial and fluvioglacial deposits or indirectly by marine and aeolian processes associated with changes in relative sea levels.

The altitude of a course can be significant in determining its character—this is particularly true for those at low altitudes at the coast (mainly links courses) and those at inland sites at high altitude (mainly moorland courses). Table 4.1 provides information on the distribution of golf courses in each of the four regions according to altitude. One third of Scotland's golf courses are below 100 feet above sea level, while 20 per cent (mainly the links courses) are below 50 feet. Fifty per cent of all courses are below 200 feet. A further 40 per cent are between 200 and 600 feet, with only ten per cent above 600 feet. Surprisingly, Scotland's highest golf course is not in the Highlands but in the central Southern Uplands at Leadhills (1,200 feet). Other high altitude courses occur at the head of the Dee Valley at Braemar (D21), in Glen Shee (C53) and in the Spey Valley at Aviemore (D15), Kingussie (D52), Carrbridge (D24) and Newtonmore (D68).

The 42 courses at altitudes above 600 feet have relatively short playing seasons either because of snow lying, frozen ground or heavy rain and strong winds. They also present particular problems for green-keeping staff. On a less severe level, similar problems occur on those 70 courses which are at altitudes between 400 and 600 feet. High altitude should not be correlated with steepness of slope. The courses at Braemar, Glen Shee, Carrbridge, Aviemore and

TABLE 4.1   THE NUMBER OF GOLF COURSES AT VARIOUS ALTITUDES IN EACH REGION

		Region					
Metres	Feet	A	B	C	D	Totals	%
360	1200					1	0.2
330	1100				1	1	0.2
300	1000			1		1	0.2
270	900				2	2	0.5
240	800	3	1		2	6	1.2
210	700	6	5		4	15	3.8
180	600	5	7	3	1	16	3.8
150	500	10	8	8	4	30	7.1
120	400	7	10	14	9	40	9.4
90	300	9	20	11	4	44	10.4
60	200	10	29	14	7	60	14.1
30	100	17	26	15	12	70	16.5
15	50	14	14	9	18	55	12.9
0	0	9	30	21	24	84	19.8

TABLE 4.2   CLASSIFICATIONS OF GOLF COURSES

Landforms	Vegetation
Undulating	Woodland
Hillside	Parkland
Drumlins	Moorland
Eskers, Kames	Links
Kame Terrace, Sandur, River Terrace	
Raised Beach/Platform	
Dunes/Sand Plain (Links)	

Newtonmore are located on valley-floor sands and gravels. However, high altitude may be correlated with high quality surrounding scenery because many such courses have spectacular views.

Another simple means of classifying golf courses is to distinguish coastal and inland courses. Thirty per cent of Scotland's golf courses (142) are located on the coast and their distribution is highly correlated with raised beaches and/or blown sand, all below 100 feet above present sea level. Not all of these courses are classic golf links as some have parkland or moorland characteristics.

The classification of golf courses used in this book is primarily based on two quite separate sets of criteria: landforms and vegetation. It should be pointed out that two courses built on the same type of landforms may have different vegetation or conversely one vegetation type (e.g. parkland) may be associated with a variety of landforms. Table 4.2 lists the landform and vegetation types used in the classification.

LANDFORMS

Any classification of the landforms occupied by golf courses will be determined by the fact that an 18-hole course only occupies between 100 and 150 acres and therefore, within the confines of any one course, it is often difficult to recognise any one landform or group of landforms. Fig 4.1 shows, in profile, the range of landforms upon which golf courses have been built in Scotland. The broad classification of landforms into mountains, valleys, plateaux and lowlands does not necessarily reveal the landscape characteristics of individual golf courses because there are numerous and significant landform variations within these broad units. Even within the next level of classification (e.g. hillside, river terrace, drumlin, raised beach,

TABLE 4.3

THE NUMBER AND PERCENTAGES OF GOLF COURSES IN EACH LANDFORM CATEGORY IN EACH REGION

Type				*Region*			
		A	*B*	*C*	*D*	*Total*	*%*
Undulating		28	41	25	23	117	28
	%	31	29	26	26		
Hillside		20	27	15	4	66	15
	%	22	17	16	5		
Drumlins		1	33	1	0	35	8
	%	1	23	1	0		
Eskers, Kames		4	2	5	0	11	3
	%	5	1	5	0		
Kame Terrace ⎫ Sandur ⎬ River Terrace ⎭	%	13 14	13 8	21 22	23 26	70	16
Raised Beaches/ ⎫ Platforms ⎬	%	12 13	10 6	11 12	3 15	46	11
Links		12	21	21	26	80	19
	%	13	15	18	28		

links) an individual golf course may be built across more than one type of landform. In assigning an individual course to a particular class, the dominant or most common landform type on that course has been used (Table 4.3 and Fig 4.2). Forty-three per cent of Scotland's golf courses occur on landform units which are larger than the individual courses and they have been classified either as 'undulating' or 'hillside' courses. Depending on the definition of these two classes, courses which occur on kames, eskers or links land could be included in the 'undulating' class and certain courses located on the sides of drumlins could be classed as 'hillside' courses. However, for the purpose of this classification, whenever a specific landform or group of landforms within a golf course have been recognised as distinctive in terms of their morphology and constituent materials, they are assigned to a specific class. The 'undulating' and 'hillside' courses are distinctive in their own right but cannot be linked to any one group of geological processes.

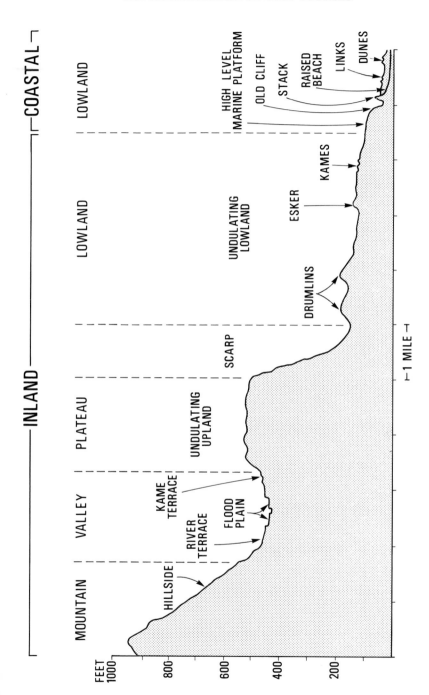

FIG4.1 Profile of the landforms which form the basis for the classification of golf courses.

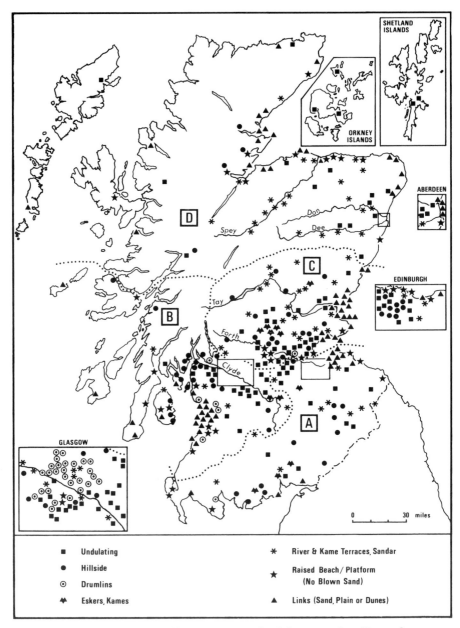

FIG4.2   The location of golf courses in each of the seven landform classes.

4.1   An 'undulating' golf course, Williamwood, Glasgow.

4.2   A 'hillside' course, Braids, Edinburgh. Tees and greens cut into a hillside underlain by lavas.

Undulating Courses

One hundred and seventeen courses (28 per cent) fall into this classification (Fig 4.3). These courses have no distinctive landform characteristics other than that they consist of assemblages of low angle slopes and no great range in altitude (usually less than 50 feet) within the course (Pl 4.1). Such courses can occur at relatively high altitudes on plateau surfaces or on lowlands. In lowland locations many of these courses have been built across areas covered by glacial till (a mixture of boulders and pebbles in a sandy-clayey matrix). This glacial deposit has buried many of the irregularities of the underlying rock surface. The main concentration of these courses is in the Central Lowlands of Scotland, with 29 per cent of Strathclyde Region's courses falling in to this category and with other concentrations in Central, Lothian and Fife Regions. Many of the landscape characteristics of these courses are determined more by their vegetation than by their landforms—they are either moorland or parkland courses. One distinctive sub group of undulating upland courses consists of those courses which occur on the plateau lavas (mainly basalts). These volcanic rocks have a very distinctive layered appearance and they have often been eroded into minor cliffs and crags. Many of these courses have a moorland vegetation because of their high altitude, the chemical characteristics of their soils and their land use history. Examples of this type of course are: Old Ranfurley (B20), Paisley (B115), Cathkin Braes (B128).

Hillside Courses

Sixty-six (15 per cent) of Scotland's golf courses are located on hillsides (Fig 4.4). Many of these hillsides are in fact valley sides which provide fine views along a strath, glen or sea loch from the higher parts of the courses (Pl 4.2). The difference in altitude between the highest and lowest points on such courses can be as much as 500 feet and to play them the golfer not only needs skill but stamina. It has also been suggested that on such courses having one leg longer than the other is a distinct advantage. Specific examples of courses dominated by steep slopes are those at Hawick (B37), Strathpeffer (D80), Tobermory (B135), the Braid Hills (B5,6), and several courses around the Firth of Clyde.

Drumlins

As previously mentioned, drumlins are elongated, streamlined hills

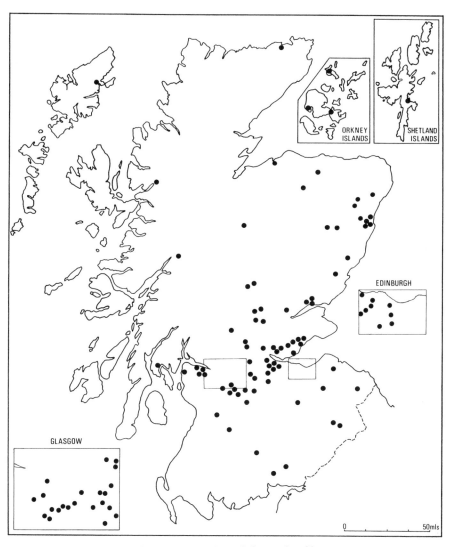

FIG4.3　The location of 'undulating' golf courses.

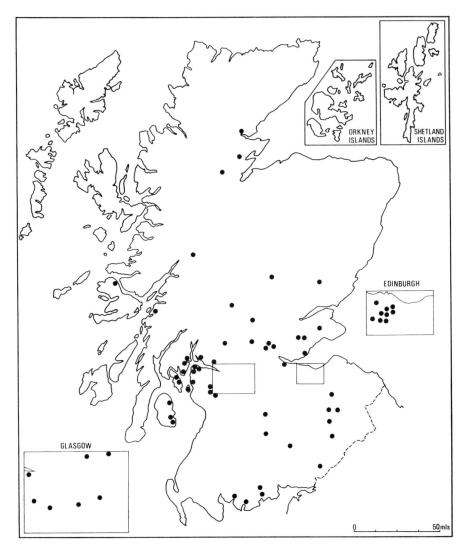

FIG4.4 The location of 'hillside' golf courses.

4.3 A green cut into the side of a drumlin, Wigtown.

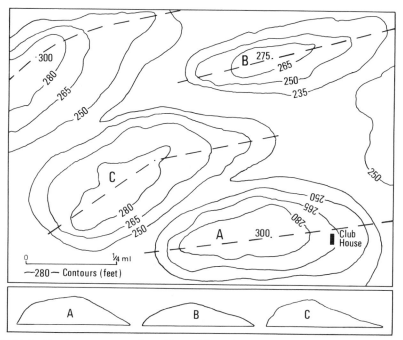

FIG4.5 Contour map and profiles of drumlins: Mount Ellon Golf Course.

(Pl 4.3), 30-100 feet high and 300-500 yards long, having the shape of an upturned spoon (Fig 4.5). They tend to occur in 'swarms' and were produced by the passage of the last ice sheet to cover Scotland (15,000-20,000 years ago). They are often not simple features, as small drumlins have been superimposed on larger ones. They vary greatly in terms of their constituent materials. Some consist entirely of glacial till while others contain beds of fluvioglacial material (sand and gravel) often with a covering of glacial till. Some drumlins have solid rock cores with only a thin cover of glacial till. Drumlins provide interesting sites for golf courses in that they provide a variety of slope angles, slope directions and slope lengths within a relatively small area.

Of the 35 golf courses (8 per cent) located on drumlins (Fig 4.6), 33 are in Strathclyde Region (Table 4.3), with the majority of these being in the Greater Glasgow area. Glasgow could well be described as the 'Drumlinoid City' as much of the late nineteenth and early twentieth-century expansion of the city took place across a drumlin field produced by the last ice sheet. Examples of golf courses on drumlins are: Balmore (B9), Bearsden (B12), Clober (B108), Clydebank (B33, 34), Crow Wood (B40), Kirkintilloch (B81), Lenzie (B92), Lethamhill (B94), Mount Ellon (B59) and Ruchill (B126). Other drumlin courses occur in Ayrshire and Dumfries and Galloway.

Eskers and Kames

Accumulations of sand and gravel deposited in close association with the glacier ice of the last ice sheet provide the nearest inland equivalent to coastal links land. When the last ice sheet melted, vast quantities of meltwater were released and these waters picked up and transported much of the rock debris which was on and in the ice. Transportation of the rock debris by the meltwater streams caused rounding and sorting of the rock particles and the debris was deposited as stratified sand and gravel. There are very large areas in Scotland covered by these sands and gravels and some of these deposits have very distinctive landforms associated with them. Because some of these deposits were accumulated actually in, on top of, or against glacier ice they acquired distinctive forms (Fig 4.7). As the ice sheet was melting, large volumes of water flowed in channels on the ice surface, in tunnels in the ice, along the side of the ice mass and away from the ice front. When debris choked the tunnels in the ice mass, new routes were found and when the ice eventually melted completely these tunnel deposits were left as upstanding ridges of sand and gravel. These ridges are known as eskers and they can occur

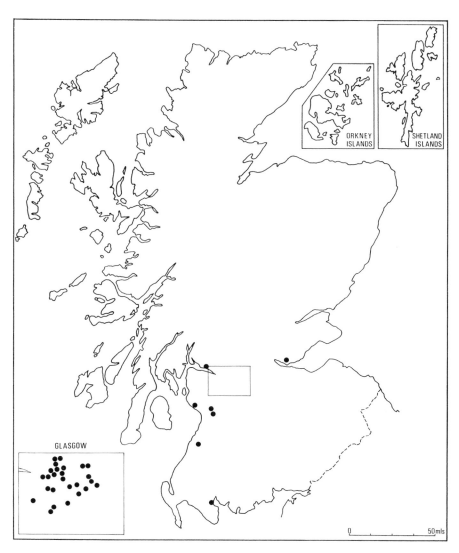

FIG4.6   The location of 'drumlin' golf courses.

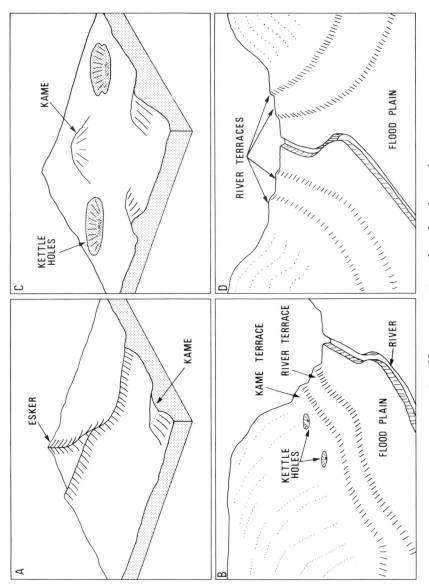

FIG4.7   Landforms consisting of sand and gravel.

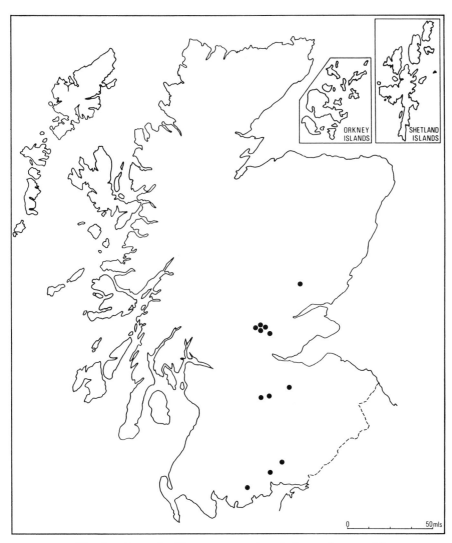

FIG4.8　The location of golf courses constructed on eskers and kames.

either as single features or as a series of sub-parallel ridges (Pl 4.4), but they all represent the former courses of meltwater streams. They range from five to 50 feet in height, often have irregular crestlines and sometimes merge with chaotic mounds or spreads of sand and gravel. Isolated mounds of sand and gravel are known as kames and may represent the deposits laid down in an individual cave under the ice. More commonly sand and gravel occurs as a series of mounds of various sizes and shapes interspersed with enclosed hollows. Such accumulations are known as kame and kettle complexes (Fig 4.7B) and originated when sand and gravel were laid down over blocks of glacier ice. When the ice blocks melted they left large enclosed depressions (kettle holes) which sometimes contain small lakes.

Ridges (eskers) and mounds (kames) of sand and gravel provide well-drained 'heath' land which has a morphology highly suited to the game of golf. There are many similarities between these areas and the ridges (dunes), hummocks and spreads of sand that form the traditional links land where so many of Scotland's early golf courses were located. Eleven golf courses (three per cent) are located on fluvioglacial sand and gravel in the form of kames or eskers (Fig 4.8). The courses at Dumfries (A20), Castle Douglas (A10), Lochmaben (A49), Carnwath (B28), Lanark (B86) and Muckhart (C75) are located on kame complexes with associated kettle holes. The course at Alyth (C7) on the edge of the Highlands is built on kames. However, it is at the famous golfing centre of Gleneagles, where four courses have been developed on a large esker and kame complex, that these sand and gravel deposits provide a distinctive golfing landscape. The ridges are 20 to 50 feet high, steepsided (20-25°) and are separated by elongated troughs or enclosed hollows (kettle holes). The ridge system splays out at its eastern end with larger flat areas separating the ridges. The golf course architects have utilised the ridges for 'rough' and tees and the inter-ridge troughs and hollows for fairways and greens.

Kame Terraces, Sandar, River Terraces

Kame terraces and sandar (outwash fans) are landforms resulting from large quantities of sand and gravel being deposited by glacier meltwaters alongside (kame terrace) or in front of (sandur) a wasting ice mass (Fig 4.7). Kame terraces are very similar to river terraces except that their scarp faces may be highly crenulated and that the upper surface may be pocked by kettle holes as a result of the burial of blocks of ice during their formation (Pl 4.5). Most river valleys in Scotland were choked by deposits of sand and gravel at the end of the

4.4 Esker ridges on either side of the 15th fairway, King's Course, Gleneagles.

4.5 Kame terrace, with kettle hole, Fort Augustus.

last Ice Age. During the past 6,000 years (a period of falling relative sea level) rivers have cut down into these deposits and in so doing produced a series of terraces representing former higher flood plains (Fig 4.7D). Where there has been a considerable amount of post-glacial erosion, only the highest parts of a kame terrace may have survived, with normal river terraces occupying the lower levels of the floor of the valley (Pl 4.6). For this reason kame terraces and river terraces are classed together as golf course sites. At Newtonmore (D68), for example, several holes of the golf course are located on an upper kame terrace which contains kettle holes, while the majority of the course is laid out on the river terrace cut during post-glacial times by the River Spey.

In locations where meltwater deposition was not confined by valley walls great fan-shaped spreads (sandar or outwash fans) were deposited. Such large sandar are not common in Scotland but the two courses at Blairgowrie (C14, 15) are located on such a feature. Its low angle slopes and free-draining soils are ideally suited to golf course construction. The old meltwater routeways (channels) across the sandur surface can be seen and there are a few kettle holes which have resulted from the melting of buried blocks of ice.

All three landforms (kame terrace, river terrace, sandur) consist of silt, sand and gravel and make excellent sites for golf courses. Seventy courses (16 per cent) are located on these landforms (Table 4.3, Fig 4.9) which are characterised by large areas of low angle slopes

4.6   River terrace, Innerleithen, Peeblesshire.

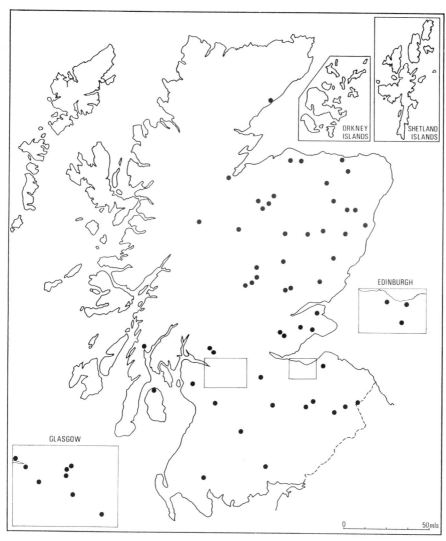

FIG 4.9 The location of golf courses constructed on river terraces, kame terraces and outwash fans (sandar).

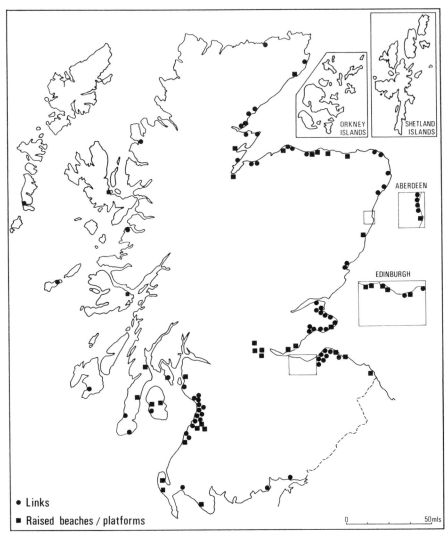

FIG 4.10 The location of golf courses constructed on links (blown sand) and raised beaches and raised marine platforms.

separated by short steep slopes (terrace scarps). Although such courses are usually well-drained, any parts of courses sited on the present flood plain can obviously be subject to flooding. Golf courses located on terraces are widespread in Scotland but there are significant concentrations of such courses in the valleys of the Tweed, Tay, Dee and Spey.

Raised Marine Platforms and Raised Beaches

One hundred and twenty six golf courses (30 per cent) are located on the Scottish coastline (Fig 4.10). They all occupy sites which have been created as a result of the relative changes in sea level which occurred during the Ice Age—mainly during the past 14,000 years (see Chapter 3). Marine erosion has produced a series of coastal platforms of unknown age at altitudes between 100 and 150 feet above present sea level. Another series of platforms at 50 to 120 feet above present sea level are believed to have been formed as the last ice sheet wasted away (14,000 to 10,000 years ago) and a period of relatively high sea level about 6,000 years ago trimmed existing platforms and cliff lines up to altitudes of 40 feet above present sea level. Some of the higher marine platforms have little or no marine or aeolian sand on their surfaces while most of the marine platforms below 100 feet have both marine sands and gravels and windblown sands on their surfaces. The almost flat or gently undulating surfaces of high level marine platforms (Pl 4.7) are in great contrast to the steep cliffs which border them or the steep valley sides of streams which cross them. A series of well-developed high-level marine platforms occur on the northern coast of Grampian Region and are sites for the golf courses at Hopeman (D42), Buckpool (D23), Cullen (D26) and Royal Tarlair (D61). The course at Cullen is a good illustration of the variety of coastal landforms which can be found in this type of environment (see Chapter 8, Fig 8.6 and Pl 4.8).

Along many parts of the Scottish coastline, raised-beach deposits form relatively narrow zones beneath former coastal cliffs (Fig 4.11A). The material in these beaches may be cobbles (e.g. Spey Bay Golf Course—D76) or gravel and sand (Brodick B22) and usually their surfaces are flat or gently undulating. Courses located on raised beaches have many of the characteristics of true links courses except that they do not have the distinctive dune ridges or hummocks. In a few locations (e.g. Spey Bay) abandoned storm-beach ridges of gravel or cobbles do provide a strong linear element to their morphology. Forty-six golf courses (11 per cent) occupy raised beaches or raised marine platforms which have little or no windblown sand on their

4.7   High level marine platform, Banffshire.

4.8   High level marine platform, abandoned cliff and sea stacks, and raised beach covered by blown sand, Cullen.

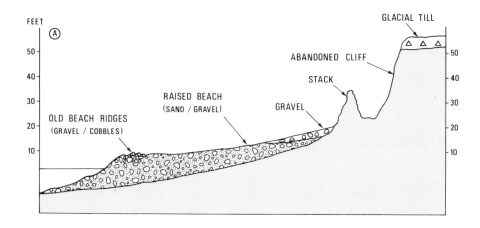

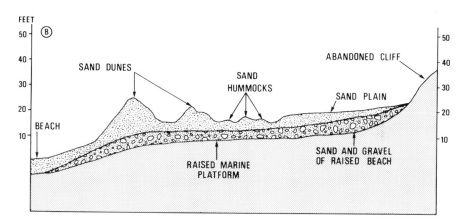

FIG 4.11   A: Section of raised beach deposits backed by abandoned stack and
cliff. B: Section of wind-blown sand forms (dunes, hummocks, plains)
covering raised-beach deposits resting on a raised marine platform.

surfaces. Courses located on high-level marine platforms are often wind swept and have a moorland vegetation.

Links

The typical Scottish links course is located on a raised beach or raised marine platform produced or at least trimmed by the relatively high sea level attained about 6,000 years ago (Fig 4.11B). The majority of these beaches or platforms are between 10 and 35 feet above present sea level. The raised beach or platform is backed by an abandoned cliff-line cut in either glacial drift (till or fluvioglacial sand and gravel) or solid rock. On top of the raised-beach or platform is a covering of windblown sand (Pl 4.9) either in the form of dune ridges, dune hummocks or as a gently undulating sand-spread (sand plain). The landward dunes and hummocks along with the sand plains are usually stabilised. The youngest dune ridges or hummocks are nearest to the present high water mark and may be still growing and subject to blow-outs (erosion). The dune ridges have been used for 'rough' and inter-dune troughs (slacks) have been used for fairways and

4.9 Typical links land—wind blown sand covering a raised beach—North Berwick.

greens for several centuries by Scottish golfers. Similarly the minor undulations associated with sand spreads over raised-beach deposits have also been traditional golfing areas. Many of Scotland's most famous golf courses—St Andrews, Carnoustie, Muirfield, Troon, Prestwick and Turnberry—make use of these natural links. Such links land was often 'common land'. It was relatively easily cleared of shrubs and rabbits and sheep produced close-cropped turf. It is interesting that the game of golf began and flourished on the youngest and in some ways most delicate of Scotland's land surfaces. Dune areas are highly unstable. They can develop very rapidly (in geological terms) over a few hundred years, and even after long periods of stability as a result of the development of a good grass cover, can easily become unstable with further sand movement. They have three characteristics which make them highly suited to the game of golf. They have a variety of slope angles and slope lengths in a small area. They are usually well-drained and they support an easily managed grass/herb/shrub vegetation.

It is perhaps a gross over-simplification to put all links courses into one class. They range from courses built on raised beaches and raised platforms with only a thin, almost flat, sand cover, through courses built on a combination of sub-parallel dune ridges and associated undulating sand spreads, to courses built entirely on sand dune ridges and hummocks. It is the morphological variety both within and between links courses that makes them so attractive to the golfer.

No other country of similar size contains 425 golf courses which, within their 45,000 acres, contain such a variety of landforms. The morphology and general scenic setting of these courses owes much to the direct and indirect effects of the environmental changes which took place during and since the last period of glaciation. The glacier ice and meltwaters moulded much of the scenery and created many of the landforms within the confines of individual golf courses. The fluctuations in relative sea level which accompanied the growth and decay of the ice sheet were responsible for all of the landforms occupied by golf courses around the Scottish coastline. It is therefore most reasonable to base a classification of Scottish golf courses primarily on their landform characteristics.

VEGETATION

Six thousand years ago virtually all of Scotland was covered by trees—oak and birch in the south and west, pine and birch in the north and north east, and birch in the far north and on the Western Isles. With the exception of the coastal links land (all developed during the last 6,000 years) the vegetation of the areas utilised for golf courses in the nineteenth and twentieth centuries was much modified from its original state by man's agricultural and industrial activities. The vegetation of golf courses falls into five classes: woodland, grassland, parkland, moorland, linksland (grass, herbs, shrubs). Many golf courses have elements of all five classes. For example, many courses are combinations of woodland, grassland and moorland vegetation. By definition, a parkland course is a combination of grass and trees and few golf courses are only grassland, there being always some attempt to introduce either trees or shrubs. For this reason the grassland classification is not used in this book, it being replaced by parkland.

Woodland Courses

The areas of extensive natural woodlands remaining in Scotland are very limited and none of them contain golf courses. However, there are a few golf courses on which most of the fairways are lined by trees. The most obvious examples are at Blairgowrie, where two courses (C14, 15) have been laid out through pine and birch forest (Pl 4.10). Even on these courses there are more open areas which are better classed as parkland. A similar set of circumstances can be found at Dougalston (B109) near Glasgow. There are many courses on which pine plantations give a woodland character to at least part of the course (e.g. Forfar C46, Ladybank C62).

Parkland Courses

Two hundred and thirty-nine (66 per cent) of the golf courses in Scotland are classed as parkland. (Fig 4.12). The classic parkland course consists of mainly deciduous trees (oak, elm, horse chestnut, birch) forming a distinctive landscape which was designed as a part of the policies of a large estate, (Pl 4.11). The golf course architect simply inherited the characteristics given to the site by landscape architects employed by the former landowner. Excellent examples of such planned parkland courses are: Ratho Park near Edinburgh (A72), Glenbervie (C47), Murrayshall (C76), Taymouth Castle (A72), Pollock (B117) and Buchanan Castle (C31). At the other end of the spectrum even the most recent parkland courses laid out within the confines of a few grassland fields usually have some planted trees

4.10 A woodland course, Rosemount, Blairgowrie.

4.11 A parkland course, Pollock, Glasgow.

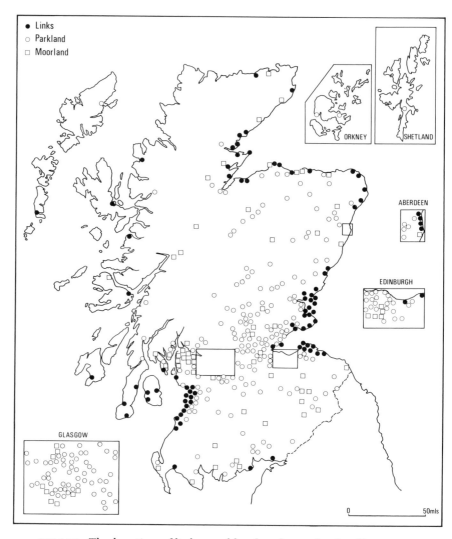

FIG 4.12   The location of links, parkland and moorland golf courses.

along the sides of fairways. Between these two extremes fall the majority of parkland courses which are characterised by a mixture of grassland and trees. The trees may be either old established oaks, elms and birch, or may be relatively new plantations of pine or birch. The more rapidly growing conifers have often been used by golf course architects in Scotland to develop the parkland character relatively quickly. On many parkland courses both rhododendrons and gorse bring great spreads of colour during spring and early summer (e.g. Gleneagles) and introduce added problems to the golfer whose shots stray from the fairway.

The trees on parkland golf courses fall into two distinct categories. Those that are integral parts of the course in that they either line the edges of fairways or are in the fairways and form golfing hazards, and those which are set back from fairways or are around the periphery of a course and add to its landscape setting. Some golf course architects have incorporated trees into the playing area and therefore they can rightly be regarded as hazards. Generally, however, trees simply add to the scenic attractiveness of a golf course.

Moorland Courses

As was explained in Chapter 3, large areas of Scotland which were formerly forest have degenerated into moorland. This is particularly true of the uplands (land over 1,000 feet) but also applies to certain areas between 500 and 1,000 feet. Typical moorland vegetation consists of tough grasses and heather plus gorse, willow and occasional trees such as birch, juniper and rowan (Pl 4.12). Even on some typical moorland courses, plantations of conifers have been used as windbreaks and to add variety to the landscape. There are 70 (16 per cent) moorland courses in Scotland (Fig 4.12). Most of them are over 300 feet above sea level and many of them (50) occur on outcrops of basalt lavas. There are numerous examples of moorland courses on the plateau basalts around Greater Glasgow (see Chapter 6). The fairways and greens on moorland courses are usually located on peaty soils which have poor drainage. Coarse grasses and mosses have been improved by seeding. The rough is generally heather and/ or coarse grass with gorse. In recent decades the replanting of moorland areas with commercial coniferous woodland has changed the general scenic setting of many moorland golf courses.

Links Land

The vegetation of sand dunes, sand spreads and raised-beaches is

4.12 A moorland course, Selkirk.

essentially grassland. The very existence of dune systems is related to
the presence of tough grasses (e.g. marram grass) which not only
survive in this very dry environment but assist in the trapping of sand
in the dune system. Because most of Scotland's sand dune systems
post-date the arrival of man in Scotland and were often the sites for
early human occupation, we have little knowledge of how the dune
vegetation would have developed without any human interference.
Whether or not, without human interference over a long period,
natural woodland would have developed on coastal dunes is a matter
of conjecture. Certainly, coniferous plantations have been used in the
last 100 years by man to stabilise dune areas (e.g. Cullbin Sands and
Tentsmuir Forest). However, over the past 5,000 years the 'natural'
vegetation (including human influences) has been grasses, herbs and
scrub (buckthorn and gorse). The contrast between the tough, long
grasses of the active dune system (marram grass) and the short
grasses and herbs of the inter-dune areas (slacks) or sand plains was
accentuated by the grazing habits of cattle, sheep and rabbits. The
development of modern green-keeping methods further modified the
vegetation into fairways and rough. On some links land, heather and
gorse has also added to the variable character of the rough. The great
variety of landforms within an area of links land produces a variety of
environments in which different types of vegetation will develop. It is

this great variety in vegetation within the area of a links course which produces such a challenge to the golfer.

Throughout the rest of this book, golf courses will be classified primarily on the basis of the dominant landforms and vegetation within the confines of a course. Apart from the rather obvious difference between inland and coastal courses (most coastal courses are on links land but a few have parkland or moorland characteristics) there are certain other important variables which should be borne in mind. There are some noticeable differences in the general environmental quality of rural golf courses compared with those located in suburban and urban environments. Poor general scenic setting, high noise levels, industrial smells and vandalism all tend to be associated with golf courses in an urban environment. However, some rural courses in Scotland (e.g. St Andrews, Carnoustie, Lossiemouth, Nairn) also have noise problems associated with low flying military aircraft. On the other hand there are some delightful parkland courses which are oases of peace in the heart of urban areas.

Wherever it is located, and whatever its landscape characteristics, the golf course is for many people the closest they get to the 'natural environment' at any time in their lives. Although tees, fairways and greens may be man-made, the general landscape produced by geological processes, the vegetation and animal life of the golf course are vital ingredients to the game of golf. It would be an interesting exercise to classify Scottish golf courses on the basis of their environmental attractions. However, for a resident of Tokyo, even a nine-hole course in the centre of Glasgow would be valued highly compared with the use of a driving range for a couple of hours per week. For Scottish golfers the fresh air (often too strong!) of a links course with countless sea-birds on the foreshore, or the sound of grouse or curlew or deer from a high moorland course would be difficult to evaluate. One of the great attractions of the game of golf is that it can be played in such a variety of environments.

Chapter 5

DUMFRIES AND GALLOWAY, THE BORDERS, LOTHIAN

REGION A

The south of Scotland has a great variety of scenery and golfing landscapes. The area can be divided into three parts (Fig 5.1) and contains some 90 golf courses. The earliest courses were established in the Lothians in the eighteenth century but between 1875 and 1899 some 30 courses were constucted throughout the area. A further seven courses were added in Dumfries and Galloway between 1900 and 1924.

DUMFRIES AND GALLOWAY

There are ten 18-hole and 14 nine-hole courses in this region (Fig 5.1). With the exception perhaps of Southerness (A81), which is a classic links course of championship standard (the Scottish Amateur Championship was played here in 1985), none of the courses is particularly famous or of very high quality. However, the variety of golfing landscapes and challenges to be found in this region is quite remarkable. Many of the courses are set in beautiful scenery with views of the Solway Firth to the south and the mountains of the western Southern Uplands to the north. The golfing climate is also relatively mild and the cost of a round of golf on many of the courses is between £3 and £6.

Coastal Courses

There are only three links courses (Fig 5.2) in this region: Wigtownshire County at Glen Luce (A32); Southerness (A81) and Powfoot (A1). Wigtownshire County is very flat, built on a raised-beach only 10–25 feet above sea level. Southerness was the first course to be built in Scotland after World War II (Pl 5.1). It is also built on a raised-beach between 20 and 35 feet above sea level. It is a course which requires accurate driving because of the presence of heather and gorse rough. Its exposed position means that wind direction and strength play an important part in determining the course's difficulty. A mere five miles to the north of the course the granite mass of Criffell rises to 1,868 feet. Powfoot (A1), some four miles west of Annan, is an undulating links course. The outer sand ridge reaches altitudes of between 23 and 46 feet above sea level and the course is built on an undulating sand plain with a relief of between six and 12 feet. The rough consists largely of gorse. The course was laid out by James Braid in 1903.

Although the courses at Stranraer (A82), Portpatrick (B69) and St Medan, Port William (B77), are located adjacent to the coast, they each have landscape characteristics which are associated with inland locations. The course at Stranraer, which was the last one designed by James Braid, is an undulating parkland course between 15 and 70 feet above sea level, built on dissected raised-beach sand and gravel. It is a good quality parkland course which owes its landscape characteristics to the fact that the isthmus between Loch Ryan and Luce Bay was once an arm of the sea and much of the land around

5.1 Southerness—a links course on the shore of the Solway Firth.

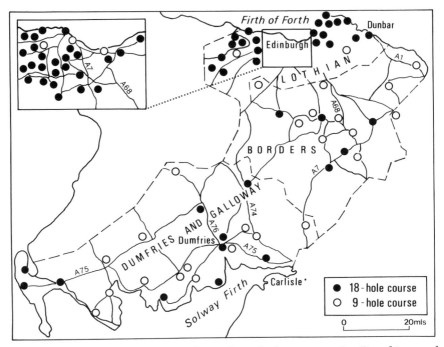

FIG 5.1 The location of nine-hole and 18-hole courses in Dumfries and Galloway, Borders and Lothian Regions (Region A).

the present shores of Loch Ryan up to an altitude of about 100 feet above present sea level is covered by marine sand and gravel.

There are two courses at Portpatrick (A69)—one of 18 holes and the other of nine holes. They are both built on a rolling upland between 150 and 200 feet above sea level. Although adjacent to the coast they are essentially moorland courses. The most spectacular hole is the 283 yards, par four, where one drives from a tee high up on the cliff edge to a green far below. Portpatrick is an excellent centre for a golfing holiday.

Another moorland course adjacent to the coast is that at St Medan (A77) some three miles south-east of Port William. This nine-hole course has fine sandy beaches on two sides but it is built between an old degraded cliff and a small rounded hill on a promontory. There are no trees and very little rough on the course. The fouth hole, the Well, is 274 yards from the tee on top of a hill down to the green amongst sand dunes some 70 feet below. The fifth, sixth and seventh holes are 'links' holes constructed on a raised beach covered by blown sand.

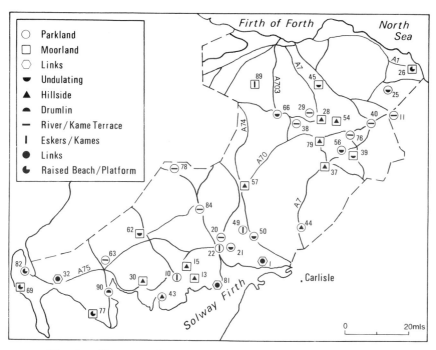

FIG 5.2   The landforms and vegetation of golf courses in Dumfries and Galloway and Borders Regions.

Although the courses at Wigtown (A90), Gatehouse of Fleet (A30), Kirkcudbright (A43) and Colvend (A13) are all within a mile of tidewater, they are all classed as inland courses.

Inland Courses

There are 17 inland courses in Dumfries and Galloway of which 12 are classed as parkland and five as moorland.

One of the most distinctive courses is that at Wigtown (A90). It is a nine-hole parkland course built on the side of drumlins (see Chapter 4). The nine-hole parkland courses at Newton Stewart (A63), Castle Douglas (A10), Thornhill (A84), Sanquhar (A78) and Lochmaben (A49) are all on undulating areas of sand and gravel, as are also the two 18-hole and one nine-hole parkland courses at Dumfries (A20, 21, 22). The 18-hole course at Kirkcudbright (A43) and the nine-hole course at Lockerbie (A50) are built on steep hillsides. Of these parkland courses the two 18-hole courses (A20, 22) at Dumfries, the

18-hole course at Thornhill (A84) and the nine-hole course at Loch-maben (A49) are the most attractive.

The five courses classed as moorland—Gatehouse of Fleet (A30); New Galloway (A62); Dalbeattie (A15); Colvend (A13); and Moffat (A57)—all present problems of classification. Only that at Moffat, which is at an altitude of between 550 and 675 feet is a true moorland course. There are spectacular views of the Annan Valley, the Tweedsmuir Hills and the town of Moffat from the eighteenth tee. This 271-yards, par four is a spectacular finishing hole with a drop from tee to green of some 75 feet. There is a similar final hole on the nine-hole moorland course at Gatehouse of Fleet (A30) but this course is only between 100 and 300 feet above sea level. The nine-hole courses at Dalbeattie (A15) and Colvend (A13) are less spectacular moorland courses.

THE BORDERS

Although this region is more famous for its rugby pitches than its golf courses, the 16 golf courses provide some interesting golfing land-scapes. Fourteen of the courses were established during the last quarter of the nineteenth century but those at Minto (A56) and Coldstream were founded in 1926 and 1948 respectively. Ten of them are of nine holes and six are 18-hole courses. On most of them a round of golf costs between £3 and £6. Although there are no so-called championship courses in the district, which is in marked contrast to the adjacent district of East Lothian, the occurrence of 16 very different courses within a 20-mile radius of St Boswells or Melrose makes these towns excellent centres for a golfing holiday. The Tweed Valley and its tributaries, the Ettrick and Teviot, provide delightful background scenery and many sites of historical interest. Although the courses may not be of the highest quality, the cheapness of the green fees, the delightful countryside and interesting towns of this area make this one of Scotland's most attractive golfing prospects. It should also be pointed out that the challenging championship courses of Gullane, North Berwick and Dunbar are only 35 miles away. All of the courses, apart from the one at Eyemouth (nine-hole, coastal moorland) are inland courses. They fall into two clear categories—seven courses (A37, 39, 79, 28, 54, 45, 89) are moorland courses often located on steep hillsides at altitudes of between 600 and 800 feet above sea level, and eight courses (A56, 66, 25, 38, 29, 76, 40, 11) are parkland courses. The parkland courses can be further subdivided between those located on the flood plains and river terraces of the rivers Tweed (A38, 29, 76, 40, 11) and those located on rolling uplands above the valley floors (A56, 66, 25).

Moorland Courses

The boundary between cultivation and rough grazing/heather moorland has varied considerably throughout history and varies from place to place within the Southern Uplands. The availability of modern machinery means that a golf course which has moorland characteristics may now be surrounded by arable land or coniferous plantations. This contrast of a moorland course with both coniferous plantations and ploughed fields around it is seen at Melrose (Pl 5.2). This course (A54) is located on the north-west flank of the Eildon Hills. The smooth conical and heather-clad summits of these hills are formed of hard volcanic rocks, sheets of lava having invaded the bedding-planes of the Old Red Sandstone sediments (see the red soil in the field to the north-east of the golf course). The Eildon Hills were made famous by the writings of Sir Walter Scott whose home at Abbotsford is only a few miles away. Although Melrose golf course has conifer plantations both on the course and around its edges, it still has many characteristics related to the heather moorland which covers the higher parts of the Eildon Hills.

The three nine-hole courses at Melrose (founded 1880), Selkirk (founded 1883) and Jedburgh (founded 1892) were all designed by Willie Park. They are all of similar length but the course at Selkirk (A79) is perched on the side of a glacially scoured hill consisting of volcanic rock (Pl 4.12). The north-east to south-west trending hill upon which the Selkirk course is built consists of a vertical sheet of volcanic rock (a dyke) intruded into Silurian shales. The north-west face of this hill has been eroded by glacier ice moving from south-west to north-east and consists of a series of minor ridges and depressions which have been utilised in the construction of the golf course. The view from the ninth tee to the ninth green demonstrates the significance of the heather-clad minor ridges in the character of this course. The course at Jedburgh (A39) is less spectacular in its morphology but is also built on the side of a hill and is an enjoyable test of golf.

There are three 18-hole moorland courses in the Borders. Those at Hawick (A37) and Galashiels (A28) are both constructed on steep hillsides with spectacular views of the surrounding countryside. The Ladhope course at Galashiels is a municipal course and as on the course at Hawick both tees and greens are often perched on hillsides.

5.2 Melrose—on the slopes of the Eildon Hills.

5.3 Torwoodlee, Galashiels—on river terraces of a tributary of the River Tweed.

The moorland course at West Linton (A89) in the far north of the district, is largely built on fluvioglacial sands and gravels and has relatively gentle undulations. There are some fine views of the Pentland Hills from this course.

Parkland Courses

There are eight parkland courses in the Borders region, only three of them (A40, 56, 66) being of 18 holes. Three of the courses are on rolling uplands—Peebles (A66), Minto (A56) four miles north-east of Hawick, and Duns (A25). There are some fine views of the Border Hills and the Tweed Valley from the Peebles course but the course at Minto is in classic deciduous parkland.

Perhaps the most distinctive type of golf course in the Borders is that built on the gravel terraces of the Tweed and its tributaries the Leithen Water, Gala Water and Leet Water (A38, 29, 76, 40, 11). During the wastage of the last ice sheet, some 15,000 years ago, these river valleys were choked with sands and gravels deposited by the meltwaters from the melting ice. Subsequently the rivers have cut down into these gravels leaving flat or gently undulating terraces which have proved excellent sites for golf courses. The nine-hole course at Innerleithen (A38) is built on flat land immediately adjacent to the river and at the foot of the smooth, rounded slopes which lead up to moorland. Since there are no trees on this course, the use of the term parkland is rather misleading. In great contrast is the parkland course at Torwoodlee, Galashiels (A29). This is one of the most beautiful courses in the Borders with some fine individual trees on the course (Pl 5.3) which is built both on the flat flood-plain and on higher river-terraces. Another pleasant nine-hole parkland course is that at St Boswells (A76) on the banks of the Tweed. The 18-hole course at Kelso (A40) is to be found in the centre of a race course and is a flat, featureless course with but few planted trees. Further down the Tweed Valley at Coldstream (A11) is a very pleasant parkland course built in the grounds of the Hirsel, the home of Sir Alec Douglas Hume.

LOTHIAN

Although only containing 52 golf courses, this region was one of the old heartlands of Scottish golf. Students of the history of the game in Scotland savour the names of the Royal Burgess Golfing Society of Edinburgh (founded 1735) and the Honourable Company of

Edinburgh Golfers (founded 1744) which established the original 13 rules of golf. Edinburgh, therefore, claims to be the 'Golf Capital of the World' on the basis of its historical links with the game and the fact that it has 25 courses within its city limits (Glasgow has 50), and that there are 86 courses within 20 miles of Princes Street (there are 90 courses within 20 miles of Sauchiehall Street). One of the earliest golf courses was at Bruntsfield Links in the heart of the city of Edinburgh, where the original six holes are now part of a 'short' course on common land where golf is still played immediately in front of the Golf Tavern (established in 1456). The other early site of golf in Edinburgh was at Leith Links which are now used as public playing fields. Although it is perhaps sad that golf is no longer played on Leith Links, the overcrowding of those links and also of the Bruntsfield Links led to a movement of the game outside of the city, first to Musselburgh (1836) and then to Muirfield, just outside Gullane, which became the home of the Honourable Company of Edinburgh Golfers in 1891.

Lothian region is divided into four districts: East Lothian; Midlothian; West Lothian and Edinburgh (Fig 5.3). The distribution of courses in Lothian region is rather uneven, with the main concentration being in Edinburgh district (25 courses) and along the East Lothian coast between Musselburgh and Dunbar (14 courses). There are two further inland courses in East Lothian, only three in Midlothian and eight in West Lothian. The majority of the courses are of 18 holes, there only being six nine-hole courses in the entire Lothian region. Apart from the 13 links courses between Dunbar and Musselburgh (Fig 5.4), six moorland courses on the south side of Edinburgh, and two moorland courses in West Lothian, the majority of courses in Lothian region are inland parkland courses.

EAST LOTHIAN

Coastal Courses

The 20-mile stretch of coastline on the south side of the Firth of Forth between Musselburgh and Dunbar contains some classic golf courses steeped in history. They all owe their existence to changes in relative sea level along the coastline during the past 6,000 years. About 6,000 years ago sea level stood some 25 feet higher against the land than it does at present. Old cliff lines and beaches associated with that higher stand of sea level have since been abandoned and large quantities of blown sand have accumulated to form dune systems and sand spreads (links). It is these blown-sand accumulations and the

1 Turnberry from the air.

2 Cruden Bay—Old Professional's shop at right.

3 Perth, Craigie Hill. A hillside course on volcanic rock.

4 Blairgowrie, Rosemount. A woodland course on a fan of sand and gravel.

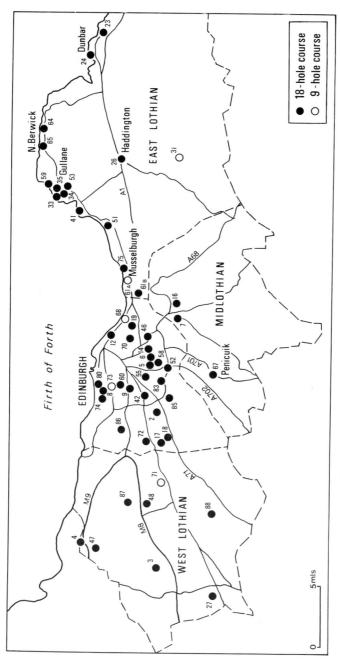

FIG 5.3   The location of nine-hole and 18-hole golf courses in Lothian.

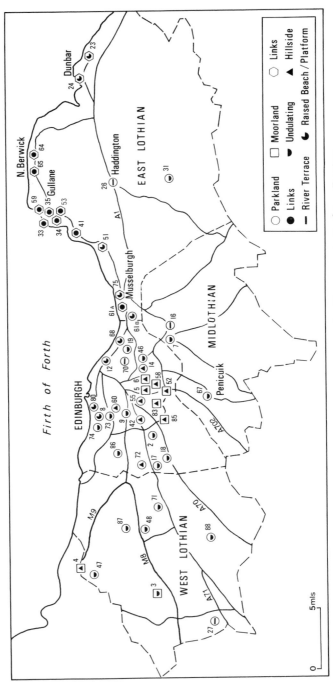

FIG 5.4   The landforms and vegetation of golf courses in Lothian Region.

underlying raised-beach deposits which have provided such good golfing country.

Golf was played on the links at Musselburgh (Pl 5.4) as early as 1672 and the earliest known trophy for stroke play was competed for by members of the Thorn Tree Golf Club on that course in 1774. Six Open Championships were played at Musselburgh links but the Honourable Company of Edinburgh Golfers, who moved to Musselburgh from Leith in 1836, subsequently moved again to Muirfield and took the Open Championship with it.

As was pointed out in Chapter 1, the date of foundation of Golf Clubs does not necessarily indicate the first date at which golf was played on a particular course. It is believed that golf has been played on Gullane Hill for over 300 years but East Lothian Golf Club was founded in 1854, Luffness Old in 1867, Kilspindie in 1867, and Gullane Golf Club in 1880. The North Berwick Golf Club was founded in 1832 and Dunbar in 1856.

There are two courses at Dunbar. The original 15 holes on the East Links (A23) were designed by Tom Morris and a further three holes added in 1880. This course is a combination of coastal links and 'inland' parkland. Holes 1, 2, 3 and 18 are in the Old Deer Park of the Duke of Roxburgh's estate, while the other 14 holes are on links land. In 1968 the Schweppes PGA Championship was held on this course. With the increase in demand for golf in the nineteen-thirties, a second course was established to the west of the town (A24) at Winterfield in 1937. The course is built on a raised marine-platform covered with sand.

There are also two golf courses at North Berwick. The North Berwick Golf Club, founded in 1832, plays over the west links (A65). A raised-beach is overlain by blown sand that forms undulating links land between 10 and 30 feet above sea level (Pl 5.5) and provides some classic links golf. Neil Elsey, writing about the course states

> Measuring 6,317 yards it's no monster in length but such is its trickery that it demands a full repertoire of shot-making. Every hole here is memorable (two of them, the 382 yards 14th named 'Perfection' and the 192 yards 15th called 'Redan' have been copied at courses all over the world) and you almost get the feeling of stepping back in time as you tackle its idiosyncrasies. There are blind shots, drives over walls and burns, shots across the bay and bunkers in which you can disappear from view. So this is how golf used to be played!

The East Links or 'Glen' course (A64) at North Berwick was

5.4 Musselburgh. A municipal course surrounded by a race-track. Six open championships were played on this course between 1874 and 1889.

5.5   North Berwick—a narrow strip of links.

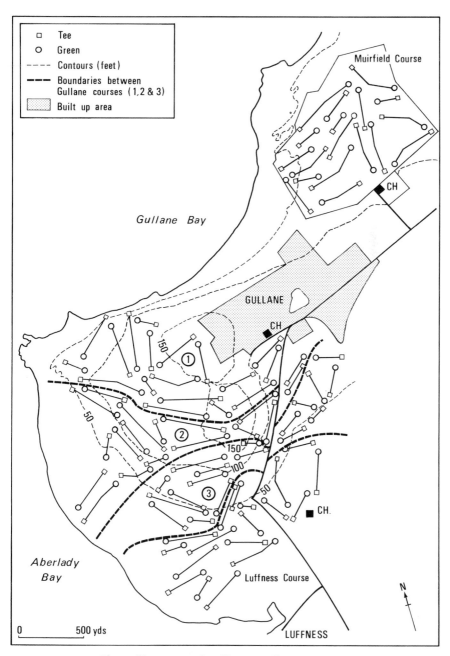

FIG 5.5 The golf courses of Gullane, Luffness and Muirfield.

originally laid out as a nine-hole course by James Braid and Ben Sayers in 1894 and extended to 18 holes in 1906. The first and 18th holes are on low lying links land developed upon a raised beach with a fossil cliff some 75 feet high on the landward side. Holes 2 to 17 are above the cliff and provide a course of gentle undulations, on an old marine platform covered with blown sand. There are excellent views across the Firth of Forth to the Kingdom of Fife and to the Bass Rock with its colony of gannets.

The small village of Gullane has been a major golfing centre for over 100 years—records show that the East Lothian Golf Club played over Gullane Hill in 1854. There are three courses at Gullane (A33, 34, 35), one at Muirfield (A59), Luffness New (A53) and Kilspindie (A41). Again, blown sand plays a major part in producing the character of all these courses but variations in relief, morphology and the underlying solid geology produce variations on the links 'theme'. Gullane Hill consists of Carboniferous sediments into which volcanic rocks (dolerite sills) have been intruded. Its summit stands 200 feet above sea level and its higher parts have a distinctly moorland appearance. However, on its northern, western and south-eastern flanks the hill has a covering of blown sand up to about 120 feet above sea level and large parts of the three courses (Fig 5.5) have been laid out on the links land. The Luffness New course was opened in 1893 and incorporates the original nine holes of Luffness Old which was founded in 1867. It is a comparatively flat course built on postglacial marine sediments and blown sand on the south-western flanks of Gullane Hill. The greens on this course were reputedly described by Gerald Micklem as the finest in Scotland. This course is used during the Oxford and Cambridge Golfing Society's Scottish tour and is also used as a qualifying course for the Open Championship.

From the top of Gullane Hill there is an excellent view north-eastwards (Pl 5.6) towards Muirfield (A59). On the sky line are the distinctive volcanic hills of Bass Rock and North Berwick Law while in the foreground is Gullane Beach backed by the high (45 feet) coastal dune ridge. Gullane Bay has a variety of dune forms and there is an extensive area of blown sand some half a mile in width underlying Muirfield golf course, upon which is a series of old dune ridges aligned west-south-west to east-north-east.

Although the links at Muirfield has been the home of the Honourable Company of Edinburgh Golfers only since 1891, the minute records of the club go back to 7 March 1744, at which time the members played on Leith Links. They subsequently moved to Musselburgh in 1836 and then to Muirfield. The Honourable Company drafted the original 'thirteen rules of golf' in 1744 and the

5.6   Muirfield from Gullane Hill.

original parchment on which these rules were written is in the Honourable Company's archives with a copy hanging in the Smoking Room of the Muirfield clubhouse.

The course is relatively flat, but the numerous hillocks, hollows and bunkers (a total of 151) and the relatively narrow fairways and fearsome rough together put a premium on length and accuracy. The ninth hole was once described by R T Jones Jnr as 'the best hole he knew in golf'. The concentric circulatory layout of the course (the back nine holes are located inside the front nine) make it an ideal course for the spectator with even the furthest points on the course being only a few minutes' walk from the clubhouse. Muirfield has been the venue for 11 Open, seven Amateur and six Scottish Amateur Championships as well as for Ryder, Walker and Curtis Cup matches.

Near Aberlady is the Kilspindie golf course (A41). Although the club was founded in 1867 the present course, which was designed by Willie Park, was opened in 1898. It is a flat links course sitting on a raised beach between 10 and 20 feet above sea level.

The Longniddry golf course (A51) is rather different from the other links courses in East Lothian. Although it sits on a sand-covered raised beach and is backed by the fossil cliff line of the postglacial sea (formed about 6,000 years ago), there are sections of the course which are of a parkland character with some fine Scots pines and various deciduous trees. Longniddry has a fine stone-built clubhouse which looks out over the course and the Firth of Forth.

The site of the Royal Musselburgh golf course (A75) at Preston Grange is difficult to classify. It is within half a mile of the coast, is built on a raised-beach and yet has all the characteristics of an inland parkland course. The forerunner of this club was the Thorntree Club which played on the links in Musselburgh—their 'Old Club Cup' for match play dating back to 1774. The present course was laid out by James Braid and opened in 1926.

The nine-hole course (A61a) in Musselburgh, mostly inside the horse racecourse is perhaps of more interest in an historical context than in its present golfing landscape. Golf was being played on these links as far back as 1672. This course was one of the original venues for the Open Championship, along with Prestwick and St Andrews, and it remained on the rota until 1891. During the mid-nineteenth century these rather inconspicuous nine holes were the focus of Scottish golf—the Honourable Company of Edinburgh Golfers, the Royal Musselburgh Golf Club, the Royal Burgess Golfers and the Bruntsfield Golfing Society all played here. Musselburgh produced champion professionals and became the centre of the golf ball and golf club manufacturing industry. Men of Musselburgh spread the game far and wide as they sought employment as golf professionals, course designers and club and ball manufacturers in many parts of the world. It was at Musselburgh that a tool to cut a standard $4\frac{1}{4}$ inch hole on the putting green was introduced in 1829. Because of the new hard paved roads to the right of the first few holes, a metal plate was fitted to produced the 'brassie' wooden club (1888) for use on these hard surfaces. The over-crowding of the links and the availability of rail transport led to the movement away from Musselburgh of the prestigious Edinburgh clubs and to the decline of Musselburgh as a major golfing centre.

Inland Courses

About a mile south of the town of Musselburgh, on the banks of the River Tyne and bissected by the main Edinburgh to London railway line, is the Monktonhall course (A61b). It is a parkland course on undulating land. This new home for the Musselburgh Golf Club was laid out by James Braid and opened in 1938.

Two other parkland courses, one at Haddington (A36) and one at Gifford (A31) add variety to the predominantly links courses of East Lothian. The 18-hole course at Haddington is run by the municipality and is located in 130 acres of fine parkland on the gravel terraces adjacent to the River Tyne. In great contrast is the nine-hole course at Gifford which sits on a rolling till-covered upland adjacent to the picturesque village with its wide main street and fine old buildings. Lord Tweedale leased a part of his estate for the construction of the course and the course was designed by the famous golfer and landscaper, Willie Watt of Royal Epsom. The course is surrounded by a fine beech hedge and mature woodland. It is indeed an interesting course, not least because it is in great contrast to the more famous links on the East Lothian coast.

MIDLOTHIAN

There are three parkland courses in Midlothian. Perhaps the least interesting is the rather flat course at Bonnyrigg (A7). To the south-east of Dalkeith is the beautiful mature parkland of Newbattle Abbey within which is to be found Newbattle Golf Club (A16). Much of the course is built on the terraces of the River South Esk with the river itself coming into play on the second and 17th holes. Glencorse Golf Club near Penicuik (A67) is partly built on the terraces of the River North Esk and also on an area of undulating upland and it therefore presents a variety of landscapes to the golfer.

WEST LOTHIAN

Many of the communities of West Lothian were associated with coal and oil shale mining during the nineteenth and early twentieth centuries. In this industrial background there are six parkland courses: Fauldhouse (A27), West Calder (A88), Linlithgow (A47), Livingston (A48), Pumpherston (A71) and Uphall (A87). The Harburn Club at West Calder is at the high altitude of 800 to 900 feet and has some characteristics of a moorland course despite the planted trees. The courses at Bathgate (A3) and Boness (A4) are moorland courses, the latter having spectacular views over the Firth of Forth.

EDINBURGH

This historic city has a long association with the game of golf. The 25 courses (only two of them being of nine holes) within the present boundaries of Edinburgh District (Fig 5.3) provide a variety of golfing landscapes with the notable lack of any true links courses. Golf was probably played within a mile of Edinburgh Castle on common land at Bruntsfield Links (not a true links course) in the fifteenth century (Fig 5.6). It was there that two of the oldest clubs in the world were established—the Royal Burgess Golfing Society (1735) and the Bruntsfield Golfing Society (1761). Edinburgh's third famous club, the Honourable Company of Edinburgh Golfers (1744) played over Leith Links (Fig 5.7). Neither the Bruntsfield Links nor the Leith Links accommodated these clubs for very long—the Royal Burgess Club moved first to Musselburgh (1836) and then to its present location (Fig 5.7) at Barnton in 1895. The Bruntsfield Golfing Society also moved to Musselburgh in the 1870s and then to its present site at Davidson's Mains in 1895, while the Honourable Company of Edinburgh Golfers moved from Leith to Musselburgh in 1836 and then on to Muirfield in East Lothian in 1891. The earliest Edinburgh clubs have therefore had associations with the flat links courses at Leith and Musselburgh before either returning to fine parkland sites to the west of the city or moving further afield, in the case of the Honourable Company, to the links at Muirfield.

Including the three famous old clubs of Edinburgh, which all moved to their present locations in the 1890s, the big expansion in the number of golf courses within Edinburgh District occurred between 1890 and 1912—16 courses being opened during this period. A further six courses (A17, 18, 46, 70, 72, 83) were opened between 1920 and 1930. Only one course has been opened since then—the municipal course at Silverknowes (A80) in 1947. The concept of providing golf 'for the people' became a strong idea at the turn of the century—courses were to be owned and run by the City Fathers in contrast to the somewhat exclusive clubs which catered for the upper classes. The earliest municipal course was opened at Craigentinny (A12) in 1891 to be followed by the two courses on the Braid Hills (A5, 6) in 1893–4 and courses at Carrickvale (A9) in 1930 and Silverknowes (A80) in 1947. The course at Portobello (A68) which dates back to 1853 is also now a municipal course. This means that nearly a quarter of Edinburgh District's golf courses are 'public' courses freely accessible to the visitor at a cost of £3 to £5 per round.

Two types of golfing landscape are to be found in Edinburgh District—moorland and parkland courses. The city of Edinburgh is built around a series of volcanic hills and uplands. The city centre is dominated by the 'crag and tail' of Castle Rock and the Royal Mile. Arthur's Seat and Salisbury Crags also bear witness to ancient volcanic action. None of these locations provide sites for golf courses. However, to the south of the city, the steep craggy slopes of the Braid

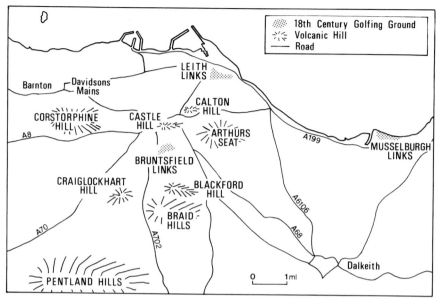

FIG 5.6   The location of the early golfing grounds of Edinburgh.

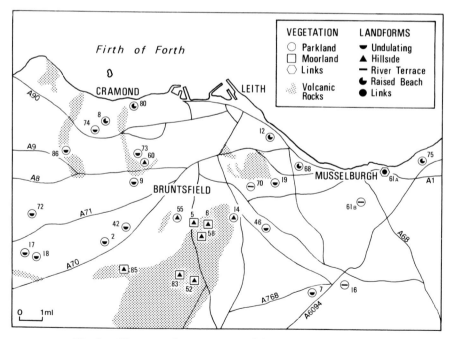

FIG 5.7   The landforms and vegetation of the golf courses of Edinburgh.

Hills and Pentland Hills produce not only sites for distinctive moorland golf courses but also magnificent views across the city to the Forth Estuary and beyond to the north. There are three courses on the north face of the Pentland Hills (A52, 83, 85). Lothianburn (A52) which was redesigned by James Braid in 1928 has been described as a good example of mountain golf—the par four ninth hole providing a particular challenge. The course at Swanston (A83) is less spectacular, but that at Torphin Hill (A85) has several steep climbs with the highest part of the course rising to over 800 feet. All three courses provide spectacular views across the city of Edinburgh to the Firth of Forth. The Braid Hills are the location of three excellent courses—the two municipal courses of Braids United (A5, 6) and Morton Hall (A58). The Braids United courses have been described as an excellent combination of hill walking and golf with drives from high crags down or across intervening valleys.

Volcanic rocks also underlie Craigmillar Park (A14), Merchants (A55), Murrayfield (A60), Ravelston (A73) and Turnhouse (A86) but none of these sites are as craggy or are at as high an altitude as the courses on the Pentland or Braid Hills. They still tend to be hilly courses but have a parkland character. Craigmillar Park golf course is situated near the Royal Observatory on Blackford Hill. This hill is a 'crag and tail' and the course is laid out along the tail and up onto the higher slopes of the volcanic crag. The Merchants course (A55) is built around ridges and valleys cut into volcanic rocks and is also quite hilly. The name of the club relates to the time when the city was divided into districts of merchants' associations. The membership of this club are proud of the fact that two of its members were awarded Victoria Crosses—one in the 1914–18 war and one in the 1939–45 war. The club records show that in 1936 James Braid redesigned four holes on the course for the sum of £5. The Murrayfield (A60) and Ravelston (A73) courses are adjacent to each other on the 'dip' slope of a volcanic sill—Corstorphine Hill. Both are hilly, parkland courses. Ravelston is a nine-hole course and once was described by a *Sunday Times* correspondent as the finest nine-hole course in Britain. The course at Turnhouse (A86) is also partly built on volcanic rock and it is adjacent to the busy Edinburgh airport.

Several of the Edinburgh courses were built in the grounds of large and distinguished 'country houses' around the periphery of the city. Baberton (A2) is an undulating parkland course originally planned by Willie Park. The club house building dates back to 1622. This club is also associated with the introduction of the steel-shafted golf club. Thomas Horsburgh, who was club captain from 1914–17 and 1929–31 made a patent application for a steel-shafted club in 1894, but it was not until November 1929 that the Royal and Ancient finally approved steel shafts. Liberton (A46) golf course was laid out around an eighteenth century mansion, Kingston Grange, which is now the club house. Just a short distance from Liberton are the ruins of Craigmillar Castle which was once the home of the first recorded lady golfer Mary Queen of Scots. On the south side of Arthur's Seat is the Prestonfield Golf Club (A70) which has a fine parkland course adjacent to Holyrood Park and Prestonfield House (now an hotel) which dates from 1687. A similar parkland course is to be found at Duddingston (A19). These courses offer high quality golf in a beautiful and historic setting in the heart of Edinburgh.

James Braid was associated with the design or alteration (redesign) of ten of Edinburgh's golf courses. Two of his finest courses are to be found at Dalmahoy (A17, 18) and a third just across the road at Ratho Park (A72). Dalmahoy, some seven miles to the west of the city centre, has two 18-hole courses (opened in 1927) in 1,000 acres of undulating parkland (Pl 5.7). They form part of a large sporting complex with facilities for squash, riding, trout fishing, archery and clay pigeon shooting. The east course is a fine test of golf and has been used for many championship events. A year after Dalmahoy opened, James Braid played a match against Harry Vardon on the nearby Ratho Park course which he had laid out among the beautiful trees in

5.7   Dalmahoy, Edinburgh—a fine parkland course.

the grounds of the Georgian mansion built in 1824. This must be one of the most beautiful courses in Scotland.

Within a one mile radius of Davidson's Mains on the west side of Edinburgh and adjacent to the shore of the Firth of Forth are to be found the two faces of Edinburgh golf. Two world-famous clubs, the Royal Burgess Golfing Society (A74) and the Bruntsfield Links Golfing Society (A8), brought their eighteenth century traditions to beautiful parkland locations in the 1890s. Both clubs maintain first-class courses and treasure their great history. Just half-a-mile towards the banks of the Forth from the Bruntsfield course is to be found Edinburgh's newest course, the Silverknowes municipal course (A80). It is a good test of golfing skills and although it does not have the great traditions of its illustrious neighbours it makes an important contribution to the Edinburgh golfing scene.

Edinburgh frequently claims to be the Golfing Capital. While other towns or cities may wish to dispute this claim, there can be no doubt that for over 300 years golf has been played in and around the city. If Edinburgh is chosen as a centre for a golfing holiday, not only do the 25 courses of Edinburgh District have much to offer but within easy access are the links of East Lothian and the numerous courses across the Forth estuary in the Kingdom of Fife.

Chapter 6

STRATHCLYDE

REGION B

Scotland's largest administrative region stretches from Loch Ryan in the south to the island of Coll in the north (over 200 miles) and from Biggar in the east to Islay in the west. Although this region contains nearly half of Scotland's population (2.4 million), 1.7 million of the region's population is concentrated in the Greater Glasgow conurbation, so that many other parts of the region have very low population densities. No other Scottish administrative area has such a variety of landscapes ranging from the urban canyons of central Glasgow to the rugged mountains of the south-west Grampians and the wind-swept shores of the Inner Hebridean Islands.

Strathclyde Region contains 150 golf courses, only 31 of which are of nine holes. For ease of reference the region is divided into seven sub-regions (Table 6.1 and Fig 6.1). Greater Glasgow consists of the City of Glasgow and its suburbs and surrounding areas from Dumbarton and Kilbirnie in the west to Kilsyth, Cumbernauld, Airdrie and Wishaw in the east, and from Milngavie in the north to Eaglesham and East Kilbride in the south. In this sub region there are 80 golf courses within a 15-mile radius of the centre of Glasgow (George Square). Within 30 miles or approximately one hour's drive by car from the centre of Glasgow, there are about 120 golf courses, which makes Glasgow the leading city in Europe in terms of accessibility to golf courses.

The distribution of golf courses in Strathclyde Region is strongly concentrated in and around Glasgow, in Lanarkshire, along the shores of the Firth of Clyde, and in Ayrshire. These four sub-regions contain 133 out of the total of 150 golf courses.

Golf was played on Glasgow Green in the seventeenth century and the first Open Championship was played at Prestwick in 1860. Glasgow Golf Club has just celebrated its 200th anniversary. There is therefore a long tradition of golf in Strathclyde, but prior to 1879

TABLE 6.1

THE POPULATION, NUMBER OF COURSES AND COURSES PER HEAD OF POPULATION IN THE
SEVEN SUB-REGIONS OF STRATHCLYDE

	Population Thousands	No of Courses 18-Hole	No of Courses 9-Hole	Total No of Courses	Courses per Head of Population
Greater Glasgow	1,700	70	10	80	1/21,000
Lanarkshire	58	7	2	9	1/6,400
Firth of Clyde	110	12	6	18	1/6,100
Ayrshire⎫	376	24	2	26⎫	1/11,400
Arran ⎬		3	4	7⎭	
Kintyre, Mid Argyll, Oban ⎫	66	3	3	6⎫	1/6,600
Islay, Jura, Mull, Coll, Tiree⎭		1	3	4⎭	

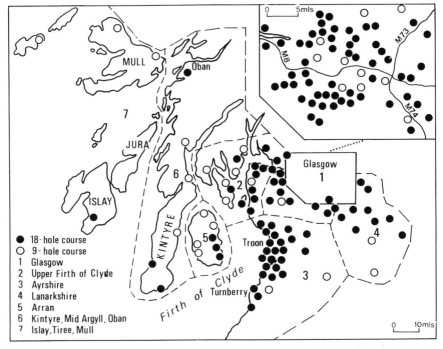

FIG 6.1 The location of nine-hole and 18-hole courses in the seven sub-
regions of Strathclyde.

(Fig 2.3) there were only five courses in existence. A major expansion took place between 1880 and 1909 (Fig 2.6) when a further 86 courses were opened.

Apart from the classic links courses at Turnberry, Prestwick, Troon, Machrihanish and Machrie (Islay), the majority of the courses in Strathclyde are inland, parkland or moorland courses. However, there is enormous variety within these two broad categories depending on the local geology, altitude and vegetation. The quality of the golf courses ranges from those of championship standard at Turnberry and Troon to unsophisticated nine-hole courses either in the heart of the City of Glasgow or amid the beautiful scenery of Argyll or the Islands.

Greater Glasgow

The City of Glasgow lies at the centre of a basin, through which the River Clyde and its tributaries flow to the Firth of Clyde. This basin is surrounded by hills which rise to over 1,000 feet in the Kilpatrick and Campsie Hills to the north (Pl 6.1), and to between 500 and 800 feet to the south-west and east of the City. There are five variables which

6.1 The Campsie Hills (plateau basalts) and drumlins in the Kelvin Valley, Kirkintilloch.

strongly influence the character of golf courses in the Greater Glasgow sub-region: solid geology; glacial history; vegetation; land use and altitude. About 300 million years ago central Scotland was located in the tropics some 600 miles south of the equator. A series of climatic changes from semi-arid to tropical resulted in the formation of the limestones and coals which were to play such a significant role in the development of Glasgow and other industrial towns in central Scotland during the nineteenth century. These sedimentary rocks underlie much of the Glasgow 'basin' while the high ground around the rim of the basin is composed of layer upon layer of volcanic rocks. The Clyde plateau basalts form a very distinctive upland landscape of rock steps and undulating plateau surfaces with a characteristic heather moorland vegetation. During the past two million years the Glasgow area has been inundated by glaciers on numerous occasions. The last great ice sheet covered the area completely 18,000 years ago and the last ice melted away about 13,000 years ago. A great glacier moved across the area from west to east, moulding the landscape by processes of erosion and deposition. The most distinctive features produced by the last ice sheet were the drumlins. These streamlined hills dominate the landscape of the lower parts of the Clyde Basin. They are a quarter to half a mile in length, 50 to 100 feet high, oval in plan shape, and usually consist of boulder clay or sand and gravel. There are some 800 drumlins in the Greater Glasgow area. After the glaciers melted away, the natural vegetation of the area would have been mixed deciduous woodland of oak, hazel, elm and birch. Little of this natural woodland survived the expansion of agriculture and industry. The deciduous trees which characterise so many parkland golf courses are the product of landscaping in the eighteenth and nineteenth centuries around large houses. Even the woodlands on the higher grounds were removed to permit grazing. Therefore, much of the present landscape of west-central Scotland reflects the changing patterns of land use which occurred during the agricultural revolution of the eighteenth and early nineteenth centuries and the industrial development of the nineteenth and twentieth centuries. There is a certain degree of altitudinal zonation in the landscape of the Greater Glasgow sub region. Below 100 feet the impact of glacial and fluvioglacial sedimentation, along with the occurrence of marine clays associated with the high stand of relative sea level about 13,000 years ago, produced relatively flat land. Between 100 and 300 feet above sea level, large numbers of drumlins produce a landscape which is strongly streamlined and dominated by short steep slopes. Above 400 feet, steep slopes are associated with the outcrops of volcanic rocks while undulating plateaus have developed on the Carboniferous sediments (limestones, sandstone, coals).

The golf courses of the Greater Glasgow sub-region strongly reflect these variations in altitude (Fig 6.2). Only ten golf courses are at altitudes of less than 100 feet. These are all parkland courses built on either river terraces or raised marine clays around the upper Firth of Clyde in the vicinity of Renfrew, Paisley and Erskine. Twenty-eight courses are between 100 and 300 feet above sea level and most of these are built on the drumlins and associated glacial and fluvioglacial deposits. The drumlin landscape produces an interesting variety of slopes in a relatively small area upon which the golf course architect can exercise his talents. There are 32 courses above 300 feet of which 15 are classed as moorland courses. All of the moorland courses are sited on outcrops of volcanic lava and they provide a most distinctive golfing environment. Six of the courses are between 500 and 750 feet above sea level and they often provide the golfer with spectacular views while at the same time exposing him to the full fury of wind and rain.

Because of the large number of golf courses in the Greater Glasgow sub-region it is further sub-divided into four quadrants (Fig 6.3)—north-west, north-east, south-east and south-west.

NORTH-WEST GREATER GLASGOW

There are 15 golf courses (three of nine-holes) on the north-west side of Glasgow (Fig 6.3). They range from Killermont (B61), the present home of the 200-year-old Glasgow Golf Club, to Ruchill, a nine-hole municipal course in the centre of a housing estate. The Glasgow Golf Club began its life on Glasgow Green alongside the River Clyde in the eighteenth century. It moved to Queens Park in 1870, to Alexandra Park in 1874, and to Blackhill in 1895 before occupying its present site at Killermont in 1904. Such movements are typical of golf clubs situated in a rapidly expanding city. The present Hilton Park Golf Club (B110, 111) was originally the Glasgow North Western Golf Club whose golf course was situated in the Ruchill district, but which was forced to give up its course because the ground was acquired by Glasgow Corporation for the purpose of building houses. At the same time the Bankhead Golf Club, whose course was at Scotstounhill had also had its ground bought by Glasgow Corporation for housing schemes. The officials of both clubs met and decided to purchase a large tract of hill land some nine miles north of the city. James Braid was commissioned to design two courses and they were opened in 1928. The migration of clubs and courses from city centre to suburban or rural sites as a result of pressure on land for uses other

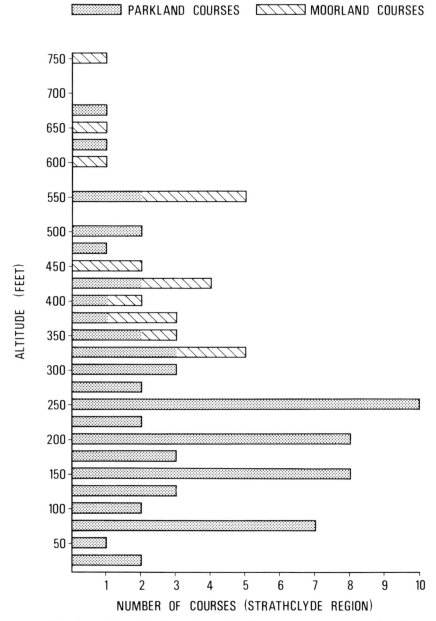

FIG 6.2 Number of parkland and moorland courses at various altitudes in Strathclyde.

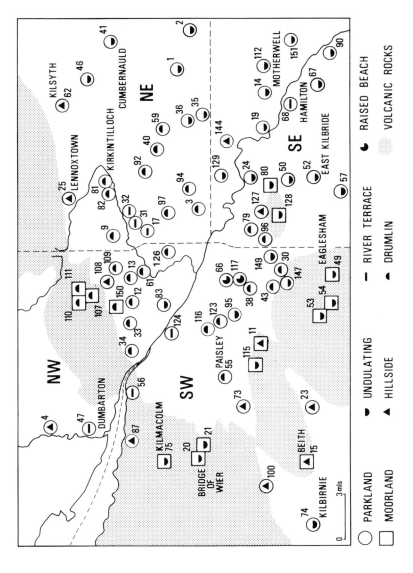

FIG6.3   The landforms and vegetation of golf courses in Greater Glasgow.

than golf has produced some fine clubs and courses. The two courses at Hilton Park command fine views across the city to the south as well as to the Highlands in the north. Since the highest part of the course is over 500 feet the golfer can experience the full impact of a south-westerly gale.

Twelve of the 15 courses to the north-west of Glasgow have been built on drumlins (Fig 6.3). They fall into two distinct groups. The group of four courses (Clober—B108; Milngavie—B107; Hilton Park—B110, 111) in the valley of the Allander Water to the north of Milngavie occur on drumlins which were formed by glacier ice which moved from north-west to south-east through a gap in the Kilpatrick Hills. Because of their high altitude (350–500 feet) the Milngavie and Hilton Park courses have a mixture of moorland and parkland while the Clober course is parkland. The eight other drumlin courses (B34,

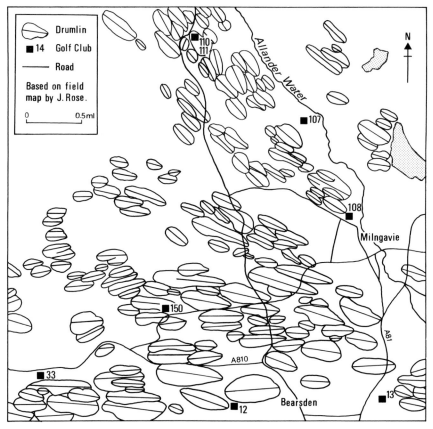

FIG 6.4   The drumlins and golf clubs of north-west Glasgow.

33, 12, 150, 109, 13, 61 and 126) are all part of the main Glasgow drumlin field which has a general west to east alignment (Fig 6.4). Although the main landform type upon which these eight courses are built produces a certain degree of similarity between the courses they also have certain distinctive characteristics. Windy Hill (B150) is a moorland course perched high on a hillside (over 400 feet) and lives up to its name with strong westerly winds funnelling up the Firth of Clyde. The public course at Dalmuir-Clydebank Overton (B34) is built on two large drumlins some 75 feet high and although the course is a parkland area it is surrounded by high-rise flats. The Clydebank and District course (B33) is at a higher altitude (250 feet) and is mainly built along the flanks of one long, narrow drumlin which has a distinctive west-east crest. The Bearsden (B12) and Douglas Park (B13) courses are similar in that they are both parkland courses built on west-east aligned drumlins with the Roman Wall (Antonine Wall) in close proximity. The newest course in this area, opened in 1978, is at Dougalston (B109). Although built across several west-east aligned drumlins the drumlinoid aspect of the course is less apparent because many of the fairways have been cut through woodland. This is the only course in the Greater Glasgow area which is dominated by tree-lined fairways. Only the northern part of the fine course of the Glasgow Golf Club at Killermont is built on drumlins. Three-quarters of this beautiful parkland course to the west and south of the clubhouse is built on gravel terraces alongside the River Kelvin. In stark contrast to the fine parkland landscape of Killermont is the nine-hole public course at Ruchill (B126) which is built across a low drumlin and surrounded by housing schemes (Pl 6.2).

Only three courses on the north-west side of Glasgow are not on drumlins. The nine-hole municipal course at Knightswood is built on raised-marine sediments (an old raised beach) and is fairly flat. Similarly the flat, parkland course at Dumbarton is built across a river terrace on the floor of the Vale of Leven. The course at Alexandria (B4) is built on a hillside with fine views to the north.

The 15 courses on the north-west side of Glasgow mainly provide golf in urban or suburban environments. Even those courses beyond the built up area (B107, 110, 111, 150) are dominated by views across the city. Only amidst the tree-lined fairways of Dougalston or on the parkland of Killermont is the presence of the city less pervasive. Even these two courses have the misfortune to be located below the main flight path to Glasgow Airport.

6.2   Ruchill—a municipal course in the heart of Glasgow.

NORTH-EAST GREATER GLASGOW

The 21 courses in this sub-region fall into three groups (Fig 6.3): the courses on the higher ground to the north (at the foot of the Campsie Hills) and east; the drumlinoid courses; the courses in the Kelvin Valley. Only two of the courses are of nine holes: Kilsyth Lennox (B62) and Alexandra Park (B3).

Two courses (B25 and B62) have been built on the lower slopes of the south-facing escarpment of the Campsie Hills. They are on the edge of the moorland although the Campsie Course at Lennoxtown has a parkland character. Another course at a relatively high altitude (400 feet) is Dullatur but it, too, has a parkland character. A new course has been built on the outskirts of Cumbernauld New Town (B41). It is a municipal course located on an undulating plateau at 500 feet to the east of the town. The industrial area of Coatbridge and Airdrie has four courses (B35, 36, 1 and 2). The Airdrie Club was established in 1871. The Coatbridge Townhead course, on the other hand, is a municipal course opened in 1970.

There are nine courses built on drumlins in this sub-region (B59, 40, 92, 97, 94, 3, 81, 82, 9). Three of them are municipal courses:

Alexandra Park (B3), Letham Hill (B94) and Little Hill (B97). All these courses are within the City of Glasgow and therefore surrounded by built-up areas. In considerable contrast are the fine parkland courses at Crow Wood (B40) and Balmore (B9). The most distinctive drumlin course is at Mount Ellon where the drumlin form is easily visible (Pl 6.3). The course at Lenzie (B92) is built over a series of three large drumlins each with a strong west to east alignment. The courses at Kirkintilloch and Hayston are built on a combination of drumlins and associated fluvioglacial sands and gravels. The drumlin forms are quite subdued and at least parts of these courses have been modified as a result of the removal of sand and gravel prior to their construction.

There are three courses (B17, 31, 32) in the Kelvin Valley, near Bishopbriggs, which owe their character to the glacial and post-glacial history of this valley. Prior to the last glaciation this valley was much deeper than it is at present. A glacier moved up the valley from west to east and deposited large quantities of debris on the valley floor. The westward flowing River Kelvin has subsequently cut into these gravel deposits and produced flat-topped river terraces upon which the Bishopbriggs course (B17) and the two courses of the Cawder Golf Club have been built. The Cawder and Kier courses are in fine

6.3 Mount Ellon—fairways across the heart of a drumlin. Note the cultivation ridges (rigs).

parkland but several of the holes are largely man-made on ground reclaimed after the commercial exploitation of sand and gravel.

While the north-east side of Glasgow cannot claim to have any courses of great distinction, there is much variety amidst the relatively large number of courses in this essentially suburban area.

SOUTH-EAST GREATER GLASGOW

The 18 golf courses (Fig 6.3) in this sub-region (four nine-hole courses) either occur in the industrialised Clyde Valley or on the high (500–600 feet) plateau which rises above the valley to the south-west. Seven of the courses are municipal—Sandyhills (B129); Kings Park (B79) and Linn Park (B96) in Glasgow, Torrance House (B52) and Langlands (B51) in East Kilbride, Strathclyde Country Park (B68) in Hamilton and Larkhall (B90). All except two of the courses are classed as parkland courses, although most of them are dominated by the urban environment which surrounds them. During the past 20 years the section of the Clyde Valley between Rutherglen and Wishaw has been transformed by the removal of much of the industrial blight which characterised this area following the decline of numerous heavy industries. The south-eastern boundary of the City of Glasgow is often remarkably sharp, the golf course at Blairbeth (B127) being bounded on the north by the housing estate of Castlemilk and on the south side by the wooded slopes of Cathkin Braes. The two municipal courses at Kings Park (B79) and Linn Park (B96), both of which are built on drumlins, are small oases of green amidst the urban landscapes of Glasgow's South Side. A mere two miles to the south-east, the fine course of Cathkin Braes Golf Club (C128) sits high on the lava plateau at an altitude of 650 feet in a moorland environment. The Kirkhill Course (B80) at Cambuslang is another moorland course on the plateau.

With the exception of the nine-hole course at Calderbraes (B144), which is a hillside course, and the nine-hole course at Strathclyde Country Park (B68), which is built on river terraces, all the other courses in the Clyde Valley are undulating parkland. In terms of quality, most of them are undistinguished although the Riccarton Course at Hamilton (B67) designed by James Braid is both a well-kept and a challenging course.

The three courses near the New Town of East Kilbride are all located on the plateau surface at between 500 and 700 feet. The East Kilbride Club has played at Nerston (B50) since 1900 and long pre-dates the New Town development. Two municipal courses—Torrance

House (B52) and Langlands (B57)—followed the expansion of the population in this area associated with the New Town development. The Langlands course was opened in 1983 and is still in an immature state.

Apart from the two courses on the Cathkin Braes (Blairbeth and Cathkin Braes Golf Clubs), Torrance House, East Kilbride, Bothwell Castle and Hamilton Riccarton, the courses to the south-east of Glasgow are neither very attractive nor of high quality. This sub-region does not have the variety of golfing landscapes which occurs in the other three Glasgow sub-regions.

SOUTH-WEST GREATER GLASGOW

It is not surprising that the south-west quadrant of Greater Glasgow has the largest number of golf courses. The 27 courses (only one of nine holes) are largely a response to the high quality of the suburban housing of the area along with the good communications network linking much of Renfrewshire with the centre of Glasgow.

The golf courses of this sub-region are of four types (Fig 6.3, Fig 6.5).

1. Those built mainly on river terraces or raised marine sediments: Erskine (B56), Haggs Castle (B65), Pollok (B117) and Renfrew (B124).
2. Those built mainly on drumlins: Cathcart Castle (B30), Cowglen (B38), Deaconsbank (B43), Elderslie (B55), Barshaw (B116).
3. Those built on hillsides or undulating land but with strong parkland characteristics: Caldwell (B23), Cochrane Castle (B73), Kilbernie (B74), Gleddoch Golf and Country Club (B87), Leverndale (B95), Lochwinnoch (B100), Whitecraigs (B147), Williamwood (B149).
4. Those built at relatively high altitude (400–600 feet) on the plateau basalts and which have a distinctive 'craggy' appearance and a dominantly moorland vegetation: Barrhead (B11), Beith (B15), Bridge of Weir—Old Ranfurley (B20), Ranfurley Castle (B21), Eaglesham (B49), East Renfrewshire (B53), Eastwood (B54), Kilmacolm (B75), Paisley-Braehead (B41).

In each of the above four types there are respectively four, six, eight and nine courses. Although the main contrast is between the

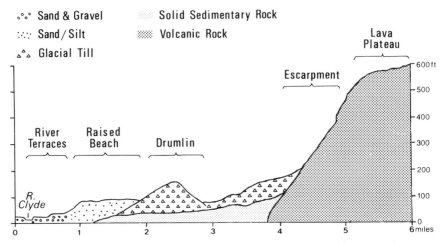

FIG 6.5   Cross-section of typical rocks and landforms in south-west Glasgow.

parkland courses of types 1, 2 and 3, and the moorland landscapes of type 4, there is considerable variety within each type.

Four courses close to the River Clyde owe their character to the changing sea levels which affected this area after the last glaciers wasted away (see Chapter 3). A relatively high stand of sea level about 13,000 years ago allowed the deposition of marine clays in the areas around Renfrew, Paisley and Pollok and these clays now underlie relatively flat land up to an altitude of about 100 feet above present sea level. In many locations the flat 'carse' lands (raised estuarine mud flats) lap against the relatively steep slopes of drumlins. Two fine golf courses were built on the relatively flat land between drumlin hills at Pollok (B117) and Haggs Castle (B65). The fine mature parkland of the Pollok estate provides a most attractive setting for a good golf course of 6,257 yards (SSS 70). Nearby are the attractions of Pollok House itself and the now world famous Burrell Museum. The Haggs Castle course is a championship course (6,464 yards, SSS 72) which for several years hosted the PGA European Tour's Glasgow Open Championship. The competition has now become the Scottish Open and has moved to Gleneagles.

As the River Clyde adjusted itself to the changing sea levels following the last glaciation, it cut terraces into the glacial, fluvioglacial and marine sediments which had choked its course to the sea. Two parkland golf courses have been developed on the Clyde terraces at Renfrew (B124) and Bishopton (B56). Both courses are of high quality.

The six courses built on drumlins in this quadrant (B30, 38, 43, 55, 116, 123) reflect the fact that the drumlins to the south-west of Glasgow tend to be larger but less numerous than those on the north side of the city and they are often surrounded by relatively flat land underlain by marine clays. The drumlin forms are often modified by the presence of outcrops of solid rock but most of them have a strong north-west to sout-east orientation. All of the golf courses built on drumlins are relatively short (circa 6,000 yards) with SSS of 67–69. The shortest course (4,600 yards) is that at Deaconsbank (B43) and it is a public course. The most attractive course in this group is that of Cathcart Castle Golf Club (B30).

In the heart of south side suburbia are located two fine parkland courses, Williamwood (B149) and Whitecraigs (B14), which are well-maintained and provide some interesting golf. They were designed respectively by James Braid and William Fernie and opened during the first decade of the nineteenth century. The course at Cochrane Castle, Johnstone (B73), is of a similar type. The parkland courses at Caldwell (B23), Kilbernie (B23) and Lochwinnoch (B100) are in a more rural setting. The most recent golfing development in this sub-region took place at Langbank with the opening of the Gleddoch Golf and Country Club (B87) in 1974. It is a parkland course (6,236 yards, SSS 71) designed by J Hamilton Stutt and built on a hillside with views across the Firth of Clyde.

There are six moorland courses in this sub-region, all of which are located on the Clyde plateau basalts (lavas) at altitudes of between 400 and 600 feet. All of these courses are characterised by their craggy outcrops and rough of heather and gorse. The course at Eaglesham (B49) and the two courses at Newton Mearns—East Renfrewshire (B53) and Eastwood (B54) are just beyond the suburban fringe of Glasgow and are of good quality. The two courses on the high lava plateau to the south of Paisley (Braehead B115 and Ferenze B11) provide spectacular views to the north-east while exposing the golfer to the full impact of inclement weather. There are two high quality moorland courses at Bridge of Weir (B20 and 21) and another at Kilmacolm (B75). The only nine-hole course in this sub-region is high up on the moorland to the south of Beith (B15). All of these moorland courses provide a distinctive golfing challenge where weather conditions are of prime concern.

THE UPPER FIRTH OF CLYDE

The pattern of the coastline in the Upper Firth, between the Kyles of

Bute in the west and Helensburgh and Greenock in the east, provides a very distinctive environment (Fig 6.6). Only occasionally are the fine views obtainable from many of the golf courses spoilt by industrial or urban development. The West Kyle, Loch Riddon, the East Kyle, Loch Striven, the Holy Loch, Loch Long and Gare Loch are glacially-scoured valleys which have been invaded by the sea. Along the shores of these sea lochs the ground rises rapidly to altitudes of between 800 and 2,000 feet. To the south of Port Glasgow, Greenock and Gourock, the plateau lavas provide high moorlands (600–900 feet) and this high ground is continued to the coast between Skelmorlie and West Kilbride. Even the island of Bute attains altitudes between 600 and 900 feet. While the industrial significance of Greenock and Port Glasgow as ports and famous centres of ship building are a part of the story of the past industrial prosperity of West Central Scotland, the rest of the Upper Firth has traditionally been a place of recreation. The development of steamer services as extensions

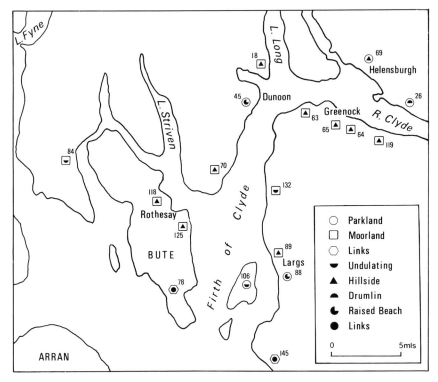

FIG 6.6 The landforms and vegetation of golf courses in the upper Firth of Clyde.

of the rail network during the second half of the nineteenth century led to the development of places such as Dunoon, Kilcreggan and Rothesay. Summer residences and holidays 'doon the water' in turn led to the opening of numerous golf courses between 1890 and 1910.

There are 18 golf courses (Fig 6.6) in this sub-region—four of nine holes, two of 13 holes and 12 of 18 holes. The majority of the courses (12) are of a moorland character but three are parkland (B45, B69, B26) and three are links courses (B88, B145, B78). None are of championship standard, few are of high quality, but most of the courses are interesting and are surrounded by fine scenery.

All of the 12 moorland courses stand on relatively high ground (300–500 feet). The four courses at Port Glasgow (B106), Greenock (B64, B65) and Gourock (B63) are all built on the Clyde Plateau lavas and therefore have a rather craggy appearance. The views northwards from these courses towards the Highlands can be spectacular (Pl 6.4). The course at Skelmorlie (B132) is distinctive in that it has 13 holes of a moorland character with excellent views across to Bute and Arran. The course at Routenburn (B89) was designed by James Braid and is located along the hillside overlooking the Firth of Clyde (Pl 6.5). Some of the holes on this course have some parkland characteristics. The two moorland courses on Bute, Port Bannantyne (B118) and Rothesay (B125) each have distinctive attributes. The Port Bannantyne course has 13 holes so that holes one to five are played twice to make up an 18-hole round—all for the price (in 1986) of a £2 day ticket. While a round at the Rothesay Golf Course (B125) cost £4.50 (1986), some stiff climbs are repaid by fine views and some very interesting golf. Each of the moorland courses at Tignabruich (B84), Inellan (B70) and Blairmore and Strone (B18) are of nine holes and all are noted for their views while providing good 'holiday golf'.

The three parkland courses at Cardross (B26), Helensburgh (B69) and Dunoon (B45) are all of good quality and each has distinctive features. The Cardross course is in fine parkland with the lower holes crossing the raised beaches which occur on the north side of the Clyde Estuary. The inland part of the course is built across drumlins and there are famous downhill drives from the 7th and 18th tees. The Helensburgh course, designed by Tom Morris in 1893, is of good quality but difficult to classify in that parts of it have a parkland aspect while other parts are moorland in character. From the higher parts of the course the Firth of Clyde can be seen to the south and Loch Lomond and the Highlands can be seen to the north.

The Cowal Golf Club at Dunoon (B45) plays on a course designed by James Braid and opened in 1890. Some of the holes cross raised-

6.4   Gourock Clubhouse and the Firth of Clyde.

6.5   Routenburn—a hillside course overlooking the Firth of Clyde.

5 Muirfield from the air at the time of an Open Championship.

6 Muirfield—the green of the short 13th hole.

7 Ratho Park. A parkland course with a fine clubhouse.

8 Braid Hills, No. 1 course: 1st green. A hillside course on volcanic rock on the south side of Edinburgh.

beach deposits and have an affinity with links land while other holes have a more inland/parkland character.

There are only three strictly coastal courses in the sub-region even though nearly all the other courses are close to the sea. Even the course at Largs (B88) is difficult to classify because although it is at a low altitude and is built across raised-beach sands and gravels and backed by a steep, wooded cliff, much of the course is of a parkland character. There is a small, nine-hole links course at Kingarth (B78) on the west side of Bute. It has small, fenced greens and is in a delightfully isolated position. The West Kilbride Golf Club (B145) plays over true links land at Seamill and the course can be regarded as the northern outpost of the string of links courses that are to be found along the Ayrshire coast between Irvine and Ayr.

AYRSHIRE

The old county name of Ayrshire tends to be used still in golfing circles rather than the more recent Kyle, Carrick and Cunninghame. Although not possessing a well-documented golfing history prior to 1851 (the founding of the Prestwick Club) to match the history of golf in East Lothian or Fife, the golf courses of Ayrshire have made and continue to make very significant contributions to Scottish golf. The 26 golf courses in this sub-region (Fig 6.7) fall clearly into two groups—the coastal courses and the inland courses (B5, B76, B77, B58, B104, B113, B105). The 19 coastal courses occur along a stretch of coastline only 30 miles long, and over one stretch of 12 miles between Irvine and Prestwick there are 13 links courses. A good drive from the extremities of one course will usually reach the adjacent golfing ground! No other county can claim to contain three venues which have been used for the Open Championship— Prestwick, where the Championship began in 1860 and was played for on 24 occasions, Troon and Turnberry. Although these championship venues naturally bring fame and fortune to the county, the 23 other courses offer a variety of golf to both locals and visitors. More golf is probably played in Troon on the five courses (three of the courses being public) than in any other town in Scotland—with the possible exception of St Andrews. In fact there are 11 public courses in the sub-region and it is probably easier to get a game of golf within a 20-mile radius of Prestwick than it is anywhere else in Britain.

Coastal Courses

The character and development of golf courses along the Ayrshire coast from Irvine in the north to Girvan in the south are the product of changing sea levels and the coming of the railway (Fig 6.8). The broad bay between Ardrossan and the Heads of Ayr and the low-level coastal platforms near Turnberry and Girvan, have been affected by major changes in sea level during the past 8,000 years (see Chapter 3). Some 6,000 years ago sea level stood between 25 and 35 feet higher than at present and as the sea fell to its present level large areas of raised beach sands and gravels were left high and dry. Along much of the coastline strong winds drove the sand into dune ridges and mounds. At some locations, golf courses have been built on relatively flat spreads of gravel and sand, while in other places these raised-beaches have been covered by blown sand and classic links and sand dunes have developed.

There is a remarkable concentration of links courses between Irvine and Prestwick. The urban development of this coastline was very

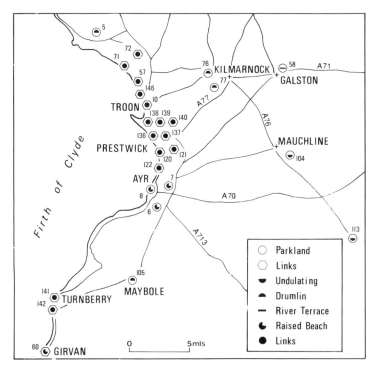

FIG 6.7   The landforms and vegetation of golf courses in Ayrshire.

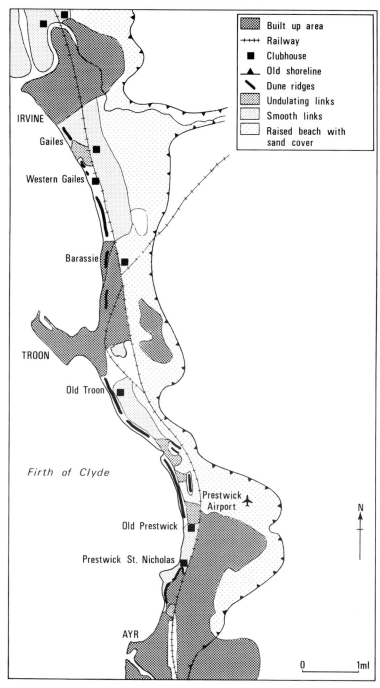

FIG6.8 The landforms of the golf courses between Ayr and Irvine.

much associated with the building of the railway in the mid nineteenth century thus linking it with Glasgow. Although relatively late starters compared with the links land of East Lothian and Fife, the Ayrshire links were to play a significant part in the development of golf in Scotland. While the links land between Irvine and Troon is of high quality and there are some fine views to the west, the industrial and urban development in this area detracts somewhat from the quality of the golfing environment.

The Prestwick Golf Club (1851) plays over what is now known as the Old Prestwick Golf Course (B120). This was the original home of the Open Championship (1860) and a stone cairn marks where the first tee used to be. From that tee, Young Tom Morris took three shots to cover 578 yards, holing out on what is now the 16th green, in one of his Championship rounds. It is interesting that the first golf course on the Ayrshire coast should be located on one of the most varied pieces of links land along this coastline (Fig 6.8). A course of some 6,544 yards (SSS 72) has been laid out between a high coastal dune ridge some 30 feet high and the railway. The ground varies between flat links, undulating links and hummocky dunes. The Prestwick St Nicholas course (B122), half a mile to the south, is built over similar terrain; a fine challenging course, it was used for qualifying rounds prior to the 1982 Open Championship at Royal Troon. The third course at Prestwick, Prestwick St Cuthbert (B121), is very flat, being built on a raised-beach with a thin covering of blown sand.

The Old Prestwick and Royal Troon courses are virtually continuous. In the 1920s the ninth green at Troon was only a short distance from the Prestwick course and members of both clubs would play from Troon to Prestwick in the morning and, having had lunch at the splendid Prestwick clubhouse, would play back to Troon in the afternoon. The Old Course (B136) at Troon (Pl 6.6) started as a five hole course in 1878. By 1883 the course had been extended to 12 holes and to 18 holes by 1886. The course is a combination of smooth undulating links on the landward side of a single dune ridge which merges into a series of dune ridges (15–30 feet high), towards the Pow Burn at the southern end of the course and a complex of hummocky dunes and undulating links in the south-east corner of the course. There are excellent views across the Firth of Clyde towards Goat Fell but the inland views are far less attractive. The Open Championship was first played here in 1923, and this course has the longest par five (577 yards, 6th hole) and the shortest par three (126 yards, 8th hole) on the Championship circuit. In the 1973 Open, Gene Sarasen had a hole-in-one on the eighth hole (the Postage Stamp) which was shown on television. The Royal Troon Club has a second course, the Portland

6.6   The Old Course, Troon. A course used for the Open Championship.

6.7   Western Gailes—a green in the midst of sand dunes.

(B137), which is a less stiff test of golf. It is built across undulating and flat links. There are also three municipal courses in Troon: Lochgreen (B138), Darley (B139), and Fullarton (B140). The Lochgreen course is the longest (6,765 yards, SSS 72) and has been used as an Open Championship qualifying course. The other courses are relatively flat and are less challenging.

On the northern edge of the town of Troon is the delightful links course of the Kilmarnock (Barassie) Golf Club (B10). This course was built by Kilmarnock merchants in 1877 and has many similarities with Old Prestwick. It is maintained to a high standard and has been used for qualifying rounds of the Open Championship.

The Barassie course is the most southerly of three courses which occupy a stretch of links land around Irvine Bay. A series of dune ridges (15–20 feet high) parallel the shore of the bay for two and a half miles and they merge into smooth links which in turn merge landward into a flat raised-beach covered with wind-blown sand. The Western Gailes Clubhouse (B146) stands on a terrace (the raised-beach) overlooking the links where fairways are often separated by marram or heather covered dune ridges (Pl 6.7). The course has no ladies' tees, there being no lady members. The course was built for Glasgow merchants, beside the railway line to Glasgow, and it is a fine example of a true links course. The club was host to the Curtis Cup in 1974, and thus allowed women into the clubhouse for the first time. Immediately to the north-east of the Western Gailes course is the Gailes Course (B57) of the Glasgow Golf Club. Somewhat less attractive than its neighbour, it is a good quality course used by the members of the Glasgow Club based in the heart of Glasgow at Killermont. One of the great attractions of the Ayrshire courses is that they usually remain playable throughout the winter at times when inland courses are closed because of frost or snow.

The two courses at Irvine, Bogside (B71) and Ravenspark (B72), are on rather flat terrain consisting of raised-beach deposits covered with blown sand. The Ravenspark course is a municipal course. Neither course is very distinguished.

The three courses in Ayr are all municipal courses and although they are near the coast and have been built on raised-beach deposits, they are all parkland courses. The mature deciduous parkland of Belleisle Park was utilised by James Braid to lay out the Belleisle (B6) and Seafield (B8) courses. The Ayr Belleisle course has been described as the best public inland course in Scotland. It has hosted the British Ladies and the Coca Cola championships, and in 1979 was a qualifying course for the European Open. The adjacent Seafield Course and the Dalmelling Course are both shorter (SSS 66) parkland courses

6.8   The 18th tee, Ailsa Course, Turnberry.

6.9   The 18th fairways of the Ailsa and Arran Courses, Turnberry.

but with green fees of less than £3 (in 1986) are pleasant alternatives to some of the more famous courses of this area.

Undoubtedly one of the most famous golf complexes in Scotland is to be found at Turnberry on the Ayrshire coast (Pls 6.8, 6.9). A first class hotel and two high quality courses, the Ailsa (B141) and the Arran (B142), in a magnificent scenic setting place Turnberry high on the list of Scotland's golfing centres. Both courses are on links land, but the championship course (the Ailsa) is partly built among the high dune ridges which fringe the bay. The Arran course is less spectacular and is located on a gently undulating raised-beach surface with a thin covering of blown-sand.

The original course at Turnberry was designed by Willie Fernie, and the Turnberry Golf Club was founded in 1902. The Arran course was opened in 1912. The development of Turnberry by the Glasgow and South-Western Railway Company not only required the building of a first-class hotel, but also the construction of an expensive railway between Ayr and Girvan. Both the hotel and railway were opened in 1906. Between 1920 and 1939 the rich and famous would travel to Turnberry by train and enter the hotel by a covered way leading from the station into the entrance lounge. Although not facing the courses and the sea, the railway entrance was known as the front of the hotel and remains so today, even though the station and line have long been closed.

During the First World War, Turnberry was used as a training station for pilots of the Royal Flying Corps and other Commonwealth Flying Units and the hotel was converted to an Officers' Mess. The damage done to the golf courses between 1914 and 1918 was very limited compared to the impact of the construction of an aerodome for RAF Coastal Command during the Second World War. The construction of concrete runways, hangars and numerous buildings virtually destroyed much of the golf courses apart from the coastal dune ridges. The hotel was used as a hospital. At a meeting in the hotel in 1946 the directors concluded that Turnberry was finished as a golfing centre. However, Frank Hole, Chairman of British Transport Hotels, who then owned the complex, convinced them that, by using the compensation due from the War Office, the rehabilitation of the golf courses and hotel was possible. Mackenzie Ross was asked to design the layout and Suttons of Reading were awarded the contract. After demolition of runways and buildings, they moved vast quantities of sand, gravel and topsoil: most of the Ailsa course was then completely re-turfed and was re-opened in 1951. This course is now ranked in the top ten of the best 50 British courses by *Golf World* and has hosted every major championship except the Ryder Cup. It

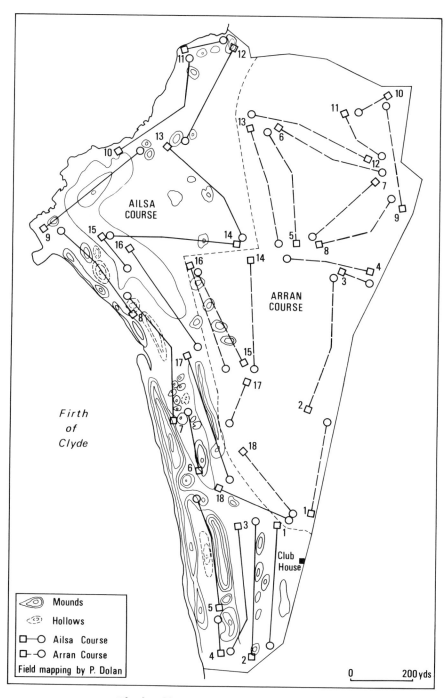

FIG 6.9　The landforms of the Turnberry golf courses.

was used for the Open Championship for the first time in 1977 when the dramatic final hole battle between Nicklaus and Watson took place.

The Ailsa course is 6,956 yards (SSS 71) of windswept links land (Fig 6.9). The course is dominated by a series of dune ridges which run parallel to the present shoreline and which reach heights of between 15 and 30 feet above the intervening hollows. Some of the fairways and greens are located in the inter-dune hollows and therefore have some protection from on-shore winds. Even such locations can suffer from a funnelling of wind, particularly when winds are blowing from the north or south. Although the Ailsa course has essentially a north-south alignment, there are five holes transverse to this alignment and therefore the golfer has to face up to a variety of wind directions during any round of golf. As on all great links courses, weather plays an important part in determining its difficulty.

The Arran course is built on gently undulating land, inland of the Ailsa course. At 6,276 yards (SSS 70) it is still a challenging course. Both courses are kept at a very high quality and attract many overseas visitors.

The southern outpost of the Ayrshire coastal courses is at Girvan (B60). It is a municipal course which has two distinct parts. Eight holes are located on a raised-marine platform covered with sand and these holes provide good links golf. Ten holes are on the flood plain adjacent to the River Girvan which crosses the course and provides a challenge at the 15th hole where a carry of 170 yards is required off the tee. The clubhouse is run as a 'public house' independently of the club, but still provides changing rooms and meals.

Inland Courses

The seven inland courses in Ayrshire are not particularly attractive or challenging, with three exceptions. The municipal courses at Kilmarnock (Annanhill, B76, and Caprington, B77) provide good parkland golf and the course of the Loudon Gowf Club at Galston is in an attractive location along a series of river terraces. The courses at Maybole (B105) and New Cumnock (B113) are both of nine holes and are of little merit.

LANARKSHIRE

The nine courses in this sub-region (Fig 6.10) have one thing in common—they are all over 500 feet above sea level and five of them are above 750 feet. One might expect that most of these courses would have a moorland character, but this is not the case. The only course classed as moorland is that at Leadhills (B91), which is Scotland's highest golf course at 1,200 feet above sea level. The relatively high altitude of all the Lanarkshire courses means that they tend to receive above average rainfall and experience more snow and frost. The growing season is shorter and they are therefore only in good condition for shorter periods than courses at lower altitudes or on the coast.

The courses at Leadhills (B91) and Douglas Water (B44) are both of nine holes. There are reasonable quality parkland courses at Strathaven (B133), Lesmahagow (B93), Carluke (B27) and Biggar (B16). The course at Biggar is a municipal course laid out on the flat-floored valley of the Biggar Gap.

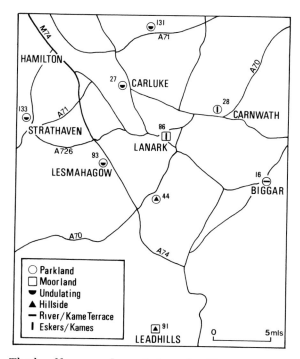

FIG 6.10 The landforms and vegetation of golf courses in Lanarkshire.

The courses at Carnwath (B28) and Lanark are built on sand and gravel laid down by the meltwaters of the last ice sheet. The Lanark Club was founded in 1851 which makes it one of the oldest clubs in the West of Scotland. The history of the club has been written by A D Robertson (*The Story of Lanark Golf Club 1851–1951*) and it makes interesting reading. The first course used by the club consisted of six holes on Lanark Moor. The course was reduced to five holes in 1853, extended to ten holes in 1857, to 13 holes in 1869, to 14 holes in 1885 and to 18 holes in 1897. The final layout was arranged by Tom Morris who received £3.10s. for his services. Ben Sayers devised a new layout in 1909 and further modifications were made by James Braid in 1926–7. The 1st and 18th holes have remained unchanged since 1851. Such additions and modifications to golf courses are probably typical of all nineteenth century Scottish golf courses but few are as well documented as the development of Lanark.

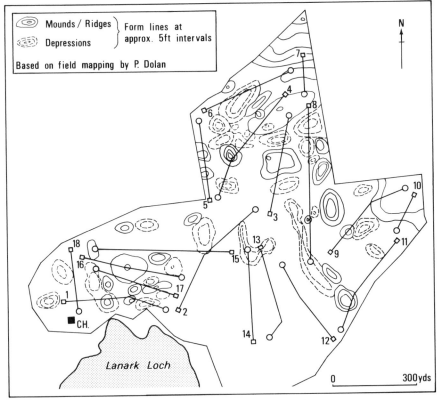

FIG 6.11 The landforms of Lanark golf course.

Lanark golf course is built on an area of undulating fluvioglacial sand and gravel. The hollows and undulations (Fig 6.11) are the product of the melting out of blocks of glacier ice buried beneath the sand and gravel spread. This type of landscape is the nearest inland equivalent to coastal links land. It is well-drained and tends to support good short grassland or moorland vegetation. In the early days the grass was kept short by the burghers' cows under the charge of a hind or cow-herd. The only implement used on the course until 1880 was a scythe. After that date, lawn mowers were acquired and a roller was bought in 1882. The first horse-drawn mower was purchased in 1897. Since the altitude of the course is some 600 feet above sea level, frosts can occur at any time of the year. Play can be interrupted both by frost, snow lying (an average of 28 days per year) and by periods of heavy rain. The course consists of a series of low mounds which rise some ten to 20 feet above the intervening hollows (Fig 6.11). The northern part of the course (holes three to eight) crosses the most complicated topography. With the exception of the greens which are generally located on elevated plateau areas, both mounds and hollows have been used for fairway and rough areas. Much of the course itself is characterised by moorland vegetation—coarse grasses, heather and whin. However, the surrounding stands of coniferous and deciduous trees tend to give the general landscape a parkland appearance. This is a good quality inland golf course maintained to a high standard.

Just a few miles east of Lanark is the Carnwath Golf Club (B28). The course is built mainly over a series of mounds (kames) and hollows underlain by sand and gravel. The course architect, Henry McKenzie, used the mounds (which rise to 10 to 50 feet) for rough, and the hollows for fairways and greens, although some greens and tees are located on a large mound (9th, 12th and 15th tees and 8th green). The deciduous and coniferous trees on the course introduce a parkland landscape but there are also strong moorland characteristics. Although the course is only 5,860 yards long (SSS 68) it is a most interesting course and well worth a visit.

Arran

The golf courses on the Island of Arran (Fig 6.12) are notable for three reasons: their fine scenic setting, their low green fees and their accessibility to visitors. No great championship courses are to be found here but the seven courses on the island provide excellent 'holiday golf'.

There are three 18-hole courses: Brodick (B102), Lamlash (B85)

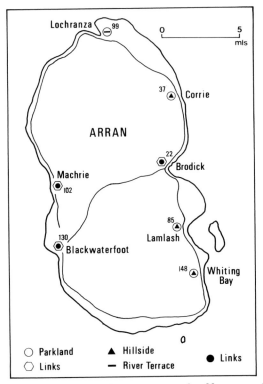

FIG 6.12   The landforms and vegetation of golf courses in Arran.

and Whiting Bay (B148). They are all short courses (less than 4,700 yards) but a round of golf cost (in 1987) less than £4. There is a 12-hole links course at Blackwaterfoot (Shiskine Golf and Tennis Club—B130) and nine-hole courses at Corrie (B37), Lochranza (B99) and Machrie (B102) on each of which a round of golf cost less than £3 (in 1987). All of Arran's golf courses occur at coastal sites but only three of them are links courses—Brodick, Machrie Bay and Blackwaterfoot.

Kintyre, Mid-Argyll, Oban

There are six golf courses between Oban and the southern tip of the Kintyre peninsula (Fig 6.13). The three nine-hole courses at Lochgilphead (B98), Tarbert (B134) and Carradale (B29) are very unsophisticated. The course at Lochgilphead was designed by the head physiotherapist at the local hospital, Dr Ian MacCammond, and the course was built by the hospital's patients and staff. The

Dunnaverty Golf Club at Southend (B48) was begun by local farmers in 1889. It is a links course, with small greens, and has some fine views. This is the home course of Belle Robertson, the Curtis Cup player and winner of many tournaments.

A very distinctive golf course is to be found in Oban (B114). Designed by James Braid, the course contains rock knolls and cliffs which provide some thrilling drives from the tees perched high on hillsides.

The last course to be described in this sub-region is often discussed in a whisper, as if those that know it simply do not wish to pass on the good news. The town of Campbeltown has two rather distinctive attributes—its nearby coalmine (now closed) and one of the finest links courses in Scotland at Machrihanish (B103). On the west shore of the Kintyre peninsula the wide sweep of Machrihanish Bay is open to the full force of the Atlantic winds and waves. A magnificent dune system backed by undulating links land has been used for golf since 1876. It has been said that had this links course of 6,228 yards (SSS 70) not been situated in such an isolated location it would have hosted many championships. Those golfers who have made the journey, either by road through the delightful scenery around Loch Fyne and down the Kintyre peninsula, or by plane from Glasgow to Campbeltown (Loganair), always speak very highly of this course.

The Islands of Islay, Colonsay, Tiree and Mull

A short flight from Campbeltown to Islay brings yet another golfing surprise. The Machrie course (B101), just outside Port Ellen, has 18 holes set amidst high dunes and rolling links land with every hole offering a challenge. There is an excellent adjoining hotel and Loganair offer various package deals from Glasgow. Not only is the golf of good quality, but Islay has many attractions including fine malt whisky, excellent fishing and a wide variety of bird life.

Although there are golf courses on the islands of Colonsay, Tiree and Mull, all but one fall into the category of 'holiday courses'. The exception is that at Tobermory, not because it is of championship standard, but because it has some very distinctive characteristics. The course is located on a hill high above the village, and it has magnificent views down the Sound of Mull and up Loch Sunart and to the surrounding mountains. It is a moorland course of nine holes with small greens and fairways which utilise the 'flats' of the step-like landscape of the basalt lavas on which the course is built. Some of the fairways are transverse to the line of the drive from tee to green and small cliffs can cause a well-hit ball to ricochet in all directions. Accuracy is more important than length on this course. A small clubhouse is only used for storage and the nearby Western Isles Hotel is used for collecting green fees (£2 per round in 1986) and for restoring the 'spirits' of golfers who have found this unique course rather more difficult than they had expected.

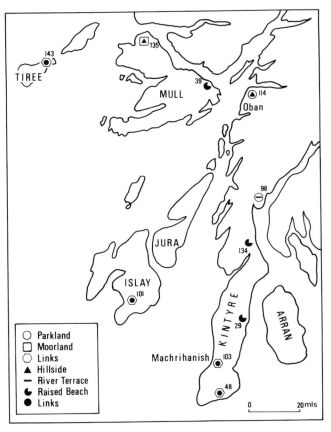

FIG 6.13   The landfoms and vegetation of golf courses in Argyll, Islay, Mull and Tiree.

Chapter 7

CENTRAL, FIFE AND TAYSIDE

REGION C

There are 96 golf courses in these three regions and together they may be regarded as the heartland of Scottish golf (Fig 7.1). This claim is based on both the antiquity of some of the clubs and courses (e.g. St Andrews 1754, Crail, 1786, Tayport 1817, Leven 1820, Royal Perth 1824, Carnoustie 1842, Earls Ferry (Elie) 1858, Lundin Links 1869, Stirling 1869) and the wide variety and large number of courses found in these regions. From St Andrews in the east to Gleneagles and Pitlochry in the west, and from Loch Lomond in the south to Montrose in the north, the golfing landscapes are full of variety and surrounded by delightful scenery. To some, the famous courses at St Andrews, Gleneagles and Carnoustie are the main attraction, but to others the delights of Ladybank, (C62), Lundin Links (C68), Elie (C42), Glenbervie (C47), Dunblane (C33), Pitlochry (C81), Forfar (C46) or Edzell (C41) are the basis for planning golfing holidays in this part of Scotland.

CENTRAL

The boundary of this region incorporates industrial areas adjacent to the Firth of Forth in the east, the shores of Loch Lomond in the west, the edge of the Highlands from Aberfoyle to Callander and the foothills of the Ochill Hills in the north-east (Fig 7.2). There are 19 golf courses in the region: six are of nine holes, 13 of 18 holes. Only two are moorland courses: Dollar (C30) and Muckart (C75), both on high ground to the south of the Ochil Hills. The other 17 courses are classed as parkland, there being no true links courses in this region.

The industrialised area of Falkirk-Grangemouth, on the south bank of the Forth Estuary, contains several interesting golf courses which owe their character to their location, either on carse clays (raised mud-flats) associated with former high sea levels, or sand and gravel

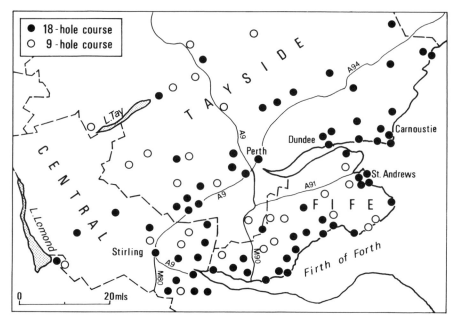

FIG 7.1 The location of nine-hole and 18-hole courses in Central, Fife and Tayside Regions.

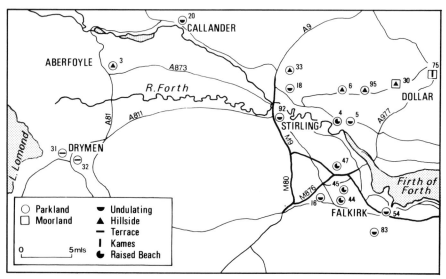

FIG 7.2 The landforms and vegetation of golf courses in Central Region.

deposited by the meltwaters of the last ice sheet (see Chapter 3). Some 6,000 years ago the Forth estuary was much wider than it is at present and the area around Falkirk, Larbert and Glenbervie was below sea level. The raised mud-flats and coastal terraces of the former estuary are now the sites of three courses: Falkirk (C44), Falkirk Tryst (C45) and Glenbervie (C47). Both Falkirk and Glenbervie are built partly on carse clays and partly on raised-beach gravels, while the Clubhouse at Glenbervie stands on the old shoreline and looks across the fairly flat carseland which has now been developed into a fine parkland course. This course hosted the Scottish PGA championship in 1986. The Falkirk Tryst course is rather flat and bears some similarities with a links course. The 18-hole municipal course at Grangemouth (C54) was opened in 1973 and is an undulating upland course. There are two rather undistinguished nine-hole courses at Polmont (C83) and Bonnybridge (C16).

There is only one golf course in Stirling (C92). It is a parkland course built on volcanic lavas in King's Park to the west of the town. However, just north of Stirling there is a nine-hole course at Bridge of Allan (C18) and an excellent 18-hole parkland course at Dunblane (C33). The Dunblane course which was opened in 1923, is built on a hillside some 250 to 400 feet above sea level. It is a well-maintained parkland course with some interesting holes and with magnificent views of the Forth Valley, the Campsie Hills and the Highlands to the north-west. Along the Highland 'edge', to the north-west, are two golf courses. The course at Callander (C20) is a good quality parkland course, while that at Aberfoyle (C3) has been extended to 18 holes and much improved in recent years.

The two courses at Drymen, near the southern shore of Loch Lomond, are really part of the Greater Glasgow golfing scene rather than a part of Central Region—Drymen is only half-an-hour's drive from the centre of Glasgow. The Buchanan Castle course (C31) is built on the flat terraces that border the River Endrick. It is a high quality course set in fine parkland. The nine-hole course of the Strathendrick Golf Club (C32) is built on silts and clays deposited in a former glacial lake.

Along the foot of the steep, southern face of the Ochil Hills is a series of four golf courses. Those at Alva (C6) and Tillicoultry (C95) are of nine holes and those at Dollar (C30) and Muckart (C75) are of 18 holes. The courses at Alva and Tillicoultry are built on hill-foot deposits of gravel and have a parkland character. The course at Dollar is built on the hill-side between 250 and 500 feet above sea level and has a moorland character, while the moorland course at Muckhart is built on an undulating upland some distance from the Ochil scarp.

The town of Alloa has two golf clubs. Alloa Braehead (C4) plays over a parkland course, to the west of the town, built on a raised-beach to the north of the River Forth. The Alloa Shawpark (C5) course is to the north-east of the town and is set in undulating parkland.

FIFE

Between the Firth of Forth and the Firth of Tay there is a 15-mile-wide peninsula which contains 33 golf courses (Fig 7.3). Several of these courses have long histories and many traditions. The game of golf during the period from the fifteenth to mid eighteenth centuries was certainly played over the fine links land at St Andrews and Elie and possibly at other locations. The game became more organised from the mid eighteenth century with the establishment of the following golf clubs in Fife: 1754, Society of St Andrews Golfers; 1786, Crail Golfing Society; 1817, Scotscraig Golf Club, Tayport; 1820, Leven Golfing Society; 1858, Earlsferry and Elie Golf Club; 1869, Lundin Links Golf Club. All of these clubs used the links land

7.1 St Andrews Courses.

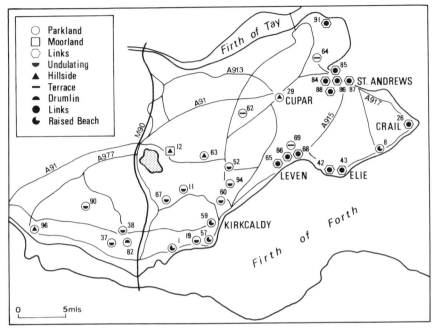

FIG 7.3 The landforms and vegetation of golf courses in Fife.

associated with the sequence of raised beaches all along the coast from Leven to Tayport—a total of some 20 miles of links land which contains 14 golf courses. Apart from Ladybank (C62) founded in 1879 and Dunfermline (C37) founded in 1887, all the inland golf courses in Fife were founded after 1890.

Coastal Courses

The history of golf at St Andrews is discussed in Chapter One. The presence of a large area of links land between the old harbour, within the estuary of the River Eden, and the ecclesiastical centre and market of the old city seems to have been significant in the early development of the game of golf. This links land was created as a result of the late-glacial and post-glacial sea level changes which are known to have occurred around the coast of Scotland during the past 13,000 years. Kincraig Point, one mile west of Elie, bears witness in the form of abandoned shore-platforms and cliffs to the former higher stand of the sea along this coast. The higher, abandoned shorelines (those over 30 feet above present sea level) were probably formed about 12-14,000 years ago. The lower raised beaches (10-30 feet above present sea levels) are related to a period of relatively higher sea

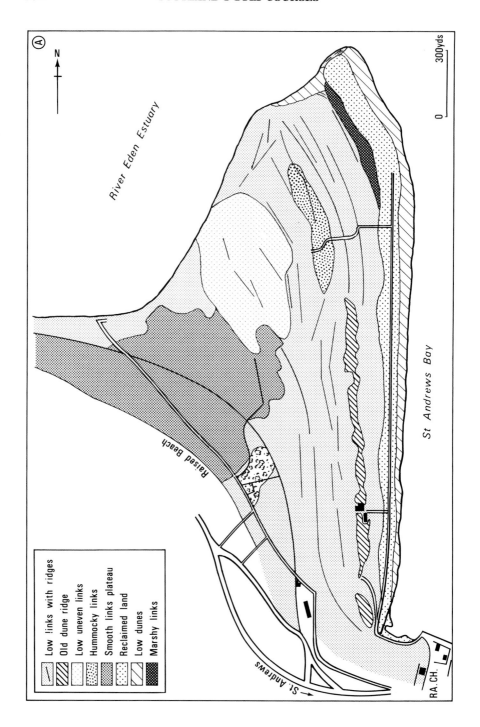

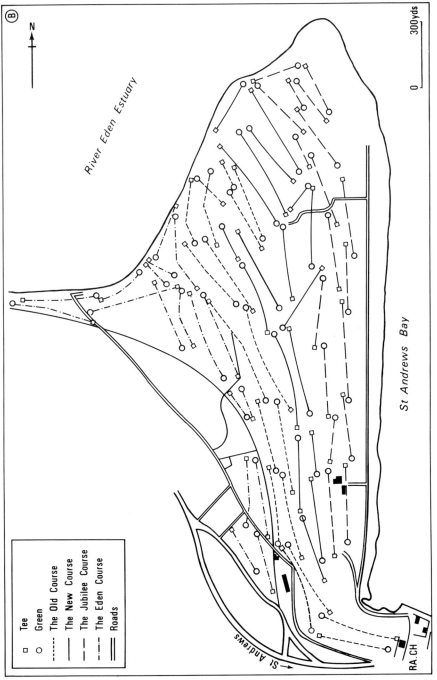

FIG 7.4 A: The landforms of the St Andrews golf courses. B: The 'Old', 'New', 'Jubilee' and 'Eden' courses at St Andrews.

level about 6,000 years ago. Since that time relative sea level has been dropping. The combination of a slowly falling sea level and the presence of large quantities of sand along the shoreline, either produced by the meltwaters of the last ice sheet or from the massive supply of sediment brought into the Tay and Eden estuaries, has permitted the development of extensive windblown sand spreads and dunes in several locations (see Chapter 3). The Pilmour Links at St Andrews are really a part of the large sand accumulation known as Tentsmuir. The area between the River Eden and St Andrews (Fig 7.4) has emerged from beneath the sea during the past 6,000 years and is underlain by a raised beach associated with a shoreline which runs roughly parallel to and just south of the main road (A91) between St Andrews and Guard Bridge. As the sea retreated eastwards from the old shoreline (at about 25 feet) large expanses of sand would dry out in the intertidal area and could be picked up and blown inshore by strong winds. Not only was the old raised beach buried by sand spreads but lines of sand dunes developed, generally aligned in a north–south direction. Most of the Old Course and Eden Course were built mainly on the gently undulating links land to the west of the main dune ridges (Pl 7.1), while the New and Jubilee Courses include dune ridges which stand 15 to 25 feet above the surrounding links and are usually covered with rough vegetation. Much of the area between the highest dune ridge and the present beach is reclaimed land.

Although the first written record of golf in the Royal Burgh of St Andrews does not occur until 1552, the game has probably been played on these links since the twelfth century. Not until after the formation of The Society of St Andrews Golfers on 14 May 1754, do we have much information about the course on the St Andrews links. The Society used the public links and even after it became the Royal and Ancient Golf Club of St Andrews in 1834 it did not, and still does not, own its own course. However, the Royal and Ancient is much concerned with the running of the five courses controlled by the St Andrews Links Trust and run by the Links Management Committee through its representatives on both bodies.

The Old Course originally consisted of 22 holes—11 out and 11 home. By the time the first survey of the course was made in 1836, it had been reduced to nine holes out and nine home, and from 1832 homeward players holed out on the same green but in a different hole. There were no tees, the player simply teeing off within two clubs' length of the previous hole. Since sand for teeing-up was obtained from the bottom of the hole, the holes became progressively deeper. Separate teeing grounds were introduced in 1846.

In 1895 the Royal and Ancient constructed the New Course (C87) on ground leased from St Andrews Town Council (Fig 7.4). The Jubilee Course (C86) was built by the Town Council in 1897 at the time of Queen Victoria's Diamond Jubilee. Originally consisting of 12 holes, it was extended to 18 in 1912. In order to accommodate the ever-increasing number of golfers, the Town Council constructed the Eden Course (C85) in 1912. Finally, the nine-hole Balgove Course (C84) was built in 1971, primarily for the use of children and beginners.

These five courses, the Royal and Ancient clubhouse, some five local clubs, several golf equipment and clothing shops, numerous first class hotels and the Old Town and university buildings make St Andrews the major and most attractive golfing centre in Scotland. There are plans to build a golfing museum adjacent to the Royal and Ancient club house and to construct another championship course in the vicinity of Strathtyrum.

Although early golf in Scotland is usually associated with St Andrews, other links in East Lothian, on the north-east coast and in other parts of Fife, were undoubtedly used by golfers in the eighteenth century. The Crail Golfing Society (C26) which now plays over the Balcomie Links was founded in 1786. This club claims to be seventeenth oldest in the world and has a complete set of minutes of the club meetings since its inception. The minute relating to the club's foundation reads as follows:

> Several gentlemen in and about the town of Crail who were fond of the diversion of Golf, agreed to form themselves into a Society. The Society was accordingly instituted upon the 23rd day of February 1786.

The Society first used a course at Sauchope before moving to its present site. Crail has one of the earliest recorded uses of iron rings to maintain the holes (1874), before the development of metal cups. The present course is built on a rock-controlled raised-platform covered by wind-blown sand which has only minor undulations and no marked dune ridges. There are no trees and very little rough vegetation.

Another early golf club was that at Tayport. The Scotscraig Golf Club (C91) was founded in 1817, making it the thirteenth oldest club in Scotland. The present lay-out was designed by James Braid. It is a gently undulating links course of 5,922 yards (SSS 71) with much heather and gorse rough and surrounded by coniferous plantations. It has similarities with a heathland course.

Between Leven and Elie, around the shores of Largo Bay there are six golf courses within an eight-mile stretch of coastline. Golf was played on the Earlsferry links in the sixteenth century and may well have been played on the Leven and Lundin links at the same time. The Leven Golfing Society (C65) was founded in 1820 and the Earlsferry and Elie Golf Club in 1858. (Elie Golf House Club 1875 and Earlsferry Thistle Club 1875). Formal golf was therefore well-established on the south coast of Fife by the mid nineteenth century. The Earlsferry links (C42) are rather similar to those at Balcomie in that they are gently undulating with no marked dune ridges except along the seaward edge of the course. The first two holes and the third tee are built on higher ground above the main links surface. The drive from the first tee is up over a ridge and the starter makes use of an old submarine periscope to ensure the fairway is clear, before permitting golfers to drive off. An excellent history of golf at Elie has been written by A M Drysdale. Iron bands to protect the holes on the course were first used in 1874 and the Club purchased its first lawn mower to cut the putting greens in 1877. The course is now kept in excellent condition.

Between Leven and Lundin Links there is a fine area of links land which has two quite distinct elements. Running parallel to the coast and extending some 400 yards inland is an area of wind-blown sand with a series of low (12–20 feet), parallel, old dune ridges. This true links land is backed by an old, abandoned cliff-line some 25 to 30 feet high, above which there is an almost flat raised beach at an altitude of between 50 and 60 feet above present sea level. The Leven Golfing Society (C65) play on the Leven Links which are in the south western part of this links system. The Leven Municipal course (The Scoonie Club, C66) is an 18-hole course, which apart from a few holes, is built mainly on the upper, flat raised beach. The Lundin Links course (C68) combines holes both on the low-level links (an extension of the Leven Links) and on the upper, flat raised beach. It is a first-class course and has been used for the qualifying rounds of the Open Championship when it has been held at St Andrews. The fourth course in this group is that played over by the Lundin Ladies Golf Club (C69) which is a nine-hole course located on the high raised beach. It is a gently undulating parkland with few trees.

There are three other courses along the south coast of Fife which, although they have coastal locations, are not typical links courses. The nine-hole course at Anstruther (C8) is built across two raised rock-platforms, both of which have a thin cover of sand. The 18-hole municipal course at Kinghorn (C57) is situated on a high coastal platform some 200 feet above sea level. It is a coastal moorland course and has fine views across the Firth of Forth. There is a delightful 18-hole course at Aberdour (C1) which is located on a series of raised marine-platforms. The first hole involves a drive across a valley to the green situated on a rocky promontary. Much of the course is parkland, developed on the sequence of raised beaches.

Although the Tulliallan course (C95) at Kincardine is primarily an inland course, with the majority of the holes on an upland some 150 to 200 feet above sea level, the first two and last two holes are in fact built across almost flat raised-beach deposits. The course is however, primarily in the parkland category.

Inland Courses

While the coastal courses of Fife may be of prime interest to the visitor, a great deal of local golf in this region is played on the 16 inland courses (six of which are nine-hole courses). It must be admitted, however, that of the 16 courses, only six can be regarded as good quality 18-hole courses—Dunfermline (C37), Burntisland, the two courses in Kirkcaldy (C59, 60), Glenrothes (C52) and Ladybank (C62). A large part of Fife, south-east of a line from Glenrothes to Kincardine, has had a long industrial history. The juxtaposition of delightful rural landscapes and attractive coastal villages with areas of both past and present industrial and mining activity is a major characteristic of this area. Perhaps the courses at Lochgelly (C67) and Auchterderran (C10) are the best examples of golf in the old industrial areas. The town of Dunfermline has three golf courses (C37, 38, 82) while Kirkcaldy has two (C59, 60), all of 18 holes and of parkland character. In a more rural setting there are interesting nine-hole courses at Saline (C90), Bishopshire (C12), Leslie (C63) and an 18-hole course at Thornton (C94).

The Dunfermline Golf Club (C37), founded in 1887, plays over some fine undulating parkland in the grounds of Pitirrane House to the west of the town. The old house is the heart of the clubhouse to which has been added a new extension. This high quality parkland course of 6,271 yards (SSS 70) is well worth a visit. Burntisland golf course (C19) is situated high above the town on an undulating upland. The two courses at Kirkcaldy are in considerable contrast. Kirkcaldy Golf Club (C59), founded in 1904, plays over hilly parkland to the south-west of the town while the municipal course (C60), opened in 1963 in the grounds of Dunnikier Park, is an undulating upland with old Scots pine plus more recently planted deciduous trees.

Another newcomer to the Fife golfing scene is the fine parkland course at Glenrothes (C52) which was developed in association with the creation of Glenrothes New Town. The 18-hole course of 6,449 yards (SSS 71) was laid out in an estate of fine mature parkland and opened in 1958.

Immediately inland from St Andrews there are three quite different golf courses and in a sense they sum up the range of inland golfing facilities throughout the region. A golf club was established in Cupar (C29) in 1855. The present course is a simple nine-hole lay-out on the side of a hill. A level stance is hard to find on this course and it is the only course where the path to the clubhouse passes through a cemetery. A little further inland is the excellent Ladybank course (C62). Tom Morris designed the original six holes and the present 18 holes constitute one of Scotland's finest inland courses. The course measures 6,617 yards (SSS 72) over fairly flat terrain. The turf has a heathland quality but there is much heather and gorse and extensive pine woods. This course was used as a qualifying course for the St Andrews Opens of 1978 and 1984.

It is perhaps appropriate to conclude this section on the golf courses of Fife with a reference to the nine-hole course at Leuchars, a mere six miles from St Andrews. Founded in 1903 the St Michaels Club plays over a nine-hole course (SSS 67) built on undulating land underlain by sand and gravel. Although this may not be a championship course, it is a pleasant golfing challenge which at £3 per round (in 1986) offers an interesting alternative to its prestigious neighbours at St Andrews.

TAYSIDE

This beautiful region of Scotland extends from Loch Tay in the west to Montrose in the east. It not only contains the famous golfing centres of Carnoustie and Gleneagles but also courses of great antiquity in places such as Montrose, Monifieth and Perth. Both along the Highland edge (Crieff, Blairgowrie, Kirriemuir, Edzell) and within the Highland glens there are numerous golf courses of a wide range of quality and difficulty, surrounded by spectacular scenery. Within Tayside region there are 43 golf courses. The nine coastal courses are all of 18 holes. Thirty-one out of the 34 inland courses are classed as parkland, there being only three moorland courses (C78, C39, C53). Twenty-three of the inland courses are of 18 holes (Fig 7.5).

Golf is known to have been played on the links at Carnoustie and Montrose, and on the gravel terraces of the Tay at Perth in the sixteenth century. It is believed by locals that golf was played in Forfar in 1651. However, the majority of the present golf courses of Tayside had their formal beginnings in the last half of the nineteenth century.

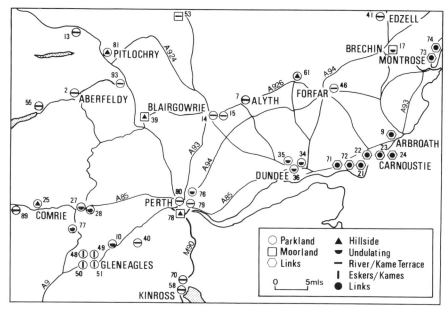

FIG 7.5 The landforms and vegetation of golf courses in Tayside.

Of more recent vintage is the complex at Gleneagles developed during the 1920s and new courses opened at Murrayshall (just outside Perth) in 1981, and the Budden course at Carnoustie also opened in 1981. There is also a new course at Letham Grange near Arbroath which was opened in 1986 with a second course under construction.

Coastal Courses

Between Monifieth, some six miles east of Dundee, and Montrose (a distance of 25 miles) there are nine links courses. Six of these are located on a triangular area of raised beach covered by blown-sand known as Barry Links. Much of this area lies a mere 10 to 20 feet above sea level with a few, old dune-ridges rising to 30 feet. The former coastline of some 6,000 years ago is located north of the A930 road between Monifieth and Carnoustie. Just to the south of this road is a strip of land about half a mile wide and four miles long, where golf has been played since 1527 and where formal golf clubs at Monifieth, Barry and Carnoustie have existed since the middle of last century. There are two 18-hole courses at Monifieth—the Medal (C71) and the Ashludie (C71). They are built over undulating links with some old dune-ridges, often covered by gorse, between the fairways. The

Monifieth Links were first formally used for golf in 1845 when Allan Robertson and Alexander Pirie of St Andrews designed a nine-hole course which was subsequently extended to 18 in 1880. Almost contiguous with the eastern end of Monifieth's Medal course is another links course played over by the Panmure Golf Club (founded 1845) of Barry (C21). The members of this club originally played over the Monifieth Links but opened their own course in 1899. This course at 6,301 yards (SSS 70) is of good quality with many low dune-ridges and numerous plateau greens. The Panmure clubhouse is of great character.

There are now three golf courses at Carnoustie—the Championship Course (C24), the Burnside Course (C23) and the newest, only opened in 1981, the Buddon Links Course (C22). The first record of golf being played at Carnoustie is dated 1650. The original ten holes of the present Championship Course were created by Allan Robertson in the mid nineteenth century and later extended to 18 holes by Tom Morris. Further modifications were made by James Braid in 1926 in the form of several new greens, tees and bunkers, but since that time the course has remained basically unchanged. Each hole is different from the next and never do more than two holes follow the same direction. This fine links course has hosted five Open Championships—the last in 1975 which was won by Tom Watson.

Two miles south-west of Arbroath, at the village of Elliot, is the clubhouse of the Arbroath Golf Club, founded in 1877. It stands on a flat terrace (probably a raised beach) with the steep slope of the abandoned shoreline leading down to an undulating links course. The course is bounded on the south-east side by the Dundee to Aberdeen railway line and beyond that is a dune-ridge some 12 to 15 feet high.

At Montrose there are two 18-hole links courses—the Medal Course (C73) and the Broomfield (C74). There is evidence to suggest that golf was played on these links in 1567 with a formal layout existing after 1810. The original course was of 17 holes but it was extended to 18 holes in 1863 and the Medal course has been changed little since that time. The undulating links upon which both courses are built are bounded to the east by a 30-foot high marram-covered dune-ridge. Five different golf clubs (The Royal Albert, The Caledonia, The Mercantile, The Victoria, The North Links Ladies) play over these courses. However, visitors are still made welcome and the courses provide good quality and relatively cheap golf.

The links courses of Tayside bear many similarities to those of Fife. In both regions there is a long history of golf being played on the links and in several towns a number of clubs play over one course. Apart from the two championship courses (St Andrews Old Course and

Carnoustie) all the links courses are easily accessible to visitors and many are surprisingly cheap for a visitor to play on.

Inland Courses

The two major urban centres in Tayside, Dundee and Perth (a combined population of some 200,000) can only muster seven golf courses between them. However, this may reflect the proximity of the two towns to a large number of golf courses throughout Tayside and Fife. The three courses in Dundee are all on the north side of the town and all, in Scottish terms, are relatively recent developments. The Downfield Course (C36) is an undulating parkland course which, although it was originally opened in 1933, was developed into its present layout in 1964. This course has hosted many amateur and professional tournaments, including the 1972 Scottish Open Championship. Peter Thomson, the five-times Open Champion, once described Downfield as '. . . one of the finest inland courses I've played anywhere in the world'. The other two courses in Dundee—Caird Park (C34) and Camperdown (C35)—are both municipal courses. The Camperdown course is set in fine mature parkland and is a stiff test of golfing skill.

Perth was once the capital of Scotland and in 1503 King James IV is known to have bought expensive golf clubs from a bow maker in Perth. The sand and gravel river-terraces on the banks of the River Tay now known as the North Inch and South Inch, were probably used as golf links in the sixteenth and seventeenth centuries. The Royal Perth Golfing Society was founded in 1824 and it still has competitions over the municipal course on the North Inch (C80). This course is fairly flat and is set in a fine mature parkland along the west bank of the Tay. The Royal Perth claims to be the oldest of the Royal clubs. When the Scottish Parliament met in Perth the Kings of Scotland would attend. The King James VI Golf Club, founded in 1858, is named in honour of the golfing King. The course now played on by the King James VI club is located on an island between two channels of the River Tay. Its mid-river location makes it unique amongst Scottish golf courses but it is also distinctive in that it can only be reached by a narrow walkway attached to the railway bridge over the River Tay. The clubhouse therefore has no adjacent car park.

Perth has a third course which is totally different from the two courses on the banks of the Tay. The Craigie Hill Course (C78) is located on volcanic rocks and is very hilly and rugged and has a moorland classification. There are some fine views from the higher parts of the course. Three miles north-east of Perth near New Scone, there is a fine modern golf development. In 1981 an undulating parkland course designed by J Hamilton Stutt was opened. It was laid out in the mature parklands of Murrayshall House, the house itself being converted to an hotel. Perth, therefore, has both the traditional North Inch municipal course with its long history, and also a modern golfing development. In many ways Perth makes an ideal centre for a golfing holiday in that within a 50-mile radius there are some 70 golf courses catering for golfers of all levels of skill and in surroundings which are of high scenic quality.

To the south-west of Perth is the district known as Strathearn. The valleys of the Earn and its tributaries provide some beautiful golfing country, the centrepiece of which is the Gleneagles complex (Pls 7.2, 7.3). It was Donald Matheson, general manager of the Caledonian Railway Company, who conceived the idea of a Grand Hotel to be built close to his company's railway line between Stirling and Perth. He was aware that the Glasgow and South-West Railway Company had already built the Turnberry Hotel and he was not to be outdone. The construction of the Gleneagles Hotel began in 1914, but was interrupted by the First World War, when part of the building was used as a hospital and rehabilitation centre for coal miners. Work was resumed in 1922 and James Braid was invited to design the King's (C48) and Queen's (C49) courses which were opened in 1924. The Prince's course (C50) was originally of nine holes but was extended to 18 holes in 1974. A fourth 18-hole course, the Glendevon, was opened in 1980. There can be few pieces of land anywhere in Scotland better suited to the construction of golf courses. Like the older links courses, the Gleneagles courses are also built on sand and gravel but instead of being the product of wave and wind action, the sand and gravel deposits of the Gleneagles area were laid down by the meltwaters of the last ice sheet. They are ice-contact, fluvioglacial (meltwater) deposits (see Chapter 3). Immense quantities of sand and gravel were brought to this site by large meltwater rivers some 15,000 years ago. They were deposited in tunnels in the ice and on top of and against large blocks of glacier ice. When all the ice melted, long sinuous ridges of sand and gravel (eskers), flat-topped mounds (kames) and enclosed hollows (kettles) were left on the south facing slope of Muir of Ochil (Fig 7.6) between 400 and 500 feet above sea level. The four golf courses have been built across this series of sub-parallel, 20 to 50 feet high, ridges and mounds which are aligned in a west-north-west to east-south-east direction. This complex land system covers an area about two miles from west to east and one mile from north to south. There are many similarities between the parallel

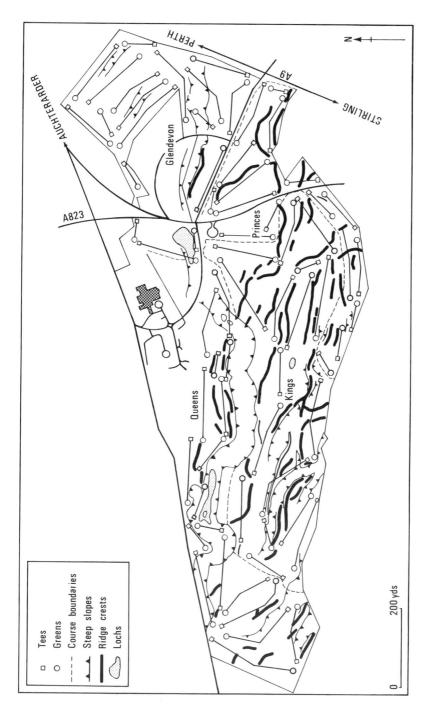

FIG 7.6   The landforms of the Gleneagles golf courses.

7.2   The First green, King's Course, Gleneagles.

7.3   Third green and 4th fairway, King's Course, Gleneagles.

ridges and hollows found on this inland site and the parallel, old dune-ridges and intervening hollows found on many coastal links courses. James Braid and subsequent golf architects made full use of these crenulations in the Gleneagles landscape. This is particularly true of the King's Course where the golfer has the luxury of the feeling of playing his own private course because so many of the fairways and greens are isolated from neighbouring holes by the high gravel ridges. The highest part of the courses is in the west, with a gentle slope down towards the south-east.

Some writers have referred to the Gleneagles courses as having a moorland or heathland character. This is understandable in that they are located on an upland plateau with firm turf and with rough of heather and gorse. However, all four courses have fine coniferous (often Scots pine) and deciduous trees and the general aspect is that of parkland.

Although the courses were designed for 'resort golf' in association with the first class hotel, they have been the venue for various championships. The King's Course has been used for the Ladies Championship and a Curtis Cup match. Both the King's and the Queen's have become internationally famous as the venues of the BBC Television, Pro-Celebrity series. The King's Course has recently been lengthened for championship play and although it hosted the Scottish Open Championship in 1987 and 1988 it is unlikely that the Open Championship will ever be played here because it is not a links course.

Golf at Gleneagles is expensive by Scottish standards but there is no other golfing complex to match it in terms of facilities, accommodation, scenery and overall quality. Even for the dedicated coastal-links golfer, Gleneagles has something special in the way the natural features have been incorporated into these inland courses.

Just a mile east of Gleneagles Hotel is the village of Auchterarder which has had its own golf club (C10) and course since 1892. The facilities and character of this course are much more in keeping with traditional Scottish golf than those of its illustrious neighbours. It is a course of 5,180 yards built over undulating parkland. There is also a nine-hole course at nearby Dunning (C40).

The view to the south from Gleneagles is dominated by a steep-sided valley which cuts through the Ochil Hills. On the north side of these hills this deep cut is known as Glen Eagles, while on the south side it is known as Glen Devon. A drive south through this beautiful country of some 16 miles (the A823 and A9) to Milnathort, will permit visits to two rather flat, parkland courses on the banks of Loch Leven. The one at Milnathort (C70) is of nine holes, but that at Kinross (The Green Hotel Golf Course—C58) is a challenging 18-hole (SSS 70) layout, again in a beautiful setting. To the north of Gleneagles (A823) there is a nine-hole course at Muthill (C77) and both an 18-hole and a nine-hole course at Crieff. The original course at Crieff was opened in 1891 but major changes have been made resulting in the present 18-hole course which opened in 1980. This new Ferntower course (C27) comprises 11 new holes and some of the original 18 holes, nine of which now make up the shorter Dornoch Course (C28). They combine to form a good quality golfing facility with magnificent views over Strathearn.

Crieff is located at the edge of the Highlands and two miles further west (on the A85) the River Earn flows through a steep-sided valley. There is an interesting nine-hole course on the north side of the Earn Valley at Comrie. Outside the small clubhouse there is a list of fauna and flora to be observed during a round of golf. Another couple of miles up the Glen there is another nine-hole course at St Fillans (C89) built on the gravel terraces and protruding rock knolls of the valley floor. The Comrie and St Fillans courses are a far cry from the sophisticated facilities of Gleneagles, but anyone who wishes to experience traditional Scottish golf should include such courses in their itinerary.

The so-called 'Highland edge' is very marked between Blairgowrie and Edzell (Fig 7.5). This is one of the very distinctive natural boundaries in Scotland which is closely associated with a geological fault (the Highland Boundary Fault). To the north and west lie the ancient metamorphic rocks of the Grampians, while to the south-east, the broad valley of Strathmore is underlain by the younger Old Red Sandstone rocks. A series of rivers (Rivers Shee, Isla, South Esk, North Esk) flow south-eastwards through deep, glacial valleys within the Grampians and suddenly emerge on to the broad plain of Strathmore. During the last glaciation (see Chapter 3) these valleys contained large glaciers and when they melted the meltwaters carried large quantities of sand and gravel which were dumped along the Highland Boundary. These gravels were either deposited as large outwash-fans, as river-terraces, or as ice-contact accumulations (eskers, kames) and it is these sand and gravel areas that provide excellent sites for golf courses at Blairgowrie, Alyth, Forfar and Edzell.

There are two fine 18-hole courses at Blairgowrie (C14, 15) built over a large, gently sloping outwash fan (sandur) of sand and gravel. The old meltwater routeways across the surface can still be seen and there are several lake-filled depressions (kettle holes). This well-drained surface has been extensively planted with pine and birch and the fairways have been developed as routeways for the golfer through the forest. Both courses are kept in fine condition, and both are stern tests of golfing skill. The Rosemount course (SSS 72) has hosted the British Boys' Championship and the Martini International, which was won in 1977 by Greg Norman.

Just a few miles to the east of Blairgowrie there is another delightful course at Alyth (C7). It is also built on undulating land consisting of sand and gravel. The pine and birch woodland does not dominate this course as it does at Blairgowrie. The Alyth course was designed by James Braid and opened in 1894. He also designed the course at Edzell (C41) in the North Esk Valley which is built on gravel terraces. Again this is a good quality parkland course (SSS 70) with some fine surrounding woodland.

The courses at Kirriemuir (C61) and Brechin (C17) were also designed by Braid but are a little different in that they are both built on rolling uplands above the floor of Strathmore. There is much less woodland on the Brechin course and therefore some excellent views across to the Highlands.

There is a delightful 18-hole course at Forfar (C46) where the locals claim golf has been played since 1651. Tom Morris was responsible for the original layout in 1871 which was added to and modified by James Braid in 1926. Today, the beautiful tree-lined fairways, many of which are crossed by old cultivation ridges constitute an interesting 6,257 yard course (SSS 69). Again, this is a course built on ridges, mounds and spreads of sand and gravel.

There are seven golf courses north-west of the Highland edge in Tayside region. The main road north (the A9) follows the deep valley of the Tay at Dunkeld. High up on a coll to the north of Dunkeld is an interesting nine-hole moorland course (C39). The course makes use of some rugged terrain with some tees placed so that the golfer is required to drive across deep ravines to small greens. This is a very different type of golf when compared to traditional links courses, but the combination of new golfing experiences and spectacular surrounding scenery make such a course well worth a visit.

The course at Pitlochry (C81), although also built across a steep rocky hillside, is more of a traditional parkland course. No two holes are alike and again there are some delightful views. There are three courses in the Tay Valley to the west of Pitlochry. There are nine-hole courses at Strathtay (C96) and Aberfeldy (C2), the latter being built on flat river terraces. Where Loch Tay empties into the River Tay at Kenmore there is another fine parkland course (C55) built on flat river terraces. The Taymouth Castle Golf Course (C55) is one of the most beautiful in the Scottish Highlands. It was designed by James Braid in 1923 and he made full use of the mature parkland surrounding the castle. Two other nine-hole courses to the north and north-east of

Pitlochry respectively, are sited on river terraces. That at Blair Atholl (C53) is rather flat and of an open parkland character, while that at the head of Glen Shee (C53) at the Dalmungie Hotel is a moorland course.

With over 40 courses ranging in type from those used for great championships to unsophisticated and yet challenging nine-hole layouts set in beautiful scenery, Tayside has a great deal to offer the golfing enthusiast. Visitors to the region should not restrict themselves to the famous golfing centres of St Andrews, Carnoustie and Gleneagles, but explore the many other delightful courses described in this chapter.

Chapter 8

HIGHLAND, GRAMPIAN AND THE ISLANDS

REGION D

For the dedicated golfing enthusiast it could be regarded as a mortal sin to provide information about this great golfing area for fear that it will become overrun by 'outsiders'. There can be nowhere else in the world where the basic simplicity of the game has been retained amidst such delightful landscapes. There are 90 golf courses in the area, one third of them being of nine holes (Fig 8.1). Apart from a few championship courses (e.g. Royal Aberdeen, Nairn, Royal Dornoch) where a round of golf may cost in excess of £12, many of the others are not only very accessible but cheap. There are numerous courses where (in 1987) a round cost £5 or less and a few at which a one pound coin deposited in an honesty box entitles you to play the course. At many courses in the north of Scotland the game is played on natural features very little modified by the golf course architect. The combination of unsophisticated courses and clubhouses and the fine surrounding scenery makes the north of Scotland a golfing region of great character. With the expansion of tourism and oil-related industry during the past two decades, many golf clubs have expanded their membership and improved their facilities but there still remain a large number of unsophisticated courses in this area.

The area dealt with in this chapter (Fig 8.2) consists of the Scottish mainland north of a line from Stonehaven in the east to Fort William in the west, plus the western islands of Skye, North and South Uist, Lewis and Harris and the northern islands of Orkney and Shetland. There is a golfing desert in the mountains to the north and west of the Great Glen.

There are records of golf having been played on the Aberdeen links in 1538 and on the Dornoch links in 1616. There is a reference in the records of the Banff magistrates for 1733 to the 'first hole of the links'. The history of the game in the north of Scotland certainly goes back to the seventeenth and possibly the sixteenth century. The oldest

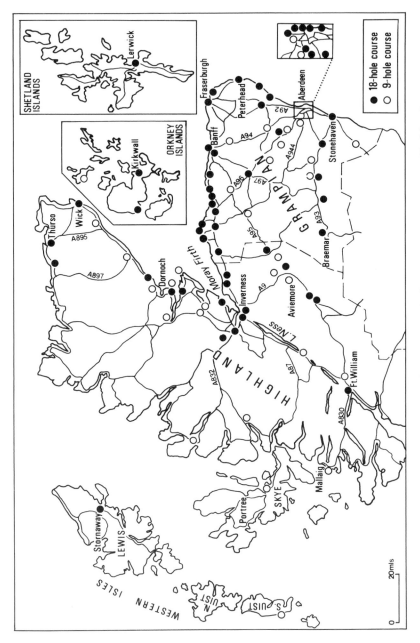

FIG 8.1 The location of nine-hole and 18-hole courses in Grampian, Highland and the Islands.

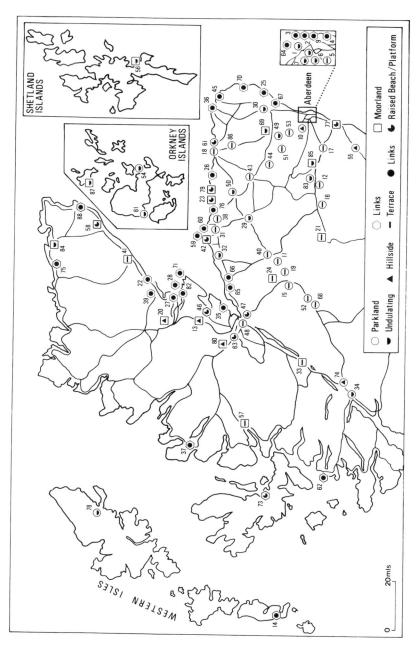

FIG 8.2 The landforms and vegetation of the golf courses of Grampian, Highland and the Islands.

formal golf club in the area is the Royal Aberdeen (1815) which was preceded by the Society of Golfers at Aberdeen (1780). Other early clubs were Cruden Bay (Port Errol 1791), Peterhead (1841), Wick (1870), Aberdeen Bon Accord (1872), Muir of Ord (1875) and Dornoch (1877). However, it was the last quarter of the nineteenth century which saw a major expansion in the number of golf clubs, some 38 clubs being established during the 25-year period. This expansion probably largely reflects the completion of the rail network between Perth, Aberdeen, Fraserburgh, Banff, Elgin, Nairn, Inverness, Wick and Thurso (Fig 2.3) by 1880. A further 12 clubs were founded between 1901 and 1910 and another ten clubs between 1920 and 1933. A further 15 courses have been opened since 1954—four in Aberdeen and one each at Invergordon (1954), Nigg Bay (1955), Inverness (1962), Keith (1963), Sconser, Skye (1964), Thurso (1964), Fort William (1976), Lossiemouth (1979), Carrbridge (1980), Aviemore (1982), Insch (1982). Most of these recent courses have been opened in response to either tourist development in the Spey Valley or population increases associated with industrial developments (Fort William, Thurso, Invergordon, Nigg Bay, Aberdeen).

The courses of this area fall into two distinct groups—those along the coastline and the inland courses. Most but not all, of the coastal courses are on links land while the inland courses are either in the undulating landscape of Buchan or in the valleys of the Dee, Spey and Great Glen.

COASTAL COURSES

Most of the coastal courses are located in the east between Stonehaven and Wick (36 courses). There are only two courses on the north coast, three on the west coast, three in the western islands and four in the islands of Orkney and Shetland.

There are 165 miles of coastline between Stonehaven and Inverness of which some 50 per cent is links land. It is almost surprising that there are only 16 golf courses built on this classic golfing landscape. Between Inverness and Brora there are a further 130 miles of coastline of which some 30 per cent is links land. North of Brora the only extensive links are to be found at Wick. The coastal courses of the north-east of Scotland either occur on platforms some 100 to 150 feet above sea level and bounded by steep cliffs, or they occur on low-lying platforms or sand accumulations, often within 20 to 50 feet of present sea level. (For explanations of the origins of these coastal features see chapter 4).

Stonehaven to Fraserburgh (including courses around Aberdeen)

Although not a long course (5,106 yards), Stonehaven (D77) produces some unusual challenges to the golfer. It is perched on a dissected platform between rocky cliffs and the railway line to Aberdeen, just north of the town. It is rather atypical of most of the coastal courses described in this section. It is perhaps best described as coastal moorland with some spectacular cliff scenery and is very exposed to winds off the North Sea.

In historical terms the King's Links at Aberdeen (D9), which form the coastline between the mouths of the Rivers Dee and Don, are one of the ancient foundations of Scottish golf. The formation of the Society of Golfers of Aberdeen in 1780, which used the King's Links, establishes that golf has been played on this site for over 200 years. The appearance of this area has been much changed by human activity over that period. Originally, both river mouths were choked by shifting sand banks and between the rivers there was a broad, low sand-plain with several small lochs, especially in the north of the area. The links merged landwards into a raised beach surface of marine sands and gravels underlain by glacial till. Between the links and the beach there used to be an extensive dune ridge but only remnants of the northern part of this system still remain. These remnants occur to the west of the main road, attaining altitudes of about 25 to 30 feet and parts of the lower back slopes of the dunes are incorporated into the design of the golf course. Much of the King's Links golf course is of a low undulating nature about 10 to 15 feet above sea level with a few sand hills and ridges up to 20 feet. The King's Links course is now a municipal course managed by Aberdeen's Department of Leisure and Recreation. The same department also manages two 18-hole and one nine-hole course at Hazlehead (D6, 7, 8), the 18-hole course at Balnagask (D4) and the nine-hole course at Auchmill (D1). The courses at Hazlehead provide over a quarter of a million rounds of golf per year. They are located on rolling uplands in some fine parkland. The Balnagask golf course lies on a promontory between Nigg Bay and Aberdeen Harbour. It is an area of undulating glacial and fluvioglacial deposits with occasional rock outcrops. There are no trees on the course and the occasional patches of heather and broom give the course a moorland appearance.

Apart from the municipal courses, Aberdeen does not have a large number of private golf courses within the city boundaries. The courses of the Royal Aberdeen Golf Club (A2, 3) will be discussed in detail below along with that of the Murcar Golf Club (A64). The Deeside Golf Club's course (D5), some three miles from the city centre, will be discussed along with the other courses to be found in the Dee Valley. There is a relatively new, 18-hole course (opened in 1977) at Westhill (D10) some six miles to the west of the city centre on the A944. It is associated with a new housing development and the course, at an altitude of between 425 and 475 feet, is a mixture of parkland and moorland.

The Aberdeen Golf Club (D2,3) was founded in 1815 and originally the club played over seven holes on the King's Links. In 1866 the club moved to Balgownie to the north of the River Don and has developed

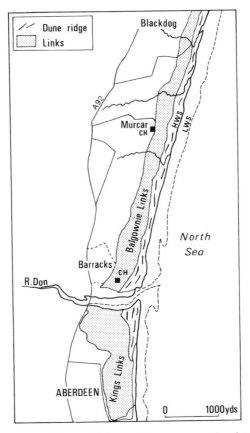

FIG 8.3 The landforms of the golf courses north of Aberdeen.

two 18-hole courses on classic links land (Fig 8.3). These links continue for some 10 miles to the north-east to the famous Sands of Forvie at the mouth of the River Ythan. Immediately adjacent to the Royal Aberdeen Club's main course is the course of the Murcar Golf Club. Both courses are characterised by a large, single coastal dune-ridge some 25 to 40 feet high, which merges inland with hillocks and ridges of sand which in turn merge into undulating links generally 20 to 50 feet above sea level. Most of these blown sand deposits are underlain by raised beach sands and gravels. The sand hills on Murcar are somewhat larger than on Royal Aberdeen. Robert Simpson was the architect who designed Royal Aberdeen and his namesake Andrew, who was the greenkeeper at the new course, designed Murcar which was opened in 1902. Both courses can be regarded as excellent examples of the golf course architects' use of links land.

The links upon which the Royal Aberdeen and Murcar courses have been constructed continue northward for a further eight miles to the mouth of the River Ythan before another golf course is encountered. At Newburgh (D67) there is a nine-hole course built on an area of low-lying links with a series of low sandhills and dunes. Most of this area is only 10 to 20 feet above sea level and the rough consists of gorse and heather. The course sits on a neck of land between the Foveran Burn and the River Ythan and there are some excellent views of the large sand hills at Forvie on the north-east side of the beautiful Ythan estuary.

At Cruden Bay (D25), some seven miles south of Peterhead, there are two courses—one of 18 holes which has been described as being of championship standard, and a nine-hole course. The Cruden Bay Golf Club started life in 1791 playing over a course at Port Errol but in 1899 a new course was opened over the large sand hills and links at the foot of the abandoned cliff on top of which the Cruden Bay Hotel had been built (Fig 8.4) by the Great North of Scotland Railway Company. The magnificent hotel was built of pink Peterhead granite and attracted wealthy golfers to travel north on the railway from Aberdeen. The new course was inaugurated by a tournament attended by Harry Vardon, James Braid and Ben Sayers. The hotel did not re-open after the Second World War and was demolished in 1947. The course was purchased by a syndicate of local people from the British Transport Commission. This organisation has established the Cruden Bay Golf and Country Club—a title which gives completely the wrong impression of what still can be regarded as a somewhat unsophisticated golfing environment for a challenging round of old-fashioned links golf. Even the arrival of the pipeline, from the Forties

Field in the North Sea, just to the south of the course has had little impact. Many of the fairways lie between 30 feet high dune ridges at the north end of the course and these give way to a single asymmetric dune ridge some 15 feet high backed by undulating links land.

The shoulder of Buchan sweeps round from Peterhead to Fraserburgh in a series of cuspate bays each of which is backed by some impressive sand dunes and links land. Some of these dunes are 30 to 40 feet high. On the north side of the town of Peterhead a golf club (D70) was established in 1841. The original clubhouse was abandoned because of the threat of erosion and the course is now served by a large modern club house. Along with the courses at Inverallochy (D45) and Fraserburgh (D36), the Peterhead course has been built on a sand-covered raised beach backed by an abandoned cliff usually cut in glacial till. The fishermen golfers of Inverallochy are believed to be the last players in the world to have given up the gutty ball.

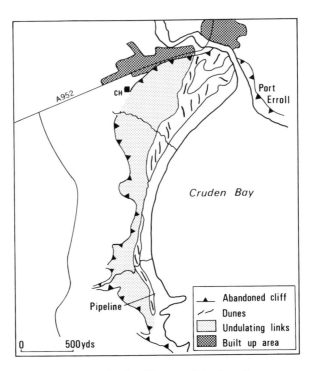

FIG 8.4   The landforms of Cruden Bay.

Fraserburgh to Nairn

Whereas much of the coastline between Fraserburgh and Aberdeen is dominated by dunes and links, that between Fraserburgh and Lossiemouth is dominated by steep rock cliffs leading up to a coastal platform some 100 to 150 feet above sea level (Fig 8.5). Only in Cullen Bay, Spey Bay and just west of Lossiemouth is there any links land. However, from Burghead to Fort George at the entrance to the Inner Moray Firth there are great expanses of sand and shingle but only the two golf courses at Nairn (D65, 66).

Between Macduff (D61) in the east and Lossiemouth (D59) in the west, a distance of some 30 miles, there are 11 coastal courses which provide a variety of golfing landscapes. Although in close proximity to the coast (the clubhouse is a mere 200 yards from the beach) the Duff House Royal course (D18) at Banff is in parkland and will be considered in the section devoted to the inland courses of Buchan.

This north-facing coast, although a relatively dry part of Scotland (annual precipitation of 22 to 30 inches) is an exposed coastline with frequent sea fogs in summer. The 11 golf courses are built on five types of coastal landforms: coastal dunes at Nairn (D65, 66) and Lossiemouth (D59, 60); raised shingle ridges at Spey Bay (D76); marine platforms and raised beach at Cullen (D26); high raised

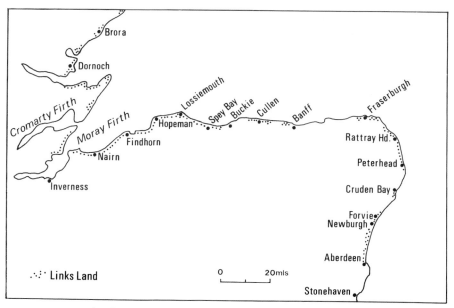

FIG 8.5 The distribution of links land in the north-east of Scotland.

marine platforms at Hopeman (D42), Buckpool (D23), Strathlene (D79) and Royal Tarlair (D61); river terraces at Garmouth and Kingston (D38). This variety of landforms provides a remarkable range of golfing landscapes within a relatively small coastal area. All the courses, except Hopeman, are of 18 holes.

Classic links courses are to be found only at Nairn and Lossiemouth (two courses at each location) and even these are in considerable contrast. The two courses at Nairn were both designed by A Simpson. The Nairn Golf Club course (D65) to the west of the town was built on a raised shingle-beach covered by blown sand. Simpson's original design (1887) was improved both by Tom Morris and James Braid and although there are no dramatic sandhills or spectacular views, it is a challenging seaside course which has been ranked in the top 40 courses in the British Isles by *Golf World*. The Ladies British Amateur Championship was held here in 1979. The Nairn Dunbar course (D66) to the east of the town lies on an elevated surface 15–30 feet above sea level, and while providing an exacting test of golf skills it has the appearance of a rather uninteresting area of links land. In great contrast are the two links courses at Lossiemouth (D59, 60) which are built on sandhills up to 25 feet high along with undulating links land. The links land consists of blown sand covering raised shingle-ridges. The Moray Golf Club was established in 1889 and the Old Course was designed by Tom Morris. A second 18-hole course (the New) was designed by Henry Cotton and opened in 1979. While both courses are very attractive, being built close to the beach and having extensive colourful areas of gorse rough, their proximity to the Lossiemouth military airfield does lead to some noisy distractions.

A different type of links course is to be found at Spey Bay (D76). An 18-hole course has been laid out on a series of raised, storm-beach ridges which accumulated during periods of higher relative sea level some 6,000 years ago. The ridges consist of boulders and pebbles and largely coincide with the rough of gorse and heather, while the fairways are to be found in the shallow 'valleys' between the ridges. Wind direction and strength obviously play an important part in determining the difficulty of this course. Just half a mile to the west of the Spey Bay golf course but on the other side of the River Spey and therefore a six-mile drive via the bridge at Fochabers is the Garmouth and Kingston course (D38). While parts of this course have the characteristic of true links (mainly built on river gravels and raised-beach gravels) other parts have fairways lined by birch and alder and have a parkland character. Both the Spey Bay and Garmouth courses provide excellent, cheap golf at under £5 per round (in 1986).

Cullen (D26) is one of the most interesting golf courses in this district. It contains two distinct golfing landscapes and provides the golfer not only with a variety of challenges but also with some fine views. It is a short course of 4,215 yards with a standard scratch score of 62, but it can be a difficult test particularly in windy conditions. The course starts out along the post-glacial raised beach and then the golfer is required to play a shot from the second tee up the face of the abandoned cliff to a green which sits up on the upper marine-platform (Fig 8.6). This platform at about 100 feet above sea level is the 'moorland' section of the course and contains holes 3, 4, 5 and 6. The seventh tee is perched on the cliff edge (Pl 8.1) with the green of this 231 yard, par three hole some 80 feet below on the links part of the course. I thoroughly enjoyed watching the result of a two wood hang in the air for several seconds before pitching on the green, on the first occasion I played the course. During two subsequent rounds in the same week it was impossible to see the green from the seventh tee because of sea fog (or 'haar') which can be another local hazard along this coastline in summer. The remainder of this course

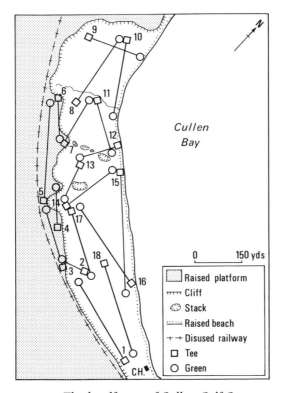

FIG 8.6   The landforms of Cullen Golf Course.

8.1   View from the 7th tee, Cullen.

8.2   Raised beach, sea stacks and old cliffline, Cullen.

(i.e. holes 8 to 18) is close to sea level and is built on the post-glacial raised beach which is fronted by a low dune-ridge and partly covered by blown sand. However, this is not typical links land because on several holes the golfer has to negotiate abandoned sea-cliffs and stacks (Pl 8.2). These upstanding rock ridges cause the player to make blind shots on the 12th, 13th and 14th holes and if the golf ball hits any of the almost vertical rock faces, it can fly in almost any direction. The last few holes are played across links land back towards the town.

There are four cliff-top courses along this coast which are located on an old raised marine-platform some 70 to 150 feet above present sea level—Hopeman (D42), Buckpool (D23), Strathlene (D79) and Royal Tarlair at Macduff (D61). They are best described as coastal moorland courses often with fine views and the occasional tricky hole which makes use of the cliff scenery. The course at Hopeman has one dramatic hole with a drop from tee to green of 100 feet and the short 13th (152 yards) at Royal Tarlair crosses a deep ravine.

The Beauly Firth to Reay (near Thurso)

This part of the Scottish coastline falls into two distinct sections. Between Inverness and Dornoch the sea penetrates far inland in the firths of Beauly (Moray), Cromarty and Dornoch. There are 11 golf courses which are either on the shores of or overlook these firths. To the north of Dornoch the character of the coastline changes with high coastal plateaux bounded by a steeply-cliffed coastline and occasional pockets of links land. In this north-east corner of Scotland there are seven golf courses.

Excellent examples of raised beaches are found around the Beauly Firth: the 18-hole course at Muir of Ord (D63) is built on one of them. It is in pleasant parkland and utilises the terrace form of the raised beaches. One of the last courses to be designed by James Braid is at Fortrose (D35): it is built on a raised beach, and raised spit which extends out into the Moray Firth and can best be described as a gentle links course.

For convenience, the very interesting inland course at Strathpeffer (D80) will be discussed in this section even though it cannot be described as a coastal course. However, from the higher parts of the course there are fine views of the Cromarty Firth. It is a very hilly, moorland course located in a col some 500 feet above sea level and surrounded by coniferous plantations. The course was opened in 1888 in association with the development of the spa town of

Strathpeffer. There are some very interesting holes on this golf course but it is its beautiful scenic setting which makes it well worth a visit.

On the north shore of the Cromarty Firth are two nine-hole courses—one at Alness (D13) and the other at Invergordon (D46). The former is a moorland course while the latter is a parkland course built on raised-beach deposits with views of the Cromarty Firth and its oil-related activities.

On the southern shore of the Dornoch Firth are two links courses— one at Tain (D82) and a nine-hole course at Portmahomack (D71). The course at Tain was designed by Tom Morris and is an interesting mixture of links and inland parkland golf. Although Tain is only some five miles from its more famous neighbour, Royal Dornoch, a 28-mile journey is required around the Firth to reach Dornoch. At Bonar Bridge at the head of the Firth there is a nine-hole moorland course (D20).

Royal Dornoch (D27, 28) is undoubtedly the most famous golf course in the north-east of Scotland (Pl 8.3). *Golf World* has ranked it in the top ten in Britain and the British Amateur Championship was played here in 1986. Tom Watson has described the course as 'one of the great courses of the five continents. I have played none finer, a natural masterpiece'. There is little doubt that the Open Championship would have been played here if the course was not

8.3   Royal Dornoch—a classic links course.

located in the north-east corner of Scotland. Although golf was probably played on the Dornoch links in the seventeenth century, the Dornoch Club was founded in 1877 and in 1886 the Club invited the veteran champion golfer, Old Tom Morris, to make a survey of the links and lay out a planned course. The club received its royal status in 1906. John Sutherland was Secretary of the club for 53 years until 1935 and had a great influence on the development of the course. By 1939 there were two 18-hole courses but the RAF requisitioned several holes for a wartime airstrip. After the war George Duncan built six new holes. The course is built on an area of blown sand resting on top of a raised beach. The combination of sand ridges, mounds and hollows, and gorse and heather rough, provides some classic links golf. This is one course where the so-called 'Scottish shot' of a pitch and run up to the hole is rarely possible as many of the greens sit on top of mounds with steep banks surrounding the putting surface. A famous son of Dornoch, Donald Ross, emigrated to America in 1898 where he designed the Seminole, Oakland Hills and Pinehurst courses among many others, and the characteristic 'perched' green so familiar in Dornoch is seen on some of his American courses—particularly at Pinehurst No 2. Not only Donald Ross but many other Scottish golfers who learned the game on the now famous links at St Andrews, Royal Dornoch, Musselburgh, Troon or Prestwick and who then emigrated to America and embarked on a career of golf course design, took with them the memory of many of the natural features of Scottish links land and incorporated them in their new man-made golfing landscapes.

After turning inland from Dornoch to pass around Loch Fleet, the main road north (A9) returns to the coast at Golspie. There is another raised beach/blown sand combination here which is the location of Golspie golf course (D39). Along with the rolling dunes and hummocks of Brora golf course (D22), some five miles further north, Golspie provides cheap and unsophisticated golfing facilities in comparison to the classic course at Dornoch. The Brora course was designed by James Braid amid a series of 20 to 40 foot high sand hills with several elevated tees and greens.

At Helmsdale (D41) and Lybster (D58) there are nine-hole courses both of moorland character although located close to the coast. North of Lybster the almost flat, wind-blown landscape of eastern Caithness is sometimes rather bleak. Three miles to the north of the town of Wick is the exposed links of the Wick Golf Club, founded in 1870 (D88). Much of the course is built on gently undulating links land which is given some protection from the easterly winds by the presence of a larger outer dune ridge. Thurso Golf Course (D84), opened in 1964, sits on the almost flat moorland surface south of the town. It can claim to be the most northerly golf course on the Scottish mainland at latitude 58° 34′ north, which is only marginally further north than the neighbouring course at Reay (D75). Golf has been played at Reay since 1893 and it is a delightful links course, the only course on the entire north coast of Scotland. One of the delights of these northern courses is to play golf late into the evening of the long summer days—it is not at all uncommon to be able to conclude an evening round at 11 p.m.

The West Coast, Western Isles (South Uist, Lewis), Orkney and Shetland

There are only three golf courses on the west coast of the Scottish mainland north of Fort William—Mallaig (D62), Loch Carron (D57) and Gairloch (D37). The courses at Mallaig and Gairloch are on links land, the latter being built across some high sand dunes. There is a nine-hole course on the east coast of Skye at Sconser (D73) and one nine-hole and one 18-hole course in the Outer Hebrides. The club at Askernish (D14) on South Uist was formed in 1891 and the course designed by Tom Morris, utilising the classic Machair sands (wind blown sand spreads) which are so extensive along the west side of the Outer Hebrides. The 18-hole course at Stornoway (D78) is a parkland course located in the castle grounds. The trees found in this parkland are a most unusual aspect of the usually treeless landscape of these islands. The Orkney Islands contain two 18-hole courses (D54, 81) and one nine-hole course (D87) and there is one 18-hole course (D56) in Shetland.

INLAND COURSES

There are four distinct areas of inland golf courses in Highland and Grampian Regions (Fig 8.1)—Buchan (the districts of Banff and Buchan, Gordon, Moray and Nairn); the Dee Valley; the Spey Valley; and the Great Glen (Fort William to Inverness).

Buchan

The series of coastal courses between Peterhead and Nairn is strongly supported by an interesting group of seven inland courses; only the course at Dufftown (D29) being of nine holes. Although located within a few hundred yards of the coastline, Duff House Royal Golf Club (D18) plays over a very fine parkland course built on the gravel terraces of the River Deveron. The history of golf in the town of Banff has a macabre beginning. In 1637 a boy was convicted and hanged for stealing golf balls. There is also a reference in the records of the Banff magistrates for 1733 to the 'first hole of the links'. It is doubtful whether these early references refer to activities on the present course which was designed by Dr A McKenzie who subsequently designed both the Augusta National and Cypress Point courses in the United States. The club was given its Royal status in 1923 and is the only club in the world to use the term as a suffix. The modern clubhouse and high quality of this parkland course make it one of the most attractive courses in this area.

Further up the valley of the River Deveron, two more courses are built on gravel terraces, one at Turriff (D86) and another at Huntly (D43). Both are pleasant parkland courses and along with the more recently developed course at Keith (D50) offer an interesting change of scene for the golfer who may have decided to visit this corner of Scotland mainly to play the coastal courses. In a similar way the two courses at Elgin (D31) and Forres (D32) offer parkland golf of a high quality to the visitors staying at Nairn and Lossiemouth.

Within a 15-mile radius to the north and north-west of Aberdeen there are six inland courses. Only two of them are of 18 holes—the courses at Ellon (D30) and Inverurie (D49) being rather flat parkland. The three nine-hole courses at Kintore (D53), Kemnay (D51) and Insch (D44) are rather uninteresting parkland courses, while the nine-hole course at Oldmeldrum (D69) is located high up on the moorland above the town.

The Dee Valley

Royal Deeside is justly famous for its beautiful scenery and for salmon fishing. Since the glaciers disappeared from this area some 10,000 years ago the River Dee has been depositing and subsequently eroding away large quantities of gravel along the valley bottom. Throughout much of the valley there are sequences of gravel terraces which have provided excellent sites for inland golf courses. All seven courses were built between 1891 and 1908 and five of them are to be found on the gravel terraces. On the outskirts of Aberdeen is the fine parkland course of the Deeside Club (D5) while a further 15 miles up the Dee Valley the course at Banchory (D17) makes full use of the stepped landscape of the river terraces. Along with the course at Aboyne

(D12) and Ballater (D16) these terraced-parkland courses provide some delightful golfing landscapes. The course at Braemar (D21) is also largely built on river gravels but it has a moorland character (Pl 8.4) in contrast to the four courses further down the valley. A second nine-hole course at Aboyne (D83) played over by the Tarland Golf Club is located in the grounds of a large mansion which was used as a wartime hospital. A nine-hole moorland course at Torphins (D85) some seven miles north-west of Banchory is not actually in the Dee Valley but it stands on an upland area some 500 feet above sea level and from the course there are excellent views of the mountains to the south of the Dee Valley.

The Spey Valley

Although the villages of Newtonmore, Kingussie, Boat of Garten, Carrbridge and Granton on Spey are most famous for their winter sports, the Spey Valley is also a major tourist attraction during the summer months and each of these villages has a golf course. Like the Dee Valley, most of the courses are built on the gravel terraces which are conspicuous features along the valley floor. The three 18-hole courses at Newtonmore (D68), Boat of Garten (D19) and Granton on

8.4 Braemar—a moorland course on the floor of the Dee Valley.

8.5   Boat of Garten.

8.6   Kingussie, built on terraced gravel along a tributary of the River Spey.

Spey (D40) as well as the two nine-hole courses at Carrbridge (D24) and Abernethy (D11) make use of these well-drained gravels. The course at Newtonmore is partly built on a kame terrace with kettle holes—that is, the gravels were deposited up against the retreating margin of a glacier and lumps of glacier ice were buried in the gravels only to melt subsequently and produce the kettle holes (depressions) in the terrace surface. There are magnificent views of the Cairngorm Mountains from this course. Many visitors have extolled the virtues of the courses at Granton on Spey and Boat of Garten (Pl 8.5). Both are characterised by rolling parkland with fine stands of conifers and birches plus heather rough. Robert Green writing in *Golf World's* 'The World of Scottish Golf' in 1985 stated that Boat of Garten '. . . is probably the finest "short" golf course I have ever played'. The one course which is markedly different from the others in the Spey Valley is that at Kingussie (D52). It is a combination of holes on terraced parkland and heather moorland with rocky outcrops (Pl 8.6).

The Great Glen

One of Scotland's most dramatic topographic features is the Great Glen. It is a long, straight and steep-sided trough resulting from many tens of millions of years of erosion by water and glacier ice along the line of a major fault (fracture) in the earth's crust. It is aligned in a south-west to north-east direction with the town of Fort William in the south-west and the town of Inverness at the north-east end.

There are five golf courses in the Great Glen. Apart from the Inverness Club (D47) which was founded in 1883, golf arrived late in the Great Glen. The interesting nine-hole course built on gravel terraces (with kettle holes) at Fort Augustus was opened in 1930. Another nine-hole course at Spean Bridge (D74) was opened in 1954. There is a fine municipal course in Inverness at Torvean (D48) built on river gravels in attractive parkland (opened 1962). The most recent course to be opened (in 1975) is to be found just north of Fort William (D34). It is built over hummocky ground created by the last glaciers to occupy this area some 10,000 years ago. It is a mixture of moorland and parkland.

The marked concentration of golf courses on the eastern side of the Scottish Highlands is probably a reflection of two sets of circumstances. Firstly, golf had its early development in the east, and the coastal and inland landscapes of Aberdeenshire, Buchan, Easter Ross and Caithness were conducive both to the expansion of the game and to the development of tourism. The climatic differences between west and east are also such that the building and upkeep of courses is easier in the east. The golfers of Fort William 'enjoy' an annual rainfall of 78 inches while those in Nairn with an annual average rainfall of 20 inches have problems in maintaining their greens through periods of drought.

APPENDIX

Key

Public/Municipal courses in italics

VISITORS   VIS
- U   Unrestricted access by visitors
- NA   No visitors allowed
- M   With a member
- I   Introduction—letter from own club, own club membership card or a handicap certificate
- WD   Weekdays
- BH   Bank Holidays

COST PER ROUND
- COST   (Cost of a weekday round, not introduced by a member. Weekend and holiday golf may be more expensive).

Category
- A   less than £3
- B   £3–£6
- C   £7–£10
- D   £11–£14
- E   £15–£18
- F   over £18

DATE   Based on date of foundation of oldest club to play on course.

ALTITUDE   ALT (ft)   Mean altitude of course (in feet) above sea level.

LANDFORMS   LAND
- U   Undulating
- H   Hillside
- D   Drumlin
- E   Esker
- K   Kame
- KT   Kame terrace
- RT   River terrace
- S   Sandur (outwash fan)
- RB   Raised beach
- RM   Raised marine platform
- L   Links

VEGETATION   VEG
- P   Parkland
- PW   Woodland
- M   Moorland
- L   Links

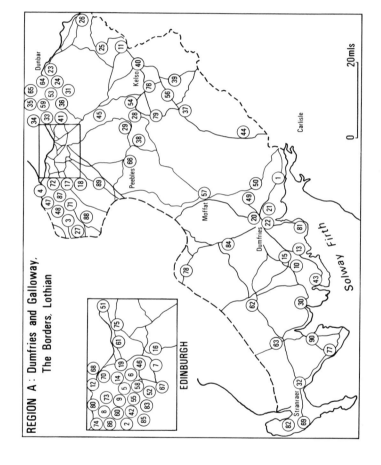

FIG A.1   Region A: Dumfries and Galloway, The Borders, Lothian.

203

REF	NAME	ADDRESS	HOLES	LENGTH (yds)	SSS	VIS	COST	DATE	ALT (ft)	LAND	VEG
A1	Annan-Powfoot	Cummertrees, Annan	18	6,283	70	U	C	1903	25	L	L
A2	Baberton	Baberton Avenue, Juniper Green, Edinburgh	18	6,140	69	M	C	1893	400	U	P
A3	Bathgate	Edinburgh Road, Bathgate, West Lothian	18	6,326	70	U	B	1892	450	U	M
A4	Bo'ness	Airngath Hill, Bo'ness, West Lothian	18	6,629	72	U	B	1892	500	H	M
A5	*Braids No. 1*	Braids Hill Approach, Edinburgh	18	5,731	68	U	A	1893	500	H	M
A6	*Braids No. 2*	See No. 1	18	4,832	63	U	A	1894	500	H	M
A7	Bonnyrigg	36 Golf Course Road, Bonnyrigg, Midlothian	18	6,046	69	U	B	1906	300	U	P
A8	Bruntsfield Links	32 Barnton Avenue, Davidson Mains, Edinburgh	18	6,407	71	Ex WE I	—	1761	125	RB	P
A9	*Carricknowe*	Glendevon Park, Edinburgh	18	6,299	70	U	A	1930	150	U	P
A10	Castle Douglas	Abercromby Road, Castle Douglas	9	5,408	66	U	B	1905	150	K	P
A11	Coldstream Hirsel	Coldstream	9	5,680	67	U	B	1948	150	T	P
A12	*Craigentinny*	Craigentinny Avenue, Lochend, Edinburgh	18	5,418	66	U	A	1891	50	RB	P
A13	Colvend	Sandyhills, by Dalbeattie, Kirkcudbrightshire	9	2,103	61	U	B	1896	150	H	M
A14	Craigmillar Park	1 Observatory Road, Edinburgh	18	5,846	68	I	C	1896	300	H	P
A15	Dalbeattie	Dalbeattie, Kirkcudbrightshire	9	4,200	61	U	A	1897	100	H	M
A16	Dalkeith Newbattle	Abbey Road, Eskbank, Dalkeith	18	6,012	69	U Ex WE	C	1934	200	T	P
A17	Dalmahoy E	Dalmahoy, Kirknewton, Midlothian	18	6,664	72	U	D	1926	325	U	P
A18	Dalmahoy W	Dalmahoy, Kirknewton, Midlothian	18	5,212	66	U	D	1926	325	U	P

Code	Club	Location				I	D				
A19	Duddingston	Duddingston Road West, Edinburgh	18	6,647	72			1897	100	U	P
A20	Dumfries and County	Edinburgh Road, Dumfries	18	5,914	68	U	C	1912	100	KT	P
A21	Dumfries Crichton Royal	Dumfries	9	3,084	69	M		1884	200	U	P
A22	Dumfries and Galloway	Laurieston Avenue, Dumfries	18	5,782	68	U	C	1880	50	K	P
A23	Dunbar E	East Links, Dunbar	18	6,426	71	U	C	1794	25	RB	L
A24	Dunbar Winterfield	North Road, Dunbar	18	5,035	65	U	B	1935	50	L	L
A25	Duns	4 Hardens Road, Duns	9	5,754	68	U	B	1898	500	U	P
A26	Eyemouth	Gunsgreen House, Eyemouth	9	5,500	67	U	B	1880	130	RB/P	M
A27	Fauldhouse, Greenburn	Bridge Street, Fauldhouse, West Lothian	18	6,210	70	U	B	1953	700	T	P
A28	*Galashiels Ladhope*	Ladhope Recreation Ground, Galashiels	18	5,309	67	U	B	1884	700	H	M
A29	Galashiels Torwoodlee	Galashiels	9	5,800	68	Ex Sat	B	1895	500	T	P
A30	Gatehouse of Fleet	Laurieston Road, Gatehouse-of-Fleet	9	2,398	63	U	B	1922	250	H	M
A31	Gifford	Gifford	9	6,138	69	U	B	1904	450	U	P
A32	Glenluce, Wigtownshire County	Mains of Park, Glenluce, Newton Stewart	9	5,726	68	U	B	1894	30	L	L
A33	Gullane 1	Gullane, East Lothian	18	6,479	71	U	D	1880	100	L	L
A34	Gullane 2	Gullane, East Lothian	18	6,127	69	U	C	1900	100	L	L
A35	Gullane 3	Gullane, East Lothian	18	5,035	64	U	B	1910	50	L	L
A36	*Haddington*	*Amisfield Course*, Haddington, East Lothian	18	6,280	70	U	B	1865	150	T	P
A37	Hawick	Vertish Hill, Hawick	18	5,929	69	U	B	1877	700	T	P
A38	Innerleithen	Leithen Road, Innerleithen	9	5,820	68	U	B	1886	500	T	P
A39	Jedburgh	Dunion Road, Jedburgh	9	5,522	67	U	B	1892	650	U	M
A40	Kelso	Racecourse Road, Kelso	18	6,066	69	U	B	1887	204	T	P
A41	Kilspindie	Aberlady, East Lothian	18	4,957	66	U	C	1867	25	L	L
A42	Kingsknowe	326 Lanark Road, Edinburgh	18	5,966	69	U	B	1908	300	U	P
A43	Kirkcudbright	Stirling Crescent, Kirkcudbright	18	5,681	67	U	B	1895	250	H	P

REF	NAME	ADDRESS	HOLES	LENGTH (yds)	SSS	VIS	COST	DATE	ALT (ft)	LAND	VEG
A44	Langholm	Whitaside, Langholm, Dumfriesshire	9	5,246	66	U	A	1892	500	H	P
A45	*Lauder*	Galashiels Road, Lauder	9	6,002	70	U	A	1896	750	U	M
A46	Liberton	297 Gilmerton Road, Edinburgh	18	5,299	66	WD	C	1920	250	U	P
A47	Linlithgow	Braehead, Linlithgow, West Lothian	18	5,858	68	U	C	1913	300	U	P
A48	Livingston	Carmondean, Livingston, West Lothian	18	6,636	72	U	B	1978	500	U	P
A49	Lochmaben	Castlehill Gate, Lochmaben, Dumfriesshire	9	5,304	66	U	B	1925	150	K	P
A50	Lockerbie	Corrie Road, Lockerbie, Dumfriesshire	9	2,614	66	U	B	1889	450	U	P
A51	Longniddry	Links Road, Longniddry, East Lothian	18	6,210	70	U	D	1921	25	L	L
A52	Lothianburn	106 Biggar Road, Edinburgh	18	5,750	69	WD	B	1893	600	H	M
A53	Luffness New	Aberlady, East Lothian	18	6,122	69	M	—	1867	50	L	L
A54	Melrose	Dingleton, Melrose	9	5,464	68	U	B	1880	550	H	M
A55	Merchants of Edinburgh	10 Craighill Gardens, Edinburgh	18	4,889	65	M	B	1907	400	H	P
A56	Minto	Minto Village, by Denholm, Hawick	18	5,460	68	U	B	1926	350	U	P
A57	Moffat	Coareshill, Moffat	18	5,218	66	WD	B	1884	750	H	M
A58	Mortonhall	231 Braid Road, Edinburgh	18	6,557	71	I	D	1892	600	H	M
A59	Muirfield Hon. Co. of Edinburgh Golfers	Gullane, East Lothian	18	6,601	73	I	F	1744	50	L	L
A60	Murrayfield	Murrayfield Road, Edinburgh	18	5,727	68	I	C	1896	300	H	P
A61a	*Musselburgh*	Silver Ring Clubhouse, Millhill, Musselburgh	9	5,380	67	U	A	1774	20	L	L
A61b	Musselburgh Monktonhall	Musselburgh, Midlothian	18	6,623	72	U	—	1938	50	T	P

Code	Name	Location	Holes	Yardage	Par			Year			
A62	New Galloway	Castle Douglas, Kirkcudbrightshire	9	5,018	64	U	B	1902	200	U	M
A63	Newton Stewart	Kirroughtree Avenue, Minnigaff, Newton Stewart	9	5,512	67	U	B	1930	75	KT	P
A64	North Berwick Glen	Tantallon Terrace, North Berwick	18	6,086	69	U	B	1906	75	RP/RB	L
A65	North Berwick	Beach Road, North Berwick	18	6,317	70	U	D	1832	25	L	L
A66	*Peebles*	Kirkland Street, Peebles	18	6,137	69	U	B	1892	650	U	P
A67	Penicuik Glencorse	Milton Bridge, Penicuik, Midlothian	18	5,205	66	WD	C	1890	500	U	P
A68	Portobello	Stanley Street, Portobello, Edinburgh	9	4,838	64	U	A	1853	50	RP	P
A69	Portpatrick Dunskey	Golf Course Road, Portpatrick	18	5,644	67	U	C	1903	100	RP	M
A70	Prestonfield	6 Prestonfield Road North, Edinburgh	18	6,216	70	WD	C	1920	200	T	P
A71	Pumpherston	Drumshoreland Road, Pumpherston, Livingston	9	5,154	65	M	B	1910	400	U	P
A72	Ratho Park	Ratho, Newbridge, Midlothian	18	6,028	69	U	C	1928	250	U	P
A73	Ravelston	Ravelston Dykes Road, Blackhall, Edinburgh	9	5,332	66	M	A	1912	300	U	P
A74	Royal Burgess Golfing Society	181 Whitehouse Road, Edinburgh	18	6,604	72	I	—	1735	150	U	P
A75	Royal Musselburgh	Prestongrange House, Prestonpans, East Lothian	18	6,237	70	WD	C	1774	50	RB	P
A76	St Boswells	St Boswells, Roxburghshire	9	5,054	65	U	B	1899	250	T	P
A77	St Medan	Monreith, Port William	9	4,554	62	U	B	1905	50	RP	M
A78	Sanquhar	Old Barr Road, Sanquhar, Dumfriesshire	9	5,144	68	U	B	1894	500	T	P
A79	Selkirk	The Hill, Selkirk	18	5,560	67	U	B	1883	800	H	M
A80	Silverknowes	Parkway, Edinburgh	18	6,210	70	U	A	1947	75	RB	P
A81	Southerness	Southerness, Dumfries	18	6,548	72	U	D	1947	30	L	L
A82	Stranraer	Creachmore, Stranraer	18	6,300	71	WD	B	1906	30	RB	P
A83	Swanston	111 Swanston Road, Fairmilehead, Edinburgh	18	5,024	65	U	B	1927	650	H	M

REF	NAME	ADDRESS	HOLES	LENGTH (yds)	SSS	VIS	COST	DATE	ALT (ft)	LAND	VEG
A84	Thornhill	Black Nest, Thornhill	18	6,011	69	U	B	1892	250	T	P
A85	Torphin Hill	Torphin Road, Edinburgh	18	5,025	66	U	B	1895	750	H	M
A86	Turnhouse	154 Turnhouse Road. Corstorphine. Edinburgh	18	6,171	69	WD	C	1909	150	U	P
A87	Uphall	Uphall. Broxburn. W. Lothian	18	5,567	67	U	B	—	400	U	P
A88	West Calder Harburn	West Calder, West Lothian	18	5,843	68	U	B	1921	800	U	P
A89	West Linton	West Linton, Peebleshire	18	6,024	69	U	B	1890	850	K	M
A90	Wigtown and Bladnoch	Wigtown	9	5,424	67	U	B	1960	75	D	P

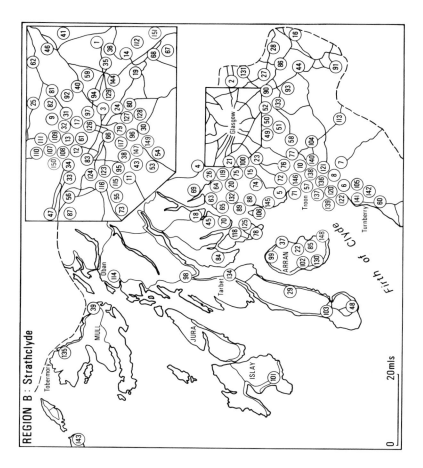

FIG A.2   Region B: Strathclyde.

REF	NAME	ADDRESS	HOLES	LENGTH (yds)	SSS	VIS	COST	DATE	ALT (ft)	LAND	VEG
B1	Airdrie	Rochsoles, Airdrie	18	6,004	69	WD	B	1877	475	U	B
B2	Airdrie Easter Moffat	Plains, Airdrie	18	6,221	70	WD	B	1922	500	U	P
B3	Alexandra Park	Alexandra Parade, Glasgow	9	3,936	60	U	A	1880	200	D	P
B4	Alexandria Vale of Leven	Bonhill, Alexandria	18	5,818	68	WD	B	1907	200	H	P
B5	Ardeer	Greenhead, Stevenston	18	6,630	72	U Ex Sat	C	1880	130	D	P
B6	Ayr Belleisle	Ayr	18	6,540	71	U	B	1927	50	RB	P
B7	Ayr Dalmilling	Westwood Avenue, Ayr	18	5,401	66	U	B	1960	60	RB	P
B8	Ayr Seafield	Belleisle Park, Ayr	18	5,244	66	U	B	1930	40	RB	P
B9	Balmore	Torrance, by Glasgow	18	5,735	67	M	C	1906	200	D	P
B10	Barrassie	Hillhouse Road, Barrassie, Troon	18	6,473	71	WD	D	1887	30	L	L
B11	Barrhead Fereneze	Barrhead	18	5,821	68	M	—	1904	350	H	M
B12	Bearsden	Thorn Road, Bearsden, Glasgow	9	5,977	68	M	—	1891	250	D	P
B13	Bearsden Douglas Park	Hillfoot, Bearsden, Glasgow	18	5,957	69	M	—	1897	200	D	P
B14	Bellshill	Orbiston, Bellshill	18	6,607	72	U	B	1905	180	U	P
B15	Beith	Bigholm Road, Beith	9	5,488	67	WD	B	1896	550	H	M
B16	Biggar	Broughton Road, Biggar	18	5,416	66	U	B	1895	650	T	P
B17	Bishopbriggs	Brackenbrae Road, Bishopbriggs, Glasgow	18	6,041	69	M	C	1906	170	T	P
B18	Blairmore and Strone	Strone, by Dunoon, Argyll	9	4,244	62	U	B	1896	300	H	M
B19	Bothwell Castle	Blantyre Road, Bothwell	18	6,312	71	WD	C	1922	160	U	P
B20	Bridge of Weir Ranfurly Old Course	Ranfurly Place, Bridge of Weir	18	6,283	70	I	D	1905	400	U	M
B21	Bridge of Weir Ranfurly Castle	Golf Road, Bridge of Weir	18	6,284	70	I	D	1889	340	U	M
B22	Brodick	Brodick, Isle of Arran	18	4,404	62	U	B	1897	40	L	L
B23	Caldwell Uplawmoor	Caldwell, Uplawmoor	18	6,046	69	WD	C	1903	350	H	P
B24	Cambuslang	Western Drive, Cambuslang	9	6,072	69	WD	C	1891	75	T	P
B25	Campsie	Crow Road, Lennoxtown	18	5,517	67	U	B	1895	350	HS	P

B26	Cardross	Cardross, Dumbarton	18	6,466	71	WD	C	1895	75	D	P
B27	Carluke	Hallcraig, Carluke	18	5,805	68	WD	B	1894	520	U	P
B28	Carnwath	Main Street, Carnwath	18	5,955	69	U	C	1907	650	K	P
B29	Carradale	Carradale	9	4,774	64	U	B	1900	65	RB	L
B30	Cathcart Castle	Mearns Road, Clarkston, Glasgow	18	5,832	68	M	—	1895	250	D	P
B31	Cawder	Cadder Road, Bishopbriggs, Glasgow	18	6,244	71	WD	D	1933	150	T	P
B32	Cawder-Kier	Cadder Road, Bishopbriggs, Glasgow	18	5,885	68	WD	D	1933	150	T	P
B33	Clydebank Dalmuir/Overtoun	Overtoun Road, Dalmuir, Clydebank	18	5,349	66	U	A	1970	150	D	P
B34	Clydebank and District, Hardgate	Hardgate, Clydebank	18	5,815	68	U	B	1905	250	D	P
B35	Coatbridge Drumpelier	Langloan, Coatbridge	18	6,227	70	I	C	1894	275	U	P
B36	Coatbridge Townhead	Townhead Road, Coatbridge	18	5,387	66	U	A	1970	300	U	P
B37	Corrie	Corrie, Isle of Arran	9	3,896	61	U	A	1892	80	H	P
B38	Cowglen	301 Barrhead Road, Glasgow	18	6,006	69	M	—	1906	100	D	P
B39	Craignure	Craignure, Mull	9	4,436	64	U	A	1981	40	RB	L
B40	Crow Wood	Muirhead, Chryston, Glasgow	18	6,249	70	M	—	1925	230	D	P
B41	Cumbernauld Palacerigg	Palacerigg, Country Park, Cumbernauld	18	6,712	71	U	B	1975	550	U	P
B43	Deaconsbank	Glasgow	18	4,800	63	U	A	1922	180	D	P
B44	Douglas Water	Douglas Water, Lanark	9	5,832	69	U	A	1922	750	H	P
B45	Dunoon Cowal	Ardenslate Road, Dunoon	18	6,251	70	U	B	1890	150	H	P
B46	Dullatur	Dullatur, Glasgow	18	6,253	70	U	C	1896	390	U	P
B47	Dumbarton	Broadmeadow, Dumbarton	18	6,157	69	WD	B	1888	20	T	P
B48	Dunaverty	Southend, Argyll	18	4,597	63	U	A	1889	40	L	L
B49	Eaglesham	Bonnyton, Eaglesham	18	6,252	71	I	C	1957	500	L	L
B50	East Kilbride	Chapelside Road, Nerston, East Kilbride	18	6,419	71	M	B	1900	500	U	P
B51	East Kilbride Langlands	Langlands, East Kilbride	18	6,153	69	U	B	1983	680	U	P
B52	East Kilbride Torrance House	Strathaven Road, East Kilbride	18	6,403	71	U	B	1969	625	U	P

REF	NAME	ADDRESS	HOLES	LENGTH (yds)	SSS	VIS	COST	DATE	ALT (ft)	LAND	VEG
B53	East Renfrewshire	Pilmuir, Newton Mearns, Glasgow	18	6,097	70	I	C	1922	550	U	M
B54	Eastwood	Muirshield, Loganswell, Newton Mearns, Glasgow	18	5,886	68	M	C	1893	600	U	M
B55	Elderslie	Elderslie, Paisley	18	6,031	69	M	C	1908	75	D	P
B56	Erskine	Bishopton	18	6,287	70	I	D	1904	75	T	P
B57	Glasgow Gailes	Gailes, Ayrshire	18	6,447	71	I	D	1892	25	L	L
B58	Galston Loudon	Galston	18	5,854	68	WD	B	1909	150	T	P
B59	Gartcosh Mount Ellen	Gartcosh, Glasgow	18	5,525	68	WD	B	1905	228	D	P
B60	*Girvan*	Golf Course Road, Girvan	18	5,075	65	U	B	1900	40	RB	L
B61	Glasgow Killermont	Killermont, Glasgow	18	5,968	69	I	D	1787	120	D	P
B62	Kilsyth Lennox	Tak-Ma-Doon Road, Kilsyth	9	5,944	69	U	B	1900	430	H	M
B63	Gourock	Cowal View, Gourock	18	6,492	71	WD	C	1896	300	H	M
B64	Greenock	Forsyth Street, Greenock	18	5,888	68	WD	C	1890	300	H	M
B65	Greenock Whin Hill	Beith Road, Greenock	18	5,454	67	U	A	1911	480	H	M
B66	Haggs Castle	70 Dumbreck Road, Glasgow	18	6,464	71	M	D	1910	70	RB	P
B67	Hamilton Riccarton	Riccarton, Ferniegair, Hamilton	18	6,255	70	M	C	1892	350	U	P
B68	*Hamilton Strathclyde Country Park*	Mote Hill, Hamilton	9	6,294	70	U	A	1920	150	RT	P
B69	Helensburgh	25 E Abercromby Road, Helensburgh	18	6,058	69	WD	C	1893	250	H	P
B70	Innellan	Innellan, Argyll	9	4,878	63	U	B	1895	210	H	M
B71	Irvine	Bogside, Irvine	18	6,454	71	U	C	1887	40	RB	L
B72	*Irvine Ravenspark*	Irvine	18	6,496	71	U	A	1907	35	RB	L
B73	Johnstone Cochrane Castle	Craigston, Johnstone	18	6,226	70	WD	C	1895	50	H	P
B74	KilbirniePlace	Largs Road, Kilbirnie	18	5,411	67	U	B	1922	250	KT	P
B75	Kilmacolm	Kilmacolm	18	5,890	68	WD	C	1891	460	U	M
B76	*Kilmarnock Annanhill*	Irvine Road, Kilmarnock	18	6,270	70	U	B	1957	120	D	P
B77	*Kilmarnock Caprington*	Ayr Road, Kilmarnock	18		69	U	B	1909	100	D	P
B78	Kingarth	Kilchattan Bay, Bute	9	4,994	64	U	A	1888	25	RB	L

B79	*King's Park*	Croftpark Avenue, Glasgow	9	6,020	U	60	A	1934	200	D	P
B80	Kirkhill	Greenlees Road, Cambuslang	18	5,889	WD	69	C	1910	430	U	M
B81	Kirkintilloch	Todhill, Campsie Road, Kirkintilloch	18	5,269	M	66	—	1895	150	D	P
B82	Kirkintilloch Hayston	Campsie Road, Kirkintilloch	18	6,042	WD	69	C	1926	150	D	P
B83	Knightswood	Lincoln Avenue, Glasgow	9	5,472	U	66	A	1929	75	U	P
B84	Kyles of Bute	Tighnabruaich, Argyll	9	4,778	U	64	B	1968	240	U	M
B85	Lamlash	Lamlash, Isle of Arran	18	4,681	U	63	B	1889	100	H	P
B86	Lanark	The Moor, Lanark	18	6,426	WD	71	C	1851	600	K	M
B87	Langbank Gleddoch Golf and Country Club	Langbank, Renfrewshire	18	6,200	WD	71	C	1974	300	H	P
B88	Largs	Irvine Road, Largs	18	6,257	U	70	C	1891	75	RB	P
B89	Largs Routenburn	Largs	18	5,650	U	67	B	1920	300	H	M
B90	*Larkhall*	Burnhead Road, Larkhall	9	6,236	U	70	A	1909	350	U	P
B91	Leadhills	Leadhills, Lanarkshire	9	4,062	U		A	1935	1200	H	M
B92	Lenzie	19 Crosshill Road, Lenzie, Glasgow	18	5,982	M	69	—	1889	250	D	P
B93	*Lesmahagow Hollandbush*	Acre Tophead, Lesmahagow	18	6,110	U	70	B	1954	750	U	P
B94	Lethamhill	Cumbernauld Road, Glasgow	18	5,946	U	68	A	1933	250	D	P
B95	Leverndale		9	—		—	B	—	100	U	P
B96	*Linn Park*	Simshill Road, Glasgow	18	4,728	U	63	A	1925	250	D	P
B97	Littlehill	Auchinairn Road, Bishopbriggs, Glasgow	18	6,199	U	69	A	1926	300	D	P
B98	Lochgilphead	Blarbuie Road, Lochgilphead, Argyll	9	4,484	U	63	B	1963	180	RT	P
B99	Lochranza	Lochranza, Isle of Arran	9	3,400	U	—	A	—	20	RT	P
B100	Lochwinnoch	Burnfoot Road, Lochwinnoch	18	6,223	WD	70	C	1897	250	H	P
B101	Machrie, Islay	Kildalton, Islay	18	6,226	U	70	B	1891	30	L	L
B102	Machrie Bay, Arran	Arran	9	4,164	U	61	A	1901	30	RB	L
B103	Machrihanish	Campbeltown, Argyll	18	6,228	U	70	C	1876	30	L	L
B104	Mauchline, Ballochmyle	Mauchline, Ayrshire	18	5,952	U	69	C	1937	400	U	P

REF	NAME	ADDRESS	HOLES	LENGTH (yds)	SSS	VIS	COST	DATE	ALT (ft)	LAND	VEG
B105	*Maybole*	Memorial Park. Maybole	9	5,270	65	U	A	1970	210	D	P
B106	Millport	Isle of Cumbrae	18	5,831	68	U	B	1888	200	U	P
B107	Milngavie	Langpark, Milngavie, Glasgow	18	5,818	68	M		1895	325	D	M
B108	Milngavie Clober	Craigton Road. Milngavie, Glasgow	18	5,068	65	U	B	1951	225	D	P
B109	Milngavie Douglaston	Milngavie, Glasgow	18	6,269	71	U	C	1978	150	D	PW
B110	Milngavie Hilton Park	Auldmarroch Estate. Stockiemuir Road. Milngavie	18	6,021	70	WD	C	1928	370	D	M
B111	Hilton Park (Allander)	Auldmarroch Estate. Stockiemuir Road. Milngavie	18	5,409	67	WD	C	1928	370	D	M
B112	Motherwell Colville Park	Jerviston Estate. Motherwell	18	6,208	70	M	C	1922	275	U	P
B113	New Cumnock	New Cumnock. Ayrshire	9	4,730	63	U	A	1901	750	D	P
B114	Oban Glencruitten	Oban	18	4,452	63	U	B	1905	100	H	P
B115	Paisley Braehead	Braehead. Paisley	18	6,424	71	I	C	1895	550	U	M
B116	*Paisley Barshaw*	Barshaw Park. Paisley	18	5,703	67	U	A	1927	100	D	P
B117	Pollok	90 Barrhead Road, Pollokshaws. Glasgow	18	6,257	70	I	D	1892	75	RB	P
B118	Port Bannantyne	Isle of Bute	13	4,654	63	U	B	1968	240	H	P
B119	Port Glasgow	Port Glasgow	18	5,712	68	U	B	1895	480	U	M
B120	Prestwick	Links Road. Prestwick	18	6,631	72	I	E	1851	30	L	L
B121	Prestwick St Cuthbert	East Road. Prestwick	18	6,470	71	WD	C	1899	35	L	L
B122	Prestwick St Nicholas	Grangemuir Road. Prestwick	18	5,926	68	I	D	1851	35	L	L
B123	Ralston	Ralston. Paisley	18	6,100	69	M	—	1904	80	D	P
B124	Renfrew	Blythswood Estate. Inchinnan Road, Renfrew	18	6,818	73	M	C	1894	30	RT	P
B125	Rothesay	Canada Hill, Rothesay. Isle of Bute	18	5,358	67	U	B	1892	350	H	M
B126	*Ruchill*	Brassey Street, Maryhill. Glasgow	9	4,480	62	U	A	1928	200	D	P

No.	Name	Location									
B127	Rutherglen Blairbeth	Burnside, Rutherglen	18	5,448	67	M	B	1910	450	H	P
B128	Rutherglen Cathkin Braes	Cathkin Braes, Rutherglen	18	6,266	71	I	C	1888	650	U	M
B129	Sandyhills	223 Sandyhills Road, Glasgow	18	6,253	70	I	C	1905	120	U	P
B130	Shiskine	Blackwaterfoot, Isle of Arran	12	3,000	41	U	A	1896	30	L	L
B131	Shotts	Blairhead, Shotts	18	6,125	70	WD	C	1895	825	U	P
B132	Skelmorlie	Skelmorlie	13	5,056	65	U	B	1890	360	U	M
B133	Strathaven	Strathaven, Lanarkshire	18	6,226	70	WD	C	1908	725	U	P
B134	Tarbert	Kilberry Road, Tarbert, Argyll	9	4,460	64	U	B	1910	50	RB	P
B135	Tobermory	Isle of Mull	9	4,920	64	U	B	1896	250	H	M
B136	Troon, Old	Craigend Road, Troon	18	6,641	73	WD / I	F	1878	30	L	L
B137	Troon, Portland	Craigend Road, Troon	18	6,274	71	WD / I	F	1894	30	L	L
B138	*Troon, Lochgreen*	Harling Drive, Troon	18	6,687	72	U	B	1907	40	L	L
B139	*Troon, Darley*	Harling Drive, Troon	18	6,327	70	U	B	1907	40	L	L
B140	*Troon, Fullarton*	Harling Drive, Troon	18	4,784	63	U	B	1907	40	L	L
B141	Turnberry, Ailsa	Turnberry, Ayrshire	18	6,950	70	H	F	1903	25	L	L
B142	Turnberry, Arran	Turnberry, Ayrshire	18	6,276	69	U / H	E	1912	25	L	L
B143	Vaul Tiree	Scarinish, Isle of Tiree	9	6,246	70	U	B	1920	60	L	L
B144	Uddingston Calderbraes	57 Roundknowe Road, Uddingston	9	5,046	67	M	B	1893	250	H	P
B145	West Kilbride	West Kilbride, Ayrshire	18	6,247	70	WD	C	1893	40	L	L
B146	Western Gailes	Gailes, Irvine	18	6,614	71	WD	D	1897	20	L	L
B147	Whitecraigs	72 Ayr Road, Giffnock, Glasgow	18	6,230	70	I	E	1905	250	U	P
B148	Whiting Bay	Isle of Arran	18	4,405	63	U	B	1895	150	H	P
B149	Williamwood	Clarkston Road, Glasgow	18	5,878	68	M	—	1906	200	U	P
B150	Windyhill	Windyhill, Bearsden, Glasgow	18	6,254	70	WD	C	1908	430	D	M
B151	Wishaw	Clelland Road, Wishaw	18	6,134	69	WD	B	1897	380	U	P

REGION C
CENTRAL, FIFE AND TAYSIDE

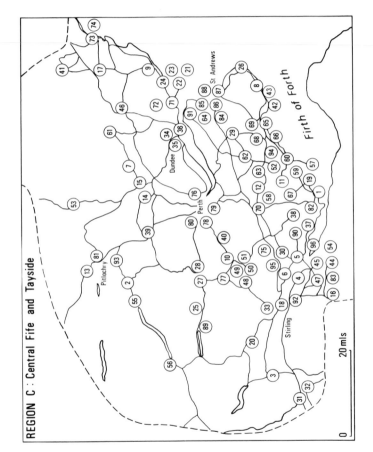

REGION C : Central Fife and Tayside

FIG A.3   Region C: Central, Fife and Tayside.

216

REF	NAME	ADDRESS	HOLES	LENGTH (yds)	SSS	VIS	COST	DATE	ALT (ft)	LAND	VEG
C1	Aberdour	Seaside Place, Aberdour	18	5,469	67	WD	B	1904	50	RB	P
C2	Aberfeldy	Taybridge Road, Aberfeldy	9	5,466	67	U	B	1895	400	RT	P
C3	Aberfoyle	Aberfoyle	18	5,204	66	U	C	1893	150	H	P
C4	Alloa Braehead	Cambus, Alloa	18	6,013	69	U	B	1891	70	RB	P
C5	Alloa	Shaw Park, Sauchie, Alloa	18	6,240	70	U	B	1891	200	U	P
C6	Alva	Beauclerc Street, Alva	9	4,814	64	U	A	1901	250	H	P
C7	Alyth	Pitcrocknie, Alyth	18	6,226	70	U	B	1894	300	K	P
C8	Anstruther	Anstruther	9	4,504	63	U	B	1890	60	RB	P
C9	*Arbroath*	Elliot, Arbroath	18	6,078	69	U	B	1877	30	L	L
C10	Auchterarder	Orchil Road, Auchterarder	18	5,741	68	U	B	1893	400	U	L
C11	Auchterderran	Woodend Road, Cardenden, Fife	9	5,400	66	U	A	1904	300	U	P
C12	Bishopshire	Kinnesswood, Perthshire	9	4,360	63	U	A	1903	600	H	M
C13	Blair Atholl	Blair Atholl, Perthshire	9	5,710	69	U	B	1892	500	RT	P
C14	Blairgowrie Rosemount	Rosemount, Blairgowrie	18	6,588	72	WD H	E	1889	180	S	PW
C15	Blairgowrie Landsdowne	Landsdowne, Blairgowrie	18	6,895	73	WD H	E	—	180	S	P
C16	Bonnybridge	Larbert Road, Bonnybridge	9	6,058	69	I	—	1924	200	U	P
C17	Brechin	Trinity, Brechin	18	5,267	66	U	B	1893	300	U	P
C18	Bridge of Allan	Sunnylaw, Bridge of Allan	9	4,900	65	WD	B	1895	450	U	P
C19	Burntisland House	Dodhead, Burntisland	18	5,865	68	U	B	1797	200	U	P
C20	Callander	Aveland Road, Callander	18	5,091	66	U	B	1890	300	U	P
C21	Carnoustie Barry Panmure	Barry, Angus	18	6,301	70	WD	C	1899	20	L	L
C22	*Carnoustie*	Carnoustie	18	6,931	74	U	E	1842	25	L	L
C23	*Carnoustie*	Buddon Links	18	6,445	71	U	B	1981	25	L	L
C24	*Carnoustie*	Burnside	18	5,935	69	U	C		25	L	L
C25	Comrie	Comrie	9	5,966	69	U	B	1891	250	H	H
C26	Crail	Balcomie Clubhouse, Crail	18	5,720	68	U	C	1786	50	L	L
C27	Crieff	Perth Road, Crieff	18	6,419	71	U	C	1891	450	U	P
C28	Crieff	Perth Road, Crieff	9	4,772	63	U	B	1980	450	U	P

REF	NAME	ADDRESS	HOLES	LENGTH (yds)	SSS	VIS	COST	DATE	ALT (ft)	LAND	VEG
C29	Cupar	Hillarvitt, Cupar	9	5,074	65	WD	B	1855	250	H	P
C30	Dollar	Brewlands House, Dollar	18	5,144	66	U	B	1896	400	H	M
C31	Drymen Buchanan Castle	Drymen	18	6,015	69	M	D	1936	40	RT	P
C32	Drymen Strathendrick	Drymen	9	4,962	65	M	B	1901	50	KT	P
C33	Dunblane	Dunblane	18	5,878	68	WD	C	1923	300	U	P
C34	Dundee Caird Park	Dundee	18	6,303	70	U	B	1926	250	D	P
C35	Dundee Camperdown	Camperdown Park, Dundee	18	6,561	72	U	A	1960	450	U	P
C36	Dundee Downfield	Turnberry Avenue, Dundee	18	6,840	73	WD	D	1932	450	U	P
C37	Dunfermline	Pitfirrane, Crossford, Dunfermline	18	6,214	70	WD	C	1887	140	U	P
C38	Dunfermline Canmore	Venturefair, Dunfermline	18	5,437	66	WD	B	1898	400	U	P
C39	Dunkeld and Burnam	Fungarth, Dunkeld	9	4,945	66	U	B	1910	500	H	M
C40	Dunning	Rollo Park, Dunning	9	4,836	64	WD	A	1953	150	RT	P
C41	Edzell	High Street, Edzell, Brechin	18	6,299	70	WD	C	1895	150	S	P
C42	Elie	Elie, Leven	18	6,241	70	U	C	1875	30	L	L
C43	Elie Sports Club	Elie, Leven	9	4,554	64	U	A	1875	30	L	L
C44	Falkirk	Stirling Road, Camelon, Falkirk	18	6,201	70	WD	C	1922	50	RB	P
C45	Falkirk, Tryst	86 Burnhead Road, Larbert	18	6,053	69	WD	B	1885	100	RB	P
C46	Forfar	Cunninghill, Forfar	18	6,255	69	WD	C	1871	250	KT	P
C47	Glenbervie	Stirling Road, Larbert	18	6,469	71	I	C	1932	120	RB	P
C48	Gleneagles Kings	Gleneagles Hotel	18	6,471	71	U	F	1924	500	E	P
C49	Gleneagles Queens	Gleneagles Hotel	18	5,965	69	U	F	1924	500	E	P
C50	Gleneagles Princes	Gleneagles Hotel	18	4,664	64	U	D	1974	500	E	P
C51	Gleneagles Glendevon	Gleneagles Hotel	18	5,719	68	U	D	1980	500	E	P
C52	Glenrothes	Golf Course Road, Glenrothes	18	6,444	71	U	A	1958	300	U	P
C53	Glenshee Dalmunzie	Glenshee, Blairgowrie	9	4,070	62	U	B	1948	1000	RT	M

	Name	Address									
C54	*Grangemouth*	Polmonthill, Grangemouth	18	6,527	71	U	B	1973	120	U	P
C55	Kenmore Taymouth Castle	Kenmore, Tayside	18	6,066	69	U	C	1923	400	RT	P
C56	Killin	Killin, Perthshire	9	4,820	65	U	B	1913	500	H	P
C57	*Kinghorn*	McDuff Crescent, Kinghorn	18	5,246	67	U	A	1887	250	RB	M
C58	Kinross Green Hotel	Beeches Park, Kinross	18	6,111	70	U	C	1900	360	RT	P
C59	Kirkcaldy	Balwearie Road, Kirkcaldy	18	6,007	70	U	B	1904	150	H	P
C60	*Kirkcaldy Kier Park*	Dunnikeir Way, Kirkcaldy	18	6,601	72	WD	A	1963	250	U	P
C61	Kirriemuir Players	Kirriemuir	18	5,541	67	WD	C	1908	500	H	P
C62	Ladybank	Annsmuir, Ladybank	18	6,617	72	WD	D	1897	150	S	P
C63	Leslie	Balsillie Laws, Leslie, Glenrothes	9	4,940	64	U	A	1898	450	H	P
C64	Leuchars St Michaels	Leuchars	9	5,510	67	WD	B	1903	100	RB	P
C65	Leven Golfing Society	Links Road, Leven	18	6,434	71	WD	C	1820	30	L	L
C66	*Leven Municipal*	Leven	18	5,403	66	U	A	1809	55	L	L
C67	*Lochgelly*	Lochore Country Park, Crosshill, Lochgelly	9	6,482	71	U	A	1910	450	U	P
C68	Lundin Links	Golf Road, Lundin Links	18	6,377	71	WD	C	1869	50	L	L
C69	Lundin Ladies	Woodielea Road, Lundin Links	9	4,730	67	U	B	1910	65	U	P
C70	Milnathort	South Street, Milnathort	9	5,918	68	U	B	1910	350	U	P
C71	*Monifieth Medal*	Princes Street, Monifieth	18	6,650	72	U	D	1858	20	L	L
C72	*Monifieth Ashludie*	Princes Street, Monifieth	18	5,123	66	WD	C	1858	20	L	L
C73	*Montrose Medal*	Traill Drive, Montrose	18	6,451	71	WD	B	1810	25	L	L
C74	*Montrose Bloomfield*	Traill Drive, Montrose	18	4,815	63	U	B	1897	25	L	L
C75	Muckhart	Muckhart, Dollar	18	6,112	70	U	B	1908	450	K	M
C76	Murrayshall	New Scone, Perth	18	6,416	71	U	C	1981	450	U	P
C77	Muthill	Peat Road, Muthill	9	4,742	63	U	B	1935	350	U	P
C78	Perth Craigie Hill	Cherrybank, Perth	18	5,379	66	U	B	1911	300	H	M
C79	Perth King James VI	Moncrieff Island, Perth	18	6,026	69	WD	C	1858	25	RT	P
C80	*Royal Perth*	North Insch, Perth	18	5,141	64	U	B	1842	20	RT	P
C81	Pitlochry	Pitlochry	18	5,811	68	U	C	1909	600	H	P
C82	Pitreavie	Queensferry Road, Dunfermline	18	6,086	69	U	B	1932	200	D	P

REF	NAME	ADDRESS	HOLES	LENGTH (yds)	SSS	VIS	COST	DATE	ALT (ft)	LAND	VEG
C83	Polmont	Manuelrigg, Maddiston, Falkirk	9	4,088	69	U	B	1901	200	U	P
C84	*St Andrews Balgove*	St Andrews	9	—		U	A	1971	15	L	L
C85	*St Andrews Eden*	St Andrews	18	5,971	69	U	C	1913	10	L	L
C86	*St Andrews Jubilee*	St Andrews	18	6,284	70	U	B	1899	10	L	L
C87	*St Andrews New*	St Andrews	18	6,604	72	U	C	1894	10	L	L
C88	*St Andrews Old*	St Andrews	18	6,566	72	H	E	1754	10	L	L
C89	StFillans	St Fillans, Tayside	9	5,268	66	U	B	1903	350	RT	P
C90	Saline	Kinneddar Hill, Saline	9	5,302	66	U	B	1912	600	U	P
C91	Scotscraig	Golf Road, Tayport	18	6,477	71	WD	C	1817	30	L	L
C92	Stirling	Queen's Road, Stirling	18	6,409	71	WD	C	1869	150	U	P
C93	Strathtay	Strathtay	9	4,082	63	U	B	1909	250	RT	P
C94	Thornton	Station Road, Thornton	18	6,175	69	U	B	1921	150	U	P
C95	Tillicoultry	Alva Road, Tillicoultry	9	5,056	66	U	B	1899	250	H	P
C96	Tulliallan	Kincardine, Alloa	18	5,982	69	U	B	1902	100	U	P

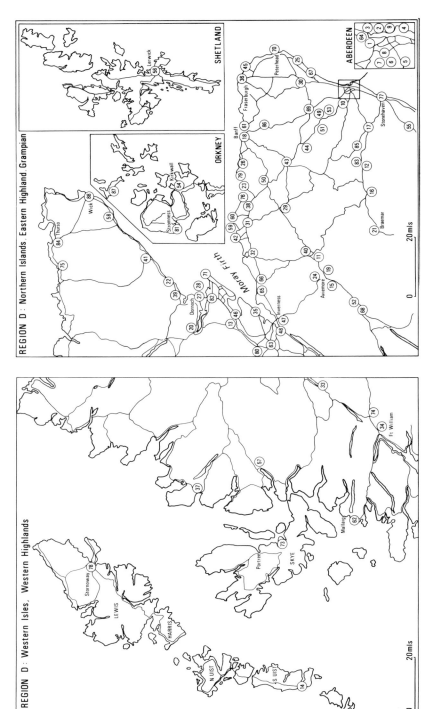

FIG A.4   Region D: Western Isles and Western Highlands.   FIG A.5   Region E: Northern Islands, Eastern Highlands, Grampian.

REF	NAME	ADDRESS	HOLES	LENGTH (yds)	SSS	VIS	COST	DATE	ALT (ft)	LAND	VEG
D1	*Aberdeen Auchmill*	Provost Rust Drive, Aberdeen	9	6,070	70	U	A	1975	300	U	P
D2	Royal Aberdeen	Balgownie, Bridge of Don	18	6,372	71	I	D	1780	30	L	L
D3	Royal Aberdeen	Balgownie, Bridge of Don	18	4,033	60	I		—	30	L	L
D4	*Aberdeen Balnagask*	St Fitticks Road, Aberdeen	18	6,055	69	U	B	1949	75	RB	P
D5	Aberdeen Deeside	Bieldside, Aberdeen	18	5,972	69	I	D	1903	75	RT	P
D6	*Aberdeen Hazlehead*	Hazlehead, Aberdeen	18	6,205	70	U	B	1927	420	U	P
D7	*Aberdeen Hazlehead*	Hazlehead, Aberdeen	18	6,045	68	U	B	1927	420	U	P
D8	*Aberdeen Hazlehead*	Hazlehead, Aberdeen	9	—		U	B	1927	420	U	P
D9	*Aberdeen King's Links*	Aberdeen	18	5,838	71	U	B	1925	30	L	L
D10	Aberdeen Westhill	Westhill, Skene, Aberdeenshire	18	5,866	69	WD	B	1977	450	H	P
D11	Abernethy	Nethy Bridge, Invernesshire	9	4,968	66	U	B	1895	725	KT	P
D12	Aboyne	Formaston Park, Aboyne	18	5,304	66	U	B	1883	430	RT	P
D13	Alness	Ardross Road, Alness	9	4,718	63	U	A	1904	200	H	M
D14	Askernish	Lochboisdale, South Uist	18	5,114	67	U	A	1891	30	L	L
D15	Aviemore	Dalfaber, Aviemore	9	4,908	64	M		1982	900	U	P
D16	Ballater	Victoria Road, Ballater	18	5,704	67	U	B	1892	700	RT	P
D17	Banchory	Kinneskie, Banchory	18	5,284	66	U	C	1905	200	RT	P
D18	Banff Duff House Royal	The Barnyards, Banff	18	6,161	69	WD	B	1909	20	RT	P
D19	Boat of Garten	Boat of Garten	18	5,690	68	U	B	1898	750	RT	P
D20	Bonar Bridge and Ardgay	Bonar Bridge	9	4,616	63	U	B	1904	200	H	P
D21	Braemar	Cluniebank Road, Braemar	18	4,916	64	U	B	1902	1150	RT	M
D22	Brora	Golf Road, Brora	18	6,110	69	U	B	1889	30	L	L
D23	Buckpool	Barhill Road, Buckie	18	6,257	70	U	B	1933	80	RM	L
D24	Carrbridge	Carrbridge	9	5,246	66	U	B	1980	880	RT	M
D25	Cruden Bay	Cruden Bay, Aberdeenshire	18	6,370	71	WD	C	1791	25	L	L
D26	Cullen	The Links, Cullen, Banffshire	18	4,610	62	U	B	1879	50	RB	L

Code	Club	Address										
D27	Royal Dornoch	Golf Road, Dornoch, Sutherland	18	6,577	72	U	D	1877	30	L	L
D28	Royal Dornoch	Golf Road, Dornoch, Sutherland	9	4,970	64	U	B	—	30	L	L
D29	Dufftown	Dufftown, Banffshire	9	4,530	63	U	B	1896	500	U	P
D30	Ellon McDonald	Ellon, Aberdeenshire	18	5,986	69	U	C	1927	100	U	P
D31	Elgin	Birnie Road, Elgin	18	6,401	71	U	C	1906	100	U	P
D32	Forres	Muiryshade, Forres	18	6,141	69	U	B	1889	100	U	P
D33	Fort Augustus	Markethill, Fort Augustus	9	5,454	68	U	B	1930	250	KT	M
D34	Fort William	North Road, Fort William	18	5,686	71	U	B	1974	100	U	M
D35	Fortrose and Rosemarkie	Ness Road East, Fortrose	18	5,973	69	U	B	1888	30	RB	L
D36	Fraserburgh	Philorth, Fraserburgh	18	6,217	70	U	B	1881	50	L	L
D37	Gairloch	Gairloch, Ross-shire	9	3,884	63	U	B	1898	40	L	L
D38	Garmouth and Kingston	Garmouth, Fochabers	18	5,637	67	U	B	1932	50	RT	P
D39	Golspie	Ferry Road, Golspie	18	5,900	68	U	B	1889	35	L	L
D40	Granton-on-Spey	Granton-on-Spey	18	5,672	67	U	B	1890	750	KT	P
D41	Helmsdale	Helmsdale, Sutherland	9	3,650	62	U	B	1894	150	RT	M
D42	Hopeman	Hopeman, Morayshire	18	5,439	66	U	B	1923	60	RM	M
D43	Huntly	Huntly, Aberdeenshire	18	5,399	66	U	B	1900	375	RT	P
D44	Insch	Golf Terrace, Insch, Aberdeenshire	9	5,488	67	U	B	1982	400	U	P
D45	*Inverallochy*	Inverallochy, Fraserburgh	18	5,137	65	U	B	1890	30	L	L
D46	Invergordon	King George Street, Invergordon	9	6,028	69	U	A	1954	50	RB	P
D47	Inverness	Inverness	18	6,226	70	WD	C	1883	80	RB	P
D48	*Inverness Torvean*	Glenurquhart Road, Inverness	18	4,308	62	U	B	1962	80	RT	P
D49	Inverurie	Blackhall Road, Inverurie	18	5,703	68	U	B	1923	425	U	P
D50	Keith	Fife Park, Keith, Banffshire	18	5,811	68	U	B	1963	450	U	P
D51	Kennay	Kennay, Aberdeenshire	9	3,730	58	WD	A	1908	300	U	P
D52	Kingussie	Gynace Road, Kingussie	18	5,408	67	U	B	1890	950	RT	M
D53	Kintore	Kintore, Aberdeenshire	9	5,367	66	WD	B	1911	200	KT	P
D54	Kirkwall	Grainbank, Kirkwall, Orkney	18	5,406	68	U	B	1889	75	U	P

REF	NAME	ADDRESS	HOLES	LENGTH (yds)	SSS	VIS	COST	DATE	ALT (ft)	LAND	VEG
D55	*Laurencekirk Auchenblae*	Auchenblae, Laurencekirk, Kincardinshire	9	4,348	60	U	A	1984	600	H	P
D56	Lerwick	PO Box 18, Lerwick	18	5,971	71	U	B	1894	30	U	M
D57	Lochcarron	Lochcarron, Ross and Cromarty	9	—	—	U	A	—	50	U	P
D58	Lybster	Main Street, Lybster	9	3,792	62	U	A	1926	200	RM	M
D59	Moray Lossiemouth Old	Stotfield Road, Lossiemouth	18	6,643	72	U	C	1889	30	L	L
D60	Moray Lossiemouth New	Stotfield Road, Lossiemouth	18	6,044	69	U	B	1979	30	L	L
D61	MacDuff Royal Tarlair	Buchan Street, MacDuff	18	5,866	68	U	B	1926	175	RM	M
D62	Mallaig Traigh	5 Back of Keppoch, Arisaig	9	4,200	68	U	A	—	40	L	L
D63	Muir of Ord	Great North Road, Muir of Ord	18	5,022	65	U	B	1875	75	RB	P
D64	Murcar	Bridge of Don, Aberdeen	18	6,226	70	U	C	1909	30	L	L
D65	Nairn	Seabank Road, Nairn	18	6,540	71	U	C	1887	30	L	L
D66	Nairn Dunbar	Lochloy Road, Nairn	18	6,431	71	U	B	1899	20	L	L
D67	Newburgh on Ythan	Newburgh, Aberdeenshire	18	6,404	71	U	B	1888	30	L	L
D68	Newtonmore	Newtonmore	18	5,890	68	U	B	1890	750	KT	P
D69	Oldmeldrum	Oldmeldrum, Aberdeenshire	9	5,252	66	U	B	1885	540	U	M
D70	Peterhead	Craigewan, Peterhead	18	6,070	69	U	B	1841	40	L	L
D71	Portmahomack Tarbat	Portmahomack, Easter Ross	9	4,656	63	U	A	1908	75	L	L
D72	Scalloway	Scalloway, Shetland	9	4,548	64	U	B	1907	75	U	M
D73	Sconser	Broadford, Skye	9	4,796	63	U	B	1964	30	RB	L
D74	Spean Bridge	Spean Bridge	18	4,406	62	U	A	1954	300	H	P
D75	Reay	Reay, Thurso	18	5,856	68	U	B	1893	25	L	L
D76	Spey Bay	Spey Bay Hotel, Spey Bay, Fochabers	18	6,059	69	U	B	1907	15	L	L
D77	Stonehaven	Cowie, Stonehaven	18	5,128	65	WD	B	1888	175	RM	M
D78	Stornoway	Lady Lever Park, Stornoway, Lewis	18	5,119	66	U	B	1947	100	U	P
D79	Strathlene	Buckie, Banffshire	18	5,957	69	U	B	1877	80	RM	M

										H	M
D80	Strathpeffer	Strathpeffer, Ross and Cromarty	18	4.792	65	U	B	1888	500		
D81	Stromness	Ness, Orkney	18	4.665	64	U	B	1890	100	L	L
D82	Tain	Tain, Ross and Cromarty	18	6.207	70	U	B	1890	25	L	L
D83	Tarland	Tarland, Aberdeenshire	9	5.812	68	U	B	1908	500	U	P
D84	*Thurso*	Newlands of Geise, Thurso	18	5.818	69	U	B	1964	150	U	M
D85	Torphins	Torphins, Aberdeenshire	9	4.660	63	U	B	1891	500	U	M
D86	Turriff	Rosehall, Turriff, Aberdeenshire	18	6.105	69	U	B	1895	150	RT	P
D87	Westray	Westray, Orkney	9	—	—	U	A	—	75	U	M
D88	Wick	Wick, Caithness	18	5.945	69	U	B	1870	50	L	L

BIBLIOGRAPHY

Alliss, P (ed), *Golf a Way of Life* (Stanley Paul, 1987)

Baird, A, *Golf on Gullane Hill* (Edinburgh, 1985)

Capital Golf (A City of Edinburgh publication)

Colville, J, *The Glasgow Golf Club* (Glasgow, 1907)

Cornish, S and Whitten, R E, *The Golf Course* (Windward, Leicester, 1981)

Crampsey, R A, *St Mungo's Gowfers—The History of Glasgow Golf Club, 1787-1987* (Glasgow, 1988)

*Darwin, B, et al., *The History of Golf in Britain* (Cassell, London, 1952)

Drysdale, A M, *The Golf House Club, Elie* (Elie, Fife, 1975)

Forgan, R, *Golfer's Handbook* (1880) (Now published annually as the *Benson and Hedges Handbook* by Macmillan)

Furnie, H B, *Golfer's Manual* (Whitehead & Orr, Cupar, Fife, 1857)

Hamilton, D, *Good Golf Guide to Scotland* (Cannongate, Edinburgh, 1982)

Hamilton, D, *Early Golf in Aberdeen* (The Partick Press, Oxford, 1985)

Hamilton, D, *Early Golf in Glasgow, 1589-1787* (The Partick Press, Oxford, 1985)

Hawtree, F W, *The Golf Course—Planning, Design, Construction* (Spon Ltd, London, 1983)

*Henderson, I and Stirk, D, *Golf in the Making* (Henderson and Stirk Ltd, Winchester, 1979)

Menzies, G (ed), *The World of Golf* (BBC Publication, London, 1982)

Price, R, *Scotland's Environment During the Last 30,000 Years* (Scottish Academic Press, Edinburgh, 1983)

Price, R, 'The Landforms of Scotland's Golf Courses', *Sport Place International*, (1988) Vol 2, No. 1, pp 2-13

Ransomes—A Great Tradition. 150 years of grasscutting technology. 1832-1982 (Ransomes Sims & Jefferies, plc, Ipswich)

Robertson, A D, *The Story of Lanark Golf Club 1851-1951* (Lanark, 1951)

Robertson, J K, *1984 St Andrews Home of Golf* (Macdonald, Edinburgh, 1984)

Scottish Tourist Board, *Golf, Staying Ahead of the Game* (Edinburgh, 1988)

Smith, R H, *Golfer's Yearbook* (Smith & Grant, Ayr, 1866)

Steel, D, *The Golf Course Guide to the British Isles* (Collins, London, 1986)

*van Hengel, S J H, *Early Golf* (F P van Eck, Vaduz, Liechtenstein, 1985)

Ward Thomas, P, et al., *The World Atlas of Golf* (Mitchell Beazley, London, 1976)

Ward Thomas, P, *The Royal and Ancient* (Scottish Academic Press, Edinburgh, 1980)

INDEX